Popular Music in Mexico

Popular Music in Mexico

Claes af Geijerstam

UNIVERSITY OF NEW MEXICO PRESS
Albuquerque

© 1976 by the University of New Mexico Press. All rights reserved.
Appendix, "Border Music of the 1970s in the Southwestern United States,"
© 1976 by Elizabeth H. Heist. All rights reserved.
Manufactured in the United States of America.
Library of Congress Catalog Card Number 75-17373
International Standard Book Number 0-8263-0414-1
First Edition

To
Carmen Sordo Sodi
and
Juan S. Garrido

Acknowledgments

The help of many people has made it possible for me to complete this book. Among those who are especially worthy of thanks is Professor Ingmar Bengtsson at the Institute of Musicology in Uppsala University; he has followed my work closely and guided me through many difficult parts. I have also had a good deal of help from Dan Malmström, without whose encouragement I would never have taken an interest in the popular music of Mexico. I would also like to thank Jean Gray for translating the first draft, Britta Wedin for typing, Regina af Geijerstam for helping me translate difficult parts of the recorded interviews, and Robert Carroll for proofreading; likewise the editor Bengt Gavell at the Esselte Studium Company, through whose initial efforts the University of New Mexico Press became interested in the book. Elizabeth H. Heist contributed the appendix, "Border Music of the 1970s in the Southwestern United States." Ingrid Nyberg transcribed the music.

I would also like to thank all of the people in Mexico with whom I had interviews, and who have been helpful in other ways. Special thanks are due to Carmen Sordo Sodi and Juan S. Garrido, the personnel at the Sección de Investigaciones Musicales, and Sociedad de Autores y Compositores de Música in Mexico City. And a final note of thanks to Dr. Gilbert Chase, who read the manuscript in its entirety and made many valuable suggestions.

Contents

Preface		ix
Introduction		1
1.	The Development of Mexican Genres	9
2.	Mariachi, Norteño, and Marimba Ensembles	41
3.	The Corrido	49
4.	The Canción	59
5.	Modern Dance Rhythms	71
6.	Popular Music Before and After the Revolution	81
7.	Composers and Musicians Up to the 1940s	93
8.	The Media	107
9.	Contemporary Trends	123
Appendix:	Border Music of the 1970s in the Southwestern United States	138
Notes		148
Bibliography		170
Comments on Recordings		177
Index		178
Illustrations after page 82		

Preface

I first became acquainted with Mexican culture, its music in particular, in the spring of 1968, when I went on a recording trip to Mexico with three colleagues of mine from Uppsala University. The main purpose of the trip was to make recordings among the Lacandón Indians, who live in Chiapas near the Guatemalan border. Our stay with the Lacandón people resulted in a number of tape recordings, and, in the course of time, a short thesis on the songs of these Indians by Dan Malmström, who initiated the trip.[1]

During our stay in Mexico, Görn Holm and I became interested in the musical instruments of the Indians. We began to gather a considerable amount of information and visual material. The main focus of our attention was the collection of instruments at the Sección de Investigaciones Musicales, which is under the control of the Instituto Nacional de las Bellas Artes (INBA), and that at the Museo Nacional de Antropología in Mexico City. We received invaluable help in our work from Mrs. Carmen Sordo Sodi, director of the Sección de Investigaciones Musicales. About a year after our return, Görn Holm and I each submitted our papers on string and wind instruments among Mexican Indians.[2]

Mexico had cast a spell on me and I was determined at first to continue my studies of the Indians. I had made all the contacts I felt I needed and was well read in this field. I would probably have continued to study the Indians if Dan Malmström had not opened my eyes to Mexican popular music as an exciting and unexplored field of research. Malmström himself was planning a thesis on modern Mexican "serious" music. Thus there was much to be gained by a change of plan for both of us. We could complement each other's research and also cooperate in the actual fieldwork.

In the summer of 1971 Dan Malmström and I undertook a journey to Mexico in order to collect material for our theses on twentieth-century Mexican music. At first my aim was to write a study dealing exclusively with the history and status of Mexican popular music in the twentieth century. During the course of the work I found it increasingly necessary to consider the rural folk music of the country, at least that part of it which has contributed to the formation of urban music culture. I therefore widened the scope of the project to include the mainstream folk music of Mexico. However, folk music of random importance to the development of recent Mexican popular music, including purely religious genres such as *alabado* and *alabanza,* were not taken into consideration.

Even with the exceptions noted above, it must be stated that this book is far from a definitive account of Mexico's folk and popular music. This is due primarily to the fact that the research of Mexican folk music is still incomplete. As yet no systematic and exhaustive investigations have been carried out, except for the fieldwork carried out in Michoacán by the Sección de Investigaciones Musicales. Published results of the research that has been done are of uneven quality. The collection of material has concentrated solely on certain dominant genres in central Mexico (such as the *son* tradition and the *corrido*).

Since I was not able to carry out any extensive field research of my own, with the exception of interviews and the examination of archives in the capital, I had to concern myself with the genres that have been most thoroughly explored. This was in line with my intentions, as I was primarily interested in that part of Mexico's folk traditions that has been most widely popularized.

It was inevitable that this study should concentrate almost exclusively on Mexico City. Nearly everything of impact in the field of popular music in Mexico emanates in some way from the capital. This limitation was also practical, since the vast collection of facts would have overwhelmed me if I had included all the various states in my study. Nevertheless, in discussing the mainstream folk music I had to broaden my outlook in regard to both the time span and the geographic area taken into consideration.

I would liken this book to an aerial photograph, taken from above the great expanse of Mexican popular music. Seen from the air, the millions of details merge into a pattern of colors and shapes. My main purpose was not to capture the individual details. I was attracted to the pattern itself, the interplay of lines.

There are bound to be those who will criticize such an overview and maintain that this is no way to carry out research. How can one survey a landscape veiled in mist? I will attempt to answer that crucial question and thereby, I trust, justify my approach to the subject.

I consider the factual material presented in this book, though incomplete, to be reliable, as it was passed on to me by informants possessing a wide knowledge of Mexican folk and popular music. My own experience in the field was slight when I began my research among institutions and individuals in Mexico City. My reliance on the informants was complete; I chose to compile the facts and base the results chiefly on their judgment. My own contribution was to adapt the material to the concepts of current ethnomusicology.

I doubt if my research could have been brought to a conclusion without the help of Carmen Sordo Sodi. Through her I met several of the country's leading experts in the sphere of Mexican music. Mrs. Sordo Sodi herself is the most outstanding of them all.

I used a cassette tape recorder for the interviews. All of them were conducted in Spanish and were transcribed after my return to Sweden, where Dr. Regina af Geijerstam helped me to decipher certain sections that were difficult to interpret. I sealed the cassettes and kept them as source material for my thesis. These interviews, as well as information derived from articles and books, and of course the music itself, provided the basis for my study.

Some form of selection was necessary in choosing informants and in evaluating their responses. I assessed the reliability of my informants according to their education and their position and experience in the musical life of Mexico. There is bound to be a certain arbitrariness involved in weighing such considerations; some judgments are inevitably subjective.

The two informants I regard as most reliable are Carmen Sordo Sodi and Juan S. Garrido. Mr. Garrido, Chilean by birth, has been involved in most of the musical events in Mexico City over the last forty years. He is generally regarded as the country's leading authority on twentieth-century popular music in Mexico. He was instrumental in forming and operating the chief radio station in Mexico, the legendary XEW, during its "golden age" (around 1935 to 1955). For many years he directed one of Mexico City's leading swing orchestras, and he was connected for a long time with the record and sheet music industry. Garrido has also been very successful as a composer, and he holds a high position in the Sociedad de Autores y Compositores de Música (SACM), the

Mexican equivalent of ASCAP. Carmen Sordo Sodi and Juan S. Garrido gave me generously of their time; I have taped interviews with them of two and one-half and three hours, respectively, filled with exciting material.

On the advice of Carmen Sordo Sodi and Dan Malmström, I chose certain other informants: Raúl Cossío, who heads Radio Universidad; Raúl Lavista, regarded as Mexico's leading composer of film music; Salvador Contreras and Luis Sandi, composers of serious music who can be considered knowledgeable on the subject; Gabriel Saldívar, the "grand old man" of Mexican musical research, who has written books on the *jarabe* and a history of Mexican music. Saldívar has studied folk music, but his chief interest lies in the history of classical music in Mexico. I also interviewed José E. Guerrero, an expert on Mexican folklore. He was formerly a lecturer on folklore at the Universidad Nacional Autónoma de México (UNAM) and is now the director of a school of music in Mexico City. Like Saldívar he represents an earlier school of thought with regard to folklore. Both men are inclined to favor ideas of national romanticism, especially in relation to ethnomusicology.

I also interviewed a younger researcher, Juan Herrejón, who was active some years ago at the Sección de Investigaciones Musicales as a collector of folk music. He is now working at the National Conservatory in Mexico City, lecturing on music theory and composition. I had short interviews with two successful composers of popular music. The first was Consuelo Velázquez, the president of SACM; she wrote "Bésame mucho," among other songs. The other was Tomás Méndez, a man of great renown in Mexico. Zeferino Nandayapa, one of the country's most skilled performers on the marimba, was kind enough to give me a long and comprehensive interview about his instrument and its role in Mexico's musical life.

Vicente T. Mendoza (1894–1964) is quoted at several points in this book. His research produced a great deal of material of rather uneven quality. Besides Mendoza and Saldívar, the most qualified writers on Mexican folk and popular music were Otto Mayer-Serra, Gerónimo Bequeiro Fóster, and Daniel Castañeda, whose names will appear frequently in the following pages.

Many problems arise when a researcher seeks an intimate knowledge of a foreign country. Apart from the language barrier, differences in life-style and attitudes make themselves felt at times and complicate the fieldwork. My efforts to meet high officials in the trade unions were not crowned with success. Mexico's largest record store, Mercado de Discos, promised me the names of the artists who had led the best-seller lists for the last ten years. Unfortunately I never received this information. In other cases it was simply impossible to make contact with people whom I wished to interview. The record companies with which I tried to get in touch erected an impenetrable telephone barrier. When, however, I did make contact with various government institutions and private individuals, I encountered a courtesy and an enthusiasm that I have rarely experienced outside of Mexico.

The informational sources of Mexico's musical development are incomplete and obscure. Isolated papers and surveys of widely varying quality have been published in different journals of a rather specialized nature. One of my major tasks was to attempt to trace these articles.[3] To study all the minor music magazines published in Mexico over the years is, however, beyond the capacity of a single individual. There are endless columns written in a somewhat gossipy tone, "weekly reviews," "celebrity reports," and the like, even in fairly specialized publications such as *Audiomúsica*. I could only skim these columns rapidly, and in many cases I was forced to leave them unread. I realize that in doing so I may well have missed the odd nugget that would have enriched my account.

The sheet music at my disposal was fairly limited. Most of it came from Juan S. Garrido and Sordo Sodi. In the use of phonograph records I concentrated on those recommended by people more knowledgeable than I am about Mexican popular music. In addition I brought back tape recordings of many hours of popular music broadcasts. On several occasions Malmström and I also recorded street musicians in Mexico City. I received valuable guidance from the "top list" of melodies and composers between 1963 and 1968 that the statistics department at SACM very kindly drew up for me.

I pondered long about the title of this book. Should it be *Mexican Popular Music*, or *Popular Music in Mexico*? This may appear to be a trivial matter, but there is a distinct difference between the first option, which is confined to native music, and the second, which covers all music launched in Mexico, including foreign music (in which the lyrics may have been translated into Spanish and the arrangement plagiarized). During the course of my work I found it difficult to maintain a clear distinction between these categories. My interest centered on works by native composers, but the thesis would have collapsed if the perspective had not been widened to include foreign products that have been introduced into the country. Non-Mexican popular music is taking a firmer hold on the taste of the Mexican public, largely because of the effects of the mass media. I therefore decided on the title *Popular Music in Mexico.*

Introduction

The terminology of music comprises a tangle of terms and concepts that are difficult to standardize. Not only is the same word used in diverse ways in different countries or in different languages; it may even vary in its meaning within the same country, and in fact be applied to different types of music. I refer to such terms as "popular music," "folk music," "traditional music," and "ethnic music."

An examination of variations in definition and usage of these and other terms within a country, or among several countries, reveals interesting tendencies in the development of concepts and classifications. Thinking it would be fruitful to test this method in the field of Mexican music, I included questions on the use of these terms in the interviews.[1] In this section I shall review the most important trends in my informants' usage of these terms, and also discuss their current meanings in Western musicology.

Tribal and Ethnic Music

The Mexican terms describing this type of music are *música tribal, música étnica, música folklórica,* and *música indígena.*[2] Both in English and Spanish, "tribal music" refers to traditions limited to certain well-defined tribes. In Mexico, for instance, there are the songs of the Lacandón Indians living in Chiapas. These songs will never be sung outside the Lacandón tribe, and they are entirely unknown except to a few anthropologists.

The term "ethnic music," which is sometimes used synonymously with tribal music, may also denote traditions in larger ethnic groups. In Mexico it refers especially to the acculturated Indians, who combine Indian and Spanish cultural traits. The ethnic situation among Mexican Indians (and among the Indians of the Latin American highlands in general) is highly complicated. The Indians and Spanish have mingled since the sixteenth century, which has resulted in the *mestizo* (mixed) race that currently predominates in the population of Mexico.

Insofar as identifiable Indian communities still exist, one may assume that they have been subject to severe cultural influence from the white and mestizo population. Nevertheless, the effect of European culture on the Indian has been uneven, and there are still tribes, primarily the Lacandones, but also the Huicholes and Coras in the mountains of Jalisco and Nayarit, who have retained their pre-Spanish traditions relatively unchanged up to the present. Yet in the overwhelming majority of cases one is dealing with communities combining Indian and Spanish cultural features, which tend to a varying extent to be mestizo. In music and dance it is often possible to see that Indian tribes have preserved dances of pre-Spanish origin but have adapted Spanish or Central European music to accompany them. Despite the European influence on style, however, the function of the music is often markedly Indian.

Consequently there is no sharp delineation between Indian (ethnic) and mestizo (folk) traditions. Moreover, in Mexico a considerable amount of ethnic music is becoming known as folk music with national cultural connotations.

A good example of Mexican music of ethnic origin that has actually become folk music is "La danza de los viejitos" (The Dance of the Little Old Men) of the Purépechas, who live in the state of Michoacán. The melody that accompanies this dance is European, probably dating from the eighteenth century, while the rhythm may be either Indian or European. The origin of the dance, however, is purely Indian. In pre-Spanish times "La danza de los viejitos" was held in honor of Tlaloc, the storm or rain god, and masks representing the face of Tlaloc are still used in this dance. Tlaloc was also named Huehuetéotl, meaning "the old god" in Nahuatl. The "viejitos" dance, though still considered typically Purépecha, has become known all over the country. It is included in the program of the Ballet Folklórico de México, and it is taught to children in schools.[3]

Folk Music

According to current definitions among ethnomusicologists, folk music should meet certain criteria: It must be transmitted orally, and it must be typical of, or peculiar to, a people, a folk group, or some other ethnically limited population group.[4] In the course of rapid industrialization, the concept of folk music has become more inclusive. K. Kos speaks as follows of the situation in Yugoslavia:

> The migration of rural populations to cities and industrial centres has forced many people to try to adapt to the new conditions of urban life. In rural areas themselves, the shift from traditional to industrial methods of farming has led to certain radical changes in the ways of living and communication. These changes . . . can be described as a kind of urbanization of the countryside and ruralization of city life.[5]

This statement also applies to Mexico. The folk music traditions grew among the mestizo population, i.e., the Spanish-Indian mixed race. The mestizo folk music, comprising Spanish, Indian, and African characteristics, was confined mainly to the countryside. Today the picture is radically changing. On the one hand, a lot of "genuine" folk music is gradually disappearing, together with the forms of life upon which it was organically dependent for its existence. This destruction is furthered by the broadcast of popular hit music by local radio stations in rural areas.[6] On the other hand, folk music styles are being greatly commercialized, largely because of the big record companies. This process has come about through imitation (as in the case of "folk rock" in the United States and "folk pop" in Sweden), and by the issue of records of particularly salable folk genres with genuine ensembles.[7] Authentic folk music is also performed by professional groups. This is the case with the Mexican group Los Folkloristas, which was formed by students in Mexico City in 1966.

In Latin America, as well as in other parts of the world, the commercialization of folk music has led to a division of genres. As a result, some folk music genres exist as two (occasionally more) parallel forms. They exist as closed, continuous traditions in rural regions, and as commercial music commissioned in the urban areas. This applies in Mexico to *mariachi* music (that is, music played by mariachi ensembles) and to *huapango*. Yet while the huapango is still mainly a folk genre with diverse regional styles, instrumental combinations, and repertoires, the mariachi music, which once belonged to the folk category, has become primarily urban popular music. There are, however, also huapangos cast in the mold of the commercial market. These may be arrangements of traditional melodies, such as "La bamba," or newly written tunes in huapango rhythm (so-called composed folk music). In the latter case there is a clear tendency toward national standardization of both melody and rhythm, which are simplified in comparison with the regional styles. The trend is toward a Mexican "standard style" within every genre, which may replace the specific regional styles and repertoires, as has already happened with the mariachi.

The term "folk music" has no real equivalent in the Spanish language, apart from the rarely used *música folk,* which is a direct translation from the English. Among Mexicans the terms *música folklórica,* and to some extent *música popular* and *música tradicional,* are used more or less as equivalents of the British or American "folk music."[8]

Traditional Music (música tradicional)

This concept has a very wide range of meanings. Generally the term covers older melodies with a firm hold on the popular consciousness, regardless of whether they were originally folk music. The repertoires of the hurdy-gurdy players and street singers are good examples of traditional melodies which may at the same time be described as popular music.

There are, in fact, two different levels in the traditional classification, one regional and one national. Authentic folk music could equally well be called "traditional regional music," as in the case of huapangos such as "Tilingo lingo" and "Ahualulco" in Veracruz. On the national level, traditional music includes well-known folk tunes, such as "La cucaracha" and "La bamba," and popular hit music written in the spirit of folk music.

Introduction

Popular Music

This is a complex concept with many possible interpretations. In an article on the popular music of Iran, Bruno Nettl says:

> Definitions are lacking in most generally used encyclopedias of music, but a working definition of popular music in Western society appears to have several ingredients: 1) it is primarily urban in provenience and audience orientation; 2) it is performed by professional but not very highly trained musicians who usually do not take an intellectual view of their work; 3) it bears a stylistic relationship to the art music of its culture, but a lower degree of sophistication; 4) in the twentieth century, at least, its diffusion has been primarily the mass media of broadcasting and recording. It is normally assumed that popular music existed before these mass media came into existence, but it is difficult, in the period before the twentieth century in Europe and America, to distinguish between the three styles [that is, art, folk, and popular music].[9]

Popular music functions in similar ways throughout the world; for producers it is an easy way to make money, and for consumers a readily digestible food for the ear. Popular music currently serves several purposes: It provides music for films, operettas, musical shows, and "pop" recordings. Light music from the classical repertoire may also be included in the popular genre. Items such as the "Prisoners' Chorus" from Verdi's *Nebuchadnezzar* and Mozart's "Eine Kleine Nachtmusik" (which was used purely as entertainment music even in its own time) are included in this category. Current arrangements of the classics continue to widen the boundaries, so that even pieces previously regarded as "difficult" can reach the best-seller lists.

The divergence of style between folk and popular music is not always evident. The differences are primarily manifested by the way in which the music is created and launched. The commercial popular music and the authentic folk music have quite different backgrounds. Popular music is primarily connected with the cities, while folk music generally belongs to rural areas.[10] Popular music, unlike folk music, is seldom based on an oral tradition. Its popularity is dependent upon commercial promotion, particularly on how well it is advertised and packaged. The latter also applies to commercialized folk music, but to a lesser extent.

Thus "popular music" has a wide range of meanings. Almost all music may be so described in some context, whether or not it was intended as such from the start. It depends entirely on the situation in which the music is used.[11] In general the term is used to describe music that has a large social and geographical range of appeal. The term frequently denotes an undertone of social or musical contempt. "Vulgar music" is often used as a synonym. *Música popular* therefore carries a strong connotation of "lower-class music." Carlos Vega, the Argentine musicologist, states:

> The term *popular* is often used disparagingly, in the sense of "inferior." In the musical order it signifies mediocre ideas and techniques, and, if the intention is pejorative, suggests means and elements of minimum quality. The expression *música popular* in Spanish (but not in the French "musique populaire") also means music that is widely diffused, and it is in this usage that we get the *outmoded* meaning of pueblo that includes all the inhabitants of a region or a country. . . .[12]

Vega expresses some significant views regarding the concepts música popular and "popular music." At the end of the quotation he also refers to a variation in the Spanish concept of the term as it relates to the English, that is, its connection with *pueblo* in the sense of *population.*

Carlos Chávez writes that música popular is the music of the people.[13] Chávez defines "the people" in this context as agricultural and industrial laborers. According to his view, música popular means everyday music at the lower levels of society. This places it on the fringe of what is usually defined as folk (or traditional) music.

José E. Guerrero has a similar definition. He states that música popular is by its nature anonymous. But in contrast to música folklórica, it is not removed from the contemporary scene.[14] He further defines música popular as the music of the people; he considers "the people" to be "the creative mass." Música popular is the work of individuals, but its character is regarded as collective. The "popular" musician/composer (*el músico popular*) lacks musical training. The popular manifestations of culture are spontaneous in nature, as opposed to the low quality commercialized music (*arte vulgar* or *populachería*), which, according to Guerrero, lacks both technique and spontaneity.

Many objections can be raised to this definition. The idea that música popular (in the sense of folk music) must always be anonymous is not accurate at all. Guerrero's way of linking the "creative mass" and the individual composer is very confusing. The idea that folk music is always a collective cultural manifestation is based on a romantic ideal.

Guerrero introduces one concept of particular interest, *música popularizada*. According to Guerrero, such music, unlike música popular, is the work of a known writer with musical training. Música popularizada, however, in contrast to música vulgar (commercial hit music), is written in a style that "gets to people" and that the majority of the public recognizes.[15] Guerrero cites two songs as examples of música popularizada, "La canción mixteca" by José López Alavez and "Diós nunca muere," composed in the mid-nineteenth century by Macedonio Alcalá, songs that came to be regarded as "regional hymns" in the state of Oaxaca. Guerrero states that the people who sing these and similar songs often do not know their origin.

There is no doubt that the definition of música popularizada is based upon qualitative judgments. Guerrero emphasizes that the composers must have "technical skill." Consequently, much of the current popular music necessarily falls outside the sphere of música popularizada.

The attempt to draw a line between popular music with folk connotations and purely commercial popular music was made in another interview. Luis Sandi, one of Mexico's most celebrated composers of serious music, makes an interesting distinction between two types of composers of popular music: those who express what the people feel, and those who write to attract the people, in other words, for profit.[16] In Sandi's estimation, Guty Cárdenas was a typical representative of those who write what the people feel. He wrote songs in the traditional style, as did Ricardo Palmerín. Agustín Lara (d. 1970), on the other hand, belonged to the second type. According to Sandi, his sole interest was "to exploit the public and the market." Sandi also feels Lara was typical in that he wrote many songs, often in a style "that is not natural to him" (*"que no es el suyo"*). Lara was a composer of commercial rather than popular music, within the terms of this definition.[17]

In conclusion, música popular is defined in a variety of ways; it is sometimes identified as folk music, at other times interpreted as popular music in the American or British sense. The second view was held by most of my informants, including Garrido and Sordo Sodi; however, they did note certain exceptions. Sordo Sodi, for instance, said that the *son* (which is a folk music genre) constitutes Mexico's most important *género popular.*

Folk and popular music are closely connected in Mexico as in all of Latin America. It may, therefore, be wise to follow Juan Herrejón's example and leave the definition of certain musical genres open to variation. The Brazilian samba, for example, belongs to both popular and folk music. Such ambivalent genres are also to be found in Mexico, in particular the son which constitutes a continuum from authentic folk music to commercial hit music. Finally, this book consists of two main parts: chapters 1–5 deal with certain genres and their history; and chapters 6–9 take a more "sociological" approach, dealing with Mexican urban culture during the last one hundred years.

1
The Development of Mexican Genres

The study of music has a long way to go in researching the cultural ties between Spanish, African, and Latin American folklore. There is material for separate studies on the assimilation of Spanish song and dance forms into Mexico and on contemporary Mexican folk music, both in their original and evolved forms. Unfortunately no reliable reference works exist in this field. The most comprehensive text that has been written on Mexican folk music is Vicente Mendoza's *Panorama de la música tradicional de México* (1956). It contains valuable details, but is not satisfactory as a whole, nor entirely accurate.[1] Due to the scarcity of adequate source material, all the information regarding the transmission of musical genres from Spain and Africa to Mexico will be presented simply as theory.[2]

Indian Roots of Mexican Folk Music

Most Mexican folk music would seem to derive from Spain, but there are a good many native elements in it. The Indian cultures, primarily the Aztecs and Mayas, were efficiently repressed from the start by the Spanish colonial authorities. The Indian music that survived gradually merged with the Spanish folklore to form one of the foundations of the country's own mestizo culture.

In attempting to distinguish between indigenous and Spanish

elements in current Indian and mestizo music, one has to take into consideration that the fiestas celebrated in fifteenth- and sixteenth-century Spain resembled in many ways those celebrated in the ancient American cultures. In both cases the people were fond of colorful dances involving many participants. For certain dances "professional" dancers and musicians were engaged, as is still the case in several Indian tribes.

Preconquest dances that seem to have no Spanish influence as far as their choreography is concerned are still performed among Indian tribes in Mexico. Two examples are "La danza del volador" and "La danza de los Quetzales" of Huastec and Totonac Indians living in the Puebla/Veracruz region.[3]

The Indians were deeply affected by Spanish music. Indians were taught Catholic church music by Franciscan friars. Soon after the Conquest (1519–21) one of these friars, Pedro de Gante, founded a "school for the teaching of European subjects in America" in Texcoco.[4] European instruments were imported, and the Indians adopted the techniques of plainsong and polyphonic music.[5] However, the conquered Indians did not by any means abandon their traditions altogether. This becomes evident when one listens to contemporary descendants of the Aztecs and Mayas. They may have accepted European string instruments and stylistic features such as functional harmony, but their way of performing is still distinctively Indian. It is, in fact, difficult to assess the Spanish influence on the Indian musical tradition, as little is known about the precise nature of their music in earlier times. The only information that exists is based on vague accounts written by Spanish friars, as well as on a good many surviving musical instruments such as drums, clay flutes, whistles, shell trumpets, rattles, and scrapers.

The Spaniards infused a considerable amount of Catholic doctrine into the Indian rituals, and current Indian fiestas can be described as a very complex blend of Indian and Catholic elements. Some fiestas are celebrated with Christian names on Christian holidays, as for example Easter, but there are no Indian fiestas that have a pure Catholic significance in religious terms. Those that appear to be Christian rituals should be viewed as Indian rituals conforming to Christian patterns (or vice-versa). Some fiestas seem to have escaped European influence altogether, such as the important rain fiesta in February which is still celebrated by the descendants of the Aztecs and Mayas. Indian elements are also present in the fiestas of the mestizos.

African Influences on Mexican Folk Music

Since the sixteenth century, African music has enriched the Spanish folk genres in Mexico. The African traditions were brought by Negro slaves who worked on haciendas in the states of Veracruz, Guerrero, and elsewhere. Gonzalo Aguirre Beltrán writes that the African traditions in New Spain survived under impossible conditions. They were virtually destroyed by pressure from the Spanish. The slaves adopted the culture of their masters, who also converted them to Catholicism.

The Spanish authorities, however, were unable to prevent the Negroes from setting their stamp on the Church's most important holy days. The element of profane dance and song was particularly apparent. There is a wealth of information concerning the official condemnation of the Negroes' degrading influence. This material dates from the mid-seventeenth century, when the importation of Negroes from Africa reached its peak. Calculations indicate that by that time there were more Negroes in Mexico than the estimated number of Spaniards.[6] The sung verses that accompanied the dances were at times hostile in content and critical of the country's colonial rulers. They coincided with the emergence of nationalistic ideas among mestizos toward the end of the seventeenth century. Sordo Sodi states that a direct line can be drawn from the forbidden dances and songs of the Negroes to the rebellious music of the mestizos.

The Negro influence spread throughout the land, but it became particularly vital in and around the urban areas: Mexico City, Puebla, Guanajuato, Morelia, Guadalajara, Pachuca, and the port city of Veracruz, the main gateway to Mexico at that time. Robert Stevenson writes that "Negroes in cities taught music and dancing, directed 'oratorios,' and ran what would now be called musical comedy theatres."[7] Aguirre Beltrán and Stevenson cite several Inquisition records from the seventeenth and eighteenth centuries, telling of Negro "excesses" in performing dances and music.

Negro dances and songs were thus assimilated into the developing Mexican culture; at the end of the eighteenth century they were included in musical comedies as an expression of the country's general opposition to Spain.[8]

Only a few studies have been made of the African influence on the "mestizo nationalism" that had its origins in the eighteenth century. There is material in both public and private archives that has not yet been examined and will assuredly shed new light on this fascinating sociocultural development. Gabriel Saldívar has a codex (in tablature) dating from the eighteenth century, which contains some musical pieces named "cumbee . . . cantos en idioma Guineo." This clearly indicates African origins in the music.[9]

Later some very influential Afro-Cuban song and dance types became popular in Mexico.[10] These cultural imports, primarily the *habanera, danzón*, and *bolero*, took root among mestizos in both the rural and urban areas, forming an important part of the commercially developed mass culture that grew up there after the mid-nineteenth century.

Spanish and Central European Roots of Mexican Folk Music

The nature of the Spanish dance and music brought to Mexico some three hundred years ago is completely unknown.[11] This is an important point to remember in constructing theories about the folk music currents between Spain and Mexico.

Is there in fact any basis to the theories concerning the Spanish origin of Mexican (and Spanish-American) folk music?[12] Gabriel Saldívar states categorically that a considerable number of the dances usually ascribed to Spain originated in Latin America soon after the conquest. These dances were then transplanted to Spain. This theory seems plausible when applied to the *sarabanda*.[13] However, in stating that the *pavane* (which occurs in a late seventeenth-century codex in Saldívar's possession) originated in Latin America, Saldívar is very likely mistaken.[14] In regard to dances, such as the *fandango* and *petenera*, there is no proof whatsoever for Saldívar's theory.[15]

Vicente Mendoza and Gilbert Chase, among others, presume that Andalusian songs and dances such as the fandango were brought to Mexico very early in the colonial period.[16] This is also simply conjecture. Carlos Vega, who gives an excellent review of South America's folk music in his *Panorama de la música popular argentina*, writes that the only established fact is that Spanish (mainly Andalusian) songs and dances came to South America as theatre music at the end of the eighteenth century; they were included in musical comedies. Vega emphasizes that far too little is known about pre-eighteenth-century music in Latin America to speculate about whether or not individual genres existed then and how they were composed.[17]

Mendoza makes the observation that the names of certain dances that were popular in Spain during the seventeenth and early eighteenth centuries still exist in Mexico. Examples include: *canario, cascabel, contradanza, fandango, malagueña, petenera, paracumbe, vaquería, zapateado,* and *zarabanda*.[18] However, due to the prevailing uncertainty about the time of transfer and the precise nature of these dances then, it is fair to assume that both the music and choreography were modified in Mexico. In time the names of these dances may have been applied to a variety of musical forms.

Very likely Mexico received Andalusian danzas cantadas earlier and in larger quantities than the rest of Spanish America, both as theatre and authentic folk music. Mexico City and Lima were the cultural centers of Spanish America during the colonial era.[19] Mexico was the country that received the largest number of immigrants from Spain, the majority coming from Andalusia and Estremadura. This fact also explains why the Veracruz area is especially rich in Andalusian tunes; Veracruz was, and still is, the largest Mexican harbor and was the natural entry point for Spanish culture. Yet Andalusian tunes and rhythms also gained a firm foothold in the states of Guanajuato, Querétaro, Michoacán, Jalisco, and Guerrero.

Spanish folk music became widely diffused throughout Mexico during the second half of the eighteenth century, being incorporated in the *tonadilla escénica*. Tonadillas were musical comedies that flourished in Madrid from the middle of the eighteenth century to the beginning of the nineteenth century. The form was refined by composers such as Luis Misón and Pablo Esteve.[20] The tonadilla originated as interludes between the acts of theatrical pieces. Eventually it developed into a type of short comic opera, twenty to thirty minutes long. Tonadillas usually consisted of three parts: an introduction presenting the characters, a series of strophic verses, and a finale. Toward the end of the century, tonadillas escénicas lasted over an hour; by then the genre was past its prime.[21]

The kind of music cultivated in the tonadilla is well defined by Roger Mindlin:

> The music of the tonadillas and sainetes of the eighteenth century was never printed and published, and thousands of scores lie moldering today in the archives of public and private libraries. The scanty fragments that did reach the general public prove, however, that it must not only have been a question of a genuine rococo music, but over and above that, also a music which exhibited true Spanish characteristics. And the music was not only full of the Spanish dance airs of the time—the *sarabanda*, the *chacona*, the *fandango* in all its varieties, and *pasacalle*, but above all, the songs give preference to the inimitable Spanish *copla* and *romanza* over the *bravura aria* in the Italian manner.[22]

Spanish tonadillas were immediately successful in Mexico, and many of them were performed in the late eighteenth and early nineteenth centuries at the Coliseo de México in the capital.[23] The production of indigenous tonadillas, such as "La Solterita," "México adorado," "El paseo de Ixtacalaco," and "La patera," became popular during the last few decades of the nineteenth century. The tonadilla reached Mexico at a time when the liberation struggle was gathering momentum, and the repression by the country's Spanish ruling class was strong. Strict censorship was applied by the Inquisition authorities. As a protest against the Spanish tunes (*peteneras, malagueñas, fandangos, olés,* [Spanish] *tangos, ayayays, cañas,* and others), native songs were included in the tonadilla, which thus became a meeting point for melody repertoires and styles.[24]

A number of tonadilla texts have been preserved in Mexican folklore, but the fate of the melodies is uncertain.[25] Mendoza believes that 60 percent of the country's treasury of folk music may consist of melodies originally derived from the tonadilla.[26] This is merely conjecture; even if certain texts have been preserved, the melodies may have been changed, or the original ones replaced. Mendoza's theory may, however, be justified in the case of melodies that resemble one another and are related by text, which implies they have a common origin. Raúl Hellmer suggests that identical text strophes are found in *sones* from Veracruz, Guerrero, Michoacán, Oaxaca, and Jalisco.[27] Unfortunately, there is no thorough reference work to consult concerning melodies.

According to Mendoza, a typical feature of the tonadilla are shouts such as *caramba, tirana, cielito, canelo, moreno, monona, mi vida, Cecilia, caray,* and so forth. These words, introduced by the tonadilla musicians to counter-balance the musical (actually textual) period of the seguidilla, are found in many Mexican folk songs.[28]

Native Mexican folk music was performed not only in tonadillas, but was also sung and played between the acts of theatrical plays.* In reference to this practice, Mayer-Serra makes the following observation:

> Towards the end of the Colonial epoch, numerous Mexican songs and dances had achieved a preeminent place, equivalent to that of the Spaniards, in the alluded interludes [between the acts of plays]. Among the Mexican songs, the forms of a Negro precedence and those of an Indian "argument" were the most popular. The most appreciated tunes were "La bamba," "La jarana," and the *sonecitos* of the Negros, such as "El bejuquito," "El chirripampli," "La indita," "El zanganito," and "La chipacuará."[29]

The performance of native music at theatres in Mexico City seems to have become more frequent in the mid-nineteenth century. In the early 1860s, when Benito Juárez led the struggle against the French intruders, many Mexican songs and dances, including the famous "Jarabe tapatío" (then known as the "Jarabe nacional") were presented in nationalist plays, and to some extent in Spanish *zarzuelas* performed in the capital. One of the men responsible for the increased popularity of native music was the Mexican opera composer Melesio Morales (1838–1908). Sordo Sodi explained that Morales started printing *sones*, calling them *aires nacionales*. They were performed in the theatre, played mostly on the piano and at times also sung. Among the sones thus promoted in the theatre were "La india frutera," "Guayabas," and "Limas."[30]

The *zarzuela*, a type of Spanish musical comedy, was introduced

---

*Many of which were colloquially called *folla*.

by visiting zarzuela troupes. According to Carlos Vega, the zarzuela reached Mexico in 1859.[31] Mayer-Serra states that during the Juárez epoch, the zarzuela sometimes presented the Mexican viewpoint, adopting native canciones as an effective means of creating a regional atmosphere. This technique was in keeping with the original development of the zarzuela in Spain; the music was always based on the folk traditions of the setting.[32] The popularity of the zarzuela in Mexico culminated in the 1880s, in the Porfirian era; by then it had lost most of its nationalistic significance.[33]

The popularity of the zarzuela has waned, but performances have not ceased altogether. In 1971 two traditional Spanish zarzuelas were performed at the Bellas Artes theatre, "La verbena de la paloma" (music by Tomás Bretón, 1894) and "La dolorosa" (music by José Serrano, 1930).[34] Both these plays belong to a kind of short zarzuela (*género chico*) that originated in Spain in the 1890s. This kind of zarzuela, which consists of only one act, was adopted by Mexican writers in the beginning of the twentieth century and renamed the *sainete*.[35] The first sainete to be performed in Mexico was called "Chin chun chan"; the music was composed by Luis G. Gorda, a Spaniard, and the text was written by a Mexican, José F. Elisondo. The plot is a comedy of errors, set in a hotel in Mexico City. The cast includes China's ambassador to Mexico.

From the late eighteenth century on, Spain was to a great extent replaced by France as an arbiter of taste, mainly among those members of Mexico's urban population who followed European cultural trends. Salon dances such as the minuet and later the waltz, polka, mazurka, and schottische, were imported from Paris. Italian opera was introduced into Mexico City in the 1820s. The *bel canto* style of singing became very popular in the capital and was also incorporated into folk music traditions.

Some Spanish Genres in Mexico

The folk traditions of Spain have changed a great deal since they were first imported to Mexico centuries ago. They have blended with Indian and African influences to become specifically Mexican.

Despite this assimilative process, some elements of the Spanish tradition appear to have been retained more or less in their original form.

Otto Mayer-Serra, the Mexican musicologist who died in 1968, explains the situation as follows in his excellent pamphlet, *The Present State of Music in Mexico:*

> Four centuries are not sufficient to integrate in folk music the elements necessary to form a wide repertory of generic types, highly original and exclusively its own. . . . Mexican folk music has hardly any musical substance that cannot be easily related to the alien materials that have formed it in the course of time. Despite this the transformation has been sufficiently vigorous to convert the quantity of assimilated elements into a new musical quality.[36]

The folk music imported from Spain during the initial colonial period was based to a great extent on genres that can be classified in literary terms, for example, the *copla, décima,* and *romance.*[37] These and other literary genres were transplanted to Mexico and there formed an important part of folk poetry.

The *copla* is a verse of four lines (occasionally as many as eight), usually consisting of eight syllables per line, with the second and fourth lines rhyming. Coplas may be sung or recited. They are often humorous and satirical. Coplas may occur independently or as part of specific musical genres. In southeastern Mexico, coplas are often improvised according to the Andalusian custom and given the name of *bomba.*[38]

Sung coplas (*coplas cantadas*) are generally set in 6/8 time, as are most folk songs of Spanish derivation.[39] The melodies are often sequential and always syllabic. The rhythm of the accompaniment is borrowed from the various regions' store of traditional rhythms. (See Example 1.)

The *décima* consists of one or more stanzas of ten octosyllabic lines, frequently introduced by a *glosa,* a quatrain establishing the basic subject.[40] Like coplas, décimas can deal with almost any aspect of human life. Décimas may be independent, but they can also be included in larger pieces. They occur in *valonas,* a genre of folk music centered in Jalisco. The texts of *huapangos* from Veracruz may also consist of décimas. The décima is a Spanish verse form of long standing; its classical rhyme scheme, which is often

Example 1. "Flor, blanca flor" from Péribán, Michoacán, (1926)—
Vicente Mendoza, *Canciones mexicanas,* pp. 3–4

used in Mexico is ABBAACCDDC.[41] (For the romance, see chapter 3.)

It is mentioned above that certain Spanish genres survive in Mexico. This is true of the fandango, which in Spain is mostly a pair dance, always in 3/4 time, whereas in Mexico it is either a pair or group dance combining 3/4 and 6/8 time.[42] In all likelihood the fandango was brought to New Spain in the eighteenth century as theatrical music and perhaps even earlier as folk music. In the nineteenth century the word fandango took on a generic significance as the designation of dance music and fiestas in the Veracruz area.[43] Today the fandango (or *fandanguito*) is still centered in the state of Veracruz. But whereas it is generally called *huapango* or *son jarocho* in northern and central Veracruz, fandango still has a generic significance in the southern part of the state.[44]

Fandangos occur in other states of Mexico as well. In Jalisco, fandango is the name generally applied to the fast ternary introductory movement of the *jarabe* dances. Téllez Girón reports that in the mountains of eastern Puebla *son de fandango* is the name traditionally given to sones played in dance halls.[45]

In Spain the malagueña is generally regarded as a variation of the fandango. According to Mendoza, four different types of malagueña have been recorded in the state of Guerrero, a region that is very rich in folklore; Mendoza gives transcriptions of two malagueñas, from Balsas and Costa Chica (See Examples 2 and 3).[46] The introduction and interlude of the malagueña from Balsas shows definite signs of Phrygian modality, typical of Andalusian folk music. Malagueñas also occur in other states, from Jalisco to Yucatán.

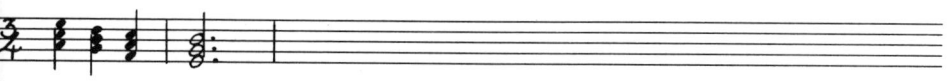

Example 2. Phrygian cadenza

Example 3. Two measures from "La malagueña," from Balsas, Guerrero—Mendoza, *Panorama de la música tradicional de México*, Ex. 185

The term *zapateado* means "heel step" (from *zapato*, "shoe"). Heel dancing; also known as *zapateo*, is typical of fandangos and huapangos from eastern Mexico and jarabes from Jalisco and other states. The following short description of the Cuban zapateo dance given by Emilio Grenet in 1939 also holds true of the Mexican zapateado or zapateo:

> The dance is executed by couples, man and woman facing each other some distance apart, marking the fluent rhythm with the feet and keeping the body motionless. The heel strikes the floor, the short steps of the dancers and the rhythm in general of the gestures which accent the dance could be no more eloquent as regards the origin of the dance. In its entirety it is a variation of the choreographic expression of Andalusia.[47]

In Mexico the name "zapateado" is sometimes applied to songs and dances displaying certain kinds of rhythm regardless of whether heel steps are used or not. In Jalisco, for example, a number of folk songs are called "zapateado." The name seems to be especially flexible in the Isthmus of Tehuantepec in Oaxaca, where almost any kind of traditional instrumental tune, above all those performed by marimba groups, may be called "zapateado."[48]

Example 4. Zapateado rhythm from Jalisco—Mendoza, "El folklore y la musicología," p. 22

A number of dances that originated in Spain later arrived in modified form from Cuba. This is the case with the tango, which exists in an Andalusian (6/8–3/4 time) and in an Afro-Cuban (2/4) version; the latter was developed in Argentina.[49] The bolero appears in Spanish 3/4 and Cuban 2/4 time. In these dances the Spanish forms are almost extinct, superseded by the Cuban versions.[50]

The *sandunga* is a melody that possesses a strong Spanish flavor, although it in no way adheres to the Andalusian style. The sandunga has long been a traditional tune in the Isthmus of Tehuantepec in the state of Oaxaca; from there its popularity spread throughout Mexico.

As is the case with so many Mexican melodies, romantic myths surround the origin of the sandunga. One of them claims that a military leader on the Isthmus, Máximo Ramón Ortiz, wrote the song in connection with his mother's death in 1853. According to Hugo de Grial, this is reflected in the following lines:

> Ay, sandunga, sandunga, mamá por diós!
> sandunga no seas ingrata
> mamá de mi corazón![51]

Another version has it that the sandunga was imported from Spain as part of a "Jaleo de Jerez" or "Jaleo Andaluz" performed at the Teatro Nacional in the capital in the early 1850s. This explanation was given by Saldívar, who considers the "nga" ending to be purely African.[52] Grial, however, suggests that the name *sandunga* is Zapotecan, "saáa" meaning music, "ndu" profound, and "ngaa" this ("this profound music").[53]

Neither of these theories appears to be wholly reliable. Saldívar's theory assumes that the melody of the sandunga has not changed since the 1850s; Grial refutes this.[54] On the other hand, Grial may be mistaken in stating that Ortiz wrote the sandunga. Although Ramón Ortiz published "La sandunga" in his name, it was most likely just his adaptation of an earlier Isthmian folk melody of Spanish origin.

A large portion of the mestizo folk music tradition in Oaxaca seems to have derived its intonation from "La sandunga" and "La llorona," tunes that closely resemble each other. In Oaxaca they act as "model melodies" for songs accompanied by guitar or marimba.

The sandunga also resembles a very well-known Basque folk melody; in recent years new lyrics attacking the late Francisco Franco ("Gallo negro") were added to this song. However, it cannot be assumed that the Basque folk song is really older than the sandunga. The only evident fact is that the sandunga obviously adheres to a Spanish melody pattern, as does "La llorona."

Mayer-Serra describes the sandunga as a mixture of the *jota* and a drawing room waltz.[55] The jota reached its peak in nineteenth-century northern Spain.[56] Radiating from Navarre, Valencia, Aragón, and parts of Castile, the local variations of the jota arrived in Latin America early in the nineteenth century. Vega states that the jota was integrated into Argentine culture in three ways: 1) as popular dance music; 2) as theatre music, and; 3) as concert performance pieces in the form of a theme with variations. This is a striking parallel to the functions of the Mexican jarabe of the same period.

The jota affected Mexican music, too. Spanish jota melodies (in modified form) can be found all the way from Jalisco to Yucatán. A certain jota influence is apparent in the jarabe and jarana dances, also. The dancers customarily lift their feet one at a time about four inches above the ground while performing slow movements; the dancers' arms are held in a raised position, and they snap their fingers like castanets. Both of these stylistic features are typical of the jota.[57] The quick and gay ternary melodies of the Yucatecan jarana also suggest a strong jota influence.[58]

To sum up, the mestizo cultural traditions developed concurrently with Mexico's struggle for independence from Spain, a movement that began gaining strength during the late eighteenth century. Yet the Spanish genres, imbued with African elements, have survived in a variety of forms, based on textual structure, rhythm, melody, or choreography. However, they have been gradually transformed. In many cases Spanish characteristics, such as certain rhythmic formulas, the Phrygian cadenza, the heel dance, and the improvisation of coplas, were taken from their original context and incorporated in the new genres that came into being in the mestizo folk music.

Moreover, the mestizos have developed their own characteristic kinds of ensemble, as for example the mariachi band, equivalents of which are not to be found in Spain. On the other hand, Spanish "flamenco" playing on the guitar, which probably developed from the sung and danced folk music of the gypsies in Andalusia in the nineteenth century, is not found in Mexico. Spanish nomenclature has survived mainly in the Veracruz area and in parts of Guerrero, where the impact of Spanish folk music has been especially strong. In other parts of Mexico, the Spanish dance names are loosely applied or totally obscured by Mexican designations such as son, huapango, jarabe, jarana, and mariachi.

The Son and the Huapango

The development of the son provides a good example of the ways in which Spanish song and dance types, combined with Indian traditions and African rhythms, have influenced Mexico's traditional folk music.[59]

As stated above, the son originated from Spanish danzas cantadas (fandango, malagueña, and others), which were brought to Mexico in the Colonial period.[60] In social terms the son shows interesting parallels to the Andalusian songs and dances. Insofar as their history can be followed, the folk music traditions of Andalusia were influenced to a great extent by gypsy music, which was a means of protest by an oppressed people. For much the same reasons the son in Mexico was originally performed by mestizos, and possibly Negroes. In the eighteenth century, both of these folk music traditions were introduced to audiences in Madrid and Mexico City, respectively, through the tonadilla escénica.[61]

The term son is not easily defined. Colloquially it is often used to denote simply an instrumental folk tune, regardless of musical style. On the other hand, musicologists such as Mendoza and Sordo Sodi define sones in accordance with specific characteristics, primarily the rhythmic complexity of the music and the subject spheres. The following discussion will deal with the son in terms of the latter definition.[62]

In the words of Sordo Sodi, the son is the heart of Mexico's instrumental folk music. Mendoza characterizes the spirit of the son as enthusiasm, liveliness, and brilliance.[63] The son is imbued with rhythmic vitality, frequently alternating between 6/8 and 3/4 time, which produces a certain "limping" effect. Stanford calls this kind of rhythm "sesquialtera" and traces it to early Mediterranean forms.[64] Similar rhythms are found in many areas of the Latin American continent.[65] Sones are most common in the tropical regions of Mexico.

Example 5. Four examples of sesquialtera—Mendoza, *Panorama de la música tradicional de México*, pp. 69–70

Sones usually begin with an instrumental section which may be called fandango or *sinfonía*. This is followed by a sung part consisting of improvised coplas, which can have a sung or purely instrumental refrain. The instrumental introduction may also serve as an interlude between the verses of the song.[66]

Sones are often imitative in regard to both vocal and instrumental effects and choreography. They imitate animals and human stereotypes. This is reflected in the titles: "Las moscas" ("The Flies"), "El mosquito," "El burro," and "El venado" ("The Stag"); among sones representing human types are: "El distinguido," "El currataco" ("The Elegant One"), and "El maracumbé."[67] Sones may also be titled after fruits and plants. Animals, as well as fruits and plants, very often symbolize women. Lovemaking is an eternal theme for sones.[68]

Sones, in the specific sense outlined above, display a rather uniform style regardless of the area in which they originate. Nevertheless, there are regional (local) characteristics relating to instrumentation, repertoire, and choreography. Sones have different names according to regions (*son veracruzano, son huasteco, son michoacano,* and so forth).[69] In the eastern parts of Mexico sones are frequently called huapango.[70]

There are different theories concerning the etymology of the word "huapango." One of them suggests that the term derives from the Aztec word *cuahpanco,* meaning the spot over which a piece of wood is placed. Another theory states that the term refers to the Huaxtecas living by the river Pango ("Panúco"), and that huapango is further used to designate the art of these aborigines. Still another theory claims that huapango is a corruption of fandango.[71]

The word huapango is used both as a designation of fiestas in eastern Mexico and of the dance music (notably sones) performed at these fiestas. Henry Schmidt states that "these huapango fiestas may go on for days and almost always last an entire night."[72]

The huapango is associated with four main regions in eastern Mexico: the Huastec region, comprising northern Veracruz, southern Tamaulipas, Hidalgo, parts of San Luis Potosí and Querétaro; central Veracruz, especially the vicinity of Alvarado and Tlacotalpán; southern Veracruz (south of Los Tuxtlas); and eastern Puebla.[73]

In central and southern Veracruz, sones are generally called *huapango, son jarocho,* or *baile de tarima. Jarocho* is the name for the people of the area; *tarima* means stage. The name derives from the fact that by tradition sones huapangos are danced on square wooden stages.[74]

The jarocho ensembles generally include a large diatonic harp, usually with thirty-two strings (*arpa grande*), which engages in intricate rhythmic interplay with the *requinto* (or *cuatro,* or *guitarra de golpe*), a small guitar used to carry the melody; it generally has four strings and is played with a plectrum. The jarocho ensembles also include the *jarana,* a small guitar found in three different sizes with five to twelve strings tuned according to the dictates of local tradition. The jarana is used to set the rhythm and to play chords. In the Alvarado region, conjuntos jarochos may include ordinary Spanish guitars and Afro-Cuban rhythms as well.[75]

The port of Veracruz has always been the main entryway for Spanish culture. It is not surprising to find a strong Spanish (especially Andalusian) flavor in the music of this state. One of the traces of Spanish culture that is found all over southeastern Mexico is the improvisation of copla verses. In huapango these artful coplas are sung or recited by a single performer; then all the musicians join in for the refrain.[76]

Huapango choreography bears a close resemblance to modern flamenco dancing; this similarity is apparent in the heel work, called zapateado. The fiery stamping of feet, creating an intense dialogue with the music, constitutes the most typical aspect of son (huapango) choreography.[77]

There are two common types of dances: couple dances for virtuosos (*bailes de pareja*), and dances for everyone (*baile de montón*). Vásquez Santa Ana has given an interesting description of a baile de montón at a huapango fiesta.

> One hour after the announcement or invitation, a huge crowd of men, women, and children gather at the spot where the event is to take place. In the grove [enramadas] large platforms [tarimas] are at times erected for the dancers. These platforms are placed over holes to act as sounding boards. The musicians begin by playing the instrumental part, then accompany the singing. During the instrumental introduction the dancers gather in files, men and women facing each other. The man invites the woman to dance by placing himself beside her, making his bow [caravana] with all possible gallantry and chivalry; the woman accepts of course, being unable to resist such an amiable invitation. The caballero, who during this act has been standing with the sombrero in his hand, now puts it on his head. The dancers begin by moving slowly, performing beautiful rhythms [stamping their feet], their faces solemn and arms dropped. During the course of the dance, the movements become more excited [*violento*]. In the first measures the music is slow. Men and women take a step forward, then a step back, moving gently to the right and then to the left. While the dance speeds up, the singers are heard at intervals, performing verses such as this:

> Sólo vestido de blanco
> a torear una ternera;
> no hablo porque no hay campo
> no porque mi amor no quiera;
> yo soy aquel que le canto
> siendo mujer, a cualquiera.

Having finished the song, which is sung falsetto, they cry out an extended "ay," smoothly and emotionally. Then the pace of the music increases. The pairs continue to stamp out the rhythm [siguen zapateando]; by and by they move forwards and backwards. Finally the dancers change places, continually renewing the pattern of the dance almost at every measure.[78]

Carmen Sordo Sodi stated that there also used to be a caller, or *conductor de huapango*, who announced the dancers' entrances in relation to the lyrics of the sones. This custom has gradually died out.[79]

Virtuoso huapango dancing was described in the late nineteenth century in an account of "La danza de la banda" given by Antonio García Cubas.[80] The dancers used their feet to turn a colorful piece of cloth lying on the ground into three rosettes, never slackening their intense zapateado. This dance is performed by the Ballet Folklórico de México to the huapango tune of "La bamba."

Huapangos performed in the jarocho area of Veracruz are among the most powerful folk music in Mexico and therefore of national interest. They are often performed in Mexico City and in other areas when events of national importance are celebrated. Some typical melodies are "La bamba," "El siguisirí," "El cascabel," and "La indita."

In the Huastec region, sones are generally called huapango or son huasteco.[81] The composition of the *conjunto huasteco* differs somewhat from that of the jarocho ensembles. In northern Veracruz the conjuntos consist of a violin (to carry the melody), a jarana, and a *guitarra quinta*, a five-coursed guitar, which is sometimes replaced by an ordinary six-stringed one. The number of instruments may be reduced by excluding either the jarana or the quinta. On the other hand, a small harp may be included in the conjunto, although at present the harp seems to be disappearing in this area.[82] The repertoire, performance techniques, and choreography have been somewhat influenced by the music of the jarocho region, but the Huastec area still has a core group of its own sones, for example, "El llorar," "El huateque," and "La chuparosa."

The huapango huastecos of Hidalgo and San Luis Potosí are generally slower than those of northern Veracruz and southern Tamaulipas, and the choreography contains less heel work. The ensembles are composed of a violin, jarana, *huapanguera* (a five-coursed instrument, usually of eight or ten strings), and an ordinary six-stringed guitar.[83] Occasionally the ensembles also include a cane flute. Among the traditional sones in San Luis Potosí are "Cielito lindo," "El agua nieve," and "El caimán."

Falsetto cries are a typical feature of the huapango huasteco, although they are becoming less common. The musicians have a characteristic way of playing the violin, straight, without a vibrato. The singers (usually two) perform in bright voices, always antiphonally. In the mountain areas, sones huastecos are played by both mestizos and Indians, since these ethnic groups live close together. The Indians pick up mestizo sones, but play them more slowly and with less rhythmic complexity. Sones are performed both at ceremonies and at social dances. Antonio Coss stated that he had heard the son "El costumbre" played by two Otomí Indians at a ceremony. He also explained that the musicians are paid only when they perform at ceremonies, not when they play for social dances.[84] In the Huastec area, sones are also played by brass bands, consisting mainly of trumpets, clarinets, cornets, and a drum. The repertoire ranges from traditional sones to recent commercial hits. The musicians have low social status, playing for money at ranches and small villages.[85]

In the western states of Mexico, the word huapango does not seem to be used as a designation for traditional sones. The son tradition of Michoacán is believed to have derived from the Spanish (Basque?) *zorzico* dance, which is composed of a mixture of 3/8 and 2/8 time, resulting in 5/8 measures. Consequently, the *son michoacano* is often called zorzico, regardless of whether or not it is composed of 5/8 measures.[86] The typical son ensemble in Michoacán, the *conjunto de arpa grande*, consists of two violins, a *vihuela* (a guitar that generally has eight strings arranged in five courses), a jarana, and a harp; a *tamboreo* (drumming effect) is performed on the soundboard of the harp by a drummer using both hands. In Guerrero, Jalisco, and some other states, the harp has been replaced by a *guitarrón* (bass guitar with four or five gut strings). This kind of ensemble is called mariachi, especially in the state of Jalisco.[87]

Thomas Stanford, who has carried out field research in these areas of Mexico, makes the following statement about sones performed in San Miguel Totolapán, Guerrero:

> As far as musical form is concerned, the sones of the area under discussion here normally contain from two to four verses, with a refrain following each one—and normally derived from it textually. The son begins with an instrumental introduction, based on the melody of the verse, which is played in thirds and sixths by the two violins. In only the malagueña and a few other pieces in the regional repertoire do the violins not play in thirds and sixths, and then they play in unison. The violins do not normally play while there is singing, or at most they may strum—more for appearance than for sound. There may be one to three voices involved in singing the verses, and these may sing in pairs (in thirds and sixths), or singly answering one another (singing in three-part harmony is an affectation, derived from the influence of radio, television, and motion pictures). Often one voice may sing nonsense syllables in the refrain, while the two voices that sing the verse answer it with fragments of the previous couplet to which the refrain is being appended. The final cadence is usually a regional stereotype, and is the same regardless of the son being performed. . . . Some few sones of the region under discussion may contain short modulations in their refrains or in a short section inserted between their refrains and the return to the instrumental introduction preceding the next verse. These modulations most often are to the subdominant, or, if the son is in a minor key, to the mediant or relatively major (the pivot chord may be the supertonic in this case). Some few sones may be in the minor turning suddenly major on the same tonic in the refrain; but this trait is far more common with the chilena. The modulation to the subdominant, however, seems to be a very special tendency of the gustos from the region of San Miguel Totolapán, Guerrero.[88]

In general the sones (huapangos) of Mexico could be characterized as extensive variations on basic melodic modal patterns.

The same tune can change considerably from one performance to the next. The harmony frequently creates two simultaneous planes, which might be described as "tonic" and "dominant." Moreover, the harmonies can give the impression of being independent of the melody line. These traits are probably derived from Spain. (See Example 6.)

The dance *jarana* (not to be confused with the instrument jarana) is sometimes considered to be a type of son, although it does not possess any of the characteristics mentioned above. Instead the

Example 6. "La malagueña," as played by Conjunto Los Madrugadores de Jesús Espinosa from Apatzingan, Michoacán. Transcribed by the author from tape 29 in INBA's files. The instruments (except for the violin) were separately recorded. Note the rhythmic complexity created by the harp; in addition, there is incidental tamboreo on the frame of the harp, a typical feature of this area of Mexico. The text of the vocal line is not included in this transcription.

etc.

choreography and music bear a certain resemblance to the jota, a quick northern Spanish folk dance in 3/4 or 3/8 time. The jarana, which has a repertoire all its own, is played by wind orchestras on the Yucatán peninsula and Tehuantepec promontory, areas that are removed from the cultural mainstream.[89]

As previously stated, the repertoires vary considerably from area to area. In some cases, however, a son that was once regional can attain nationwide popularity and be molded into a single standard version. This happened to "La bamba" from Veracruz, which was launched by jarocho groups in Mexico City in 1945.[90] On the other hand, songs that have a standard title and text may differ greatly as far as the lyrics and melody are concerned. Such is the case with "Cielito lindo."

According to Sordo Sodi, the earliest reference made to "Cielito lindo" dates from the end of the eighteenth century. "Cielito lindo" may have been performed in tonadillas at the Coliseo Theatre in Mexico City, as was the tune "El butaquito," to which "Cielito lindo" is said to be related. Nowadays "Cielito lindo" is a popular son in Guerrero and the Huastec area.[91]

In the twentieth century a commercial waltz canción based on the traditional text has become immensely popular all over America and Europe. The melody bears no resemblance at all to the huapango "Cielito lindo." There are several composers who claim to have written the canción "Cielito lindo." In Mexico Quirino F. Mendoza is generally regarded as its composer. According to Juan S. Garrido, however, that is highly unlikely. In fact, some doubt arises as to whether the melody is Mexican at all. Garrido believes it was originally a Spanish song.

In addition to the traditional sones that have been discussed, a number of Mexican songs are colloquially called *canciones huapangueadas* or *huapangos lentos*.[92] These are songs of fairly recent composition, written in huapango rhythm, that preserve to an extent the gay and picaresque character of sones. Huapangos lentos are performed by commercial groups in a variety of "authentic" styles, and by troubadours with guitar accompaniment. "La cuera," "Traicionera," and "Serenata huasteca" are three very well-known Mexican canciones performed in huapango rhythm.[93]

Mexican composers have a natural tendency to write in the musical style that prevails in their home territory. Lorenzo

Barcelata from Veracruz writes and performs his tunes in the jarocho style; in his huapangos Nicandro Castillo draws on the Huastec tradition. Barcelata and Castillo perform both traditional and modern huapangos with their orchestras.[94] It is nearly impossible for an outsider to determine whether these tunes are newly composed or not.

During the last few decades, sones have been incorporated into the repertoire of trumpet mariachi bands with increasing frequency and success. For studio recordings the bands are generally enlarged with entire string sections and instruments alien to the traditional sones, such as the saxophone and marimba. In these modernized sones, the element of improvisation, so important in the authentic folk music, is totally eliminated.

The kind of huapango that is performed in the Huastec area of Mexico generally provides the rhythm for these "meso-huapangos," unless otherwise stated in the score.[95] However, son rhythms do not differ much from region to region. The rhythmic beat of the bass in "Tata Dios" by Valeriano Trejo is certainly very characteristic of the huapango huasteco; this beat is also common in troubadour singing of huapango lento (then accentuated on the guitar). It is also found in South America, for example, in the Argentine *zamba* and the Chilean *cueca*. (See Example 7.)

The distinctive feature of this type of rhythm is the simultaneous use, the synthesis, of duple and triple time. (See Examples 8 and 9.) The resulting complexity, which also involves constant alternations between 6/8 and 3/4 time, can hardly be described in words—it must be experienced!

The son rhythms have not been studied in depth. Further examination (which is beyond the scope of this survey) reveals a number of problems. In transcribing a piece, the mere choice of time signature can cause difficulty. The polyrhythms often make it impossible to distinguish the anacrusis from the first beat in the measure. The polyrhythmic layering of duple and triple time is accentuated by varying stress. The guitarist(s) draws attention to unstressed beats by rapidly scraping his fingers over the strings, then immediately dampening the tone with the palm of his hand; the interrupted chord is heard as if it were emphasized. This effect is often used on the fifth quaver in 6/8 time.

Juan S. Garrido expressed the opinion that the complicated

Example 7. "Tata Dios," huapango by Valeriano Trejo. Measures 9 through 16 of the verse. Note the last two measures which recall the style of authentic haupango huasteco. This song more properly belongs to the meso-huapango category.

rhythms of the huapango have prevented it from attaining real success, both within Mexico and beyond its borders.[96] I, however, believe that the vigorous rhythms are the life force of this music. My view is reinforced by the real success of several huapango recordings that have been made in other countries.

Live and studio recordings of authentic huapango groups are made regularly. A number of groups work on a commercial basis yet retain their traditional performance techniques and repertoires, which consist of older sones as well as newer ones. Thus even modern huapangos, played by commercial groups, may be recorded in traditional styles. Live performances of sones are becoming rare. Fifteen years ago jarocho bands played on every street corner in the city of Veracruz. Nowadays a jarocho band is hardly to be found in that town, and authentic haupango music can only be heard in certain villages.[97]

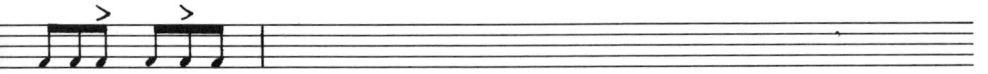

Example 8. Typical rhythm of Mexican sones.

Example 9. Two examples of rhythm in Jaliscian sones—Paul Bowles, "On Mexico's Popular Music," p. 227

The Jarabe and the Valona

The jarabe is a choreographic genre consisting of a series of dances.[98] The melodies vary according to local tradition, but a core group of tunes seems to be standard throughout the country. Originally the jarabe may have consisted exclusively of sones in the sense defined in the previous section. In the course of the nineteenth century, however, the repertoire was renovated in accordance with the latest musical imports from Europe and Cuba, especially the waltz. The Spanish jota was probably also influential.

The jarabe as a folk music form is most firmly established in the state of Jalisco. The famous jarabes include "Jarabe de la botella" and "Jarabe largo," also known as "Jarabe jalisciense."[99] Yet Jalisco is by no means the only region to cultivate the jarabe; many other Mexican states have their jarabes, for example, Oaxaca, with its famous "Jarabe mixteco," Michoacán, with the "Jarabe michoacano," and Coahuila, with the "Jarabe pateño."[100]

In all its varieties the jarabe is a courtship dance. The woman dancer, dressed in a *vestido de china poblana*, taps her feet to entice her partner; at the same time she avoids him with grace and agility.[101] The zapateado is the same as that performed in the huapango dance.[102]

The name *jarabe* actually means "syrup"; it may be related to *charape*, a drink from Michoacán made from brown sugar.[103] It may also derive from the Arabic *xarape*. The latter theory is supported by the association with the "Jarabe gatuno" ("Gypsy Jarabe") of Spain, which is regarded as the ancestor of the Mexican jarabe. Saldívar claims that in mid-eighteenth-century Spain the "Jarabe gatuno" was a degenerate version of the *seguidilla*, both in words and movements. Saldívar further suggests that the name *jarabe gatuno* was (and is?) also used in Mexico.[104]

The term jarabe occurs in late eighteenth-century Mexican sources. In 1778 the texts of a "Pan de jarabe" from Veracruz and a "Jarabe de manteca" from Pachuca were confiscated by the Spanish authorities. They are included in the Inquisition records at the Archivo General de la Nación in Mexico City. This is, in fact, the earliest mention of the jarabe in Mexico that exists. The Inquisition files of 1796 show a jarabe text, "Viaje al infierno," and in 1805 the following jarabe gatuno was confiscated:

> Veinte reales he de dar
> contados uno por uno
> sólo por verte bailar
> el jarabito gatuno.[105]

During the nineteenth century, the jarabe became widely diffused throughout Mexico; it radiated from two centers, the capital and Jalisco. In diverse regions it was acclimatized to local conditions by incorporating traditional tunes. According to Mendoza, the jarabe's development toward a chain of dances seems to have been gradual, but this theory may not be entirely correct.

At the turn of the nineteenth century, the jarabe evidently consisted of an instrumental introduction (called fandango or sinfonía) and sung copla verses with a refrain. The sung part could be repeated innumerable times. In his *Memoria de mi tiempo,* an important document concerning the cultural and political events of the early nineteenth century, Don Guillermo Prieto states that by 1830 jarabes consisted of an instrumental introduction, a copla, a zapateo (in fast tempo), a *descanso* (during which the dancers rested), and in conclusion a refrain. Thus the complete jarabe was made up of five parts.[106]

A significant collection of twenty-four *canciones* and *jarabes mexicanos,* published by J. Böhme in Hamburg around 1830, contains the following jarabe tunes: "El palomo," "Los enanos," "El perico," "El aforrado," "El ahualulco," and "La tapatía" (in subsequent collections called "El tapatío").[107] Some of these jarabe "airs" are mentioned by Calderón de la Barca around 1840 in her book, *La vida en México.*[108] Antonio García Cubas gives an account of current jarabe melodies in *Libro de mis recuerdos.*[109] Important collections that include jarabe tunes were published by Niceto Zamacois (1861), M. Murguía (1858), and Miguel Ríos Toledano (1884). Juan N. Cordero, who published *Música razonada* in 1897, listed the best-known jarabe tunes of his time: "El palomo," "El atole," "Los enanos," "El perico," and "La Diana." Cordero states that the latter tune used to be repeated in the chain of jarabe tunes, recurring as a kind of rondo.[110]

Most of the jarabes to which these authors refer can be considered as parts of the "nationalized" jarabe that apparently developed during the nineteenth century. The jarabe actually became a national dance. During Benito Juarez's campaign against Maximilian in the mid-1860s, elaborate performances of the jarabe were given in theatres in the French-held capital. At that time it was called the "Jarabe nacional" or the "Jarabe oficial."[111] Later the name was changed to "Jarabe tapatío."[112]

The term *"tapatío"* always refers to the people or events of Guadalajara, the state capital of Jalisco and Mexico's second city. By extension, the term is also applied to the entire state. The name "Jarabe tapatío" would suggest that this national dance, popularized in the theatre, originated in Jalisco. According to Saldívar, this is probably not so. Instead, he states, this "Jarabe tapatío" appears to be a chain of folk tunes from all over central Mexico; it used to include tunes such as "El palomo" and "Los enanos," which do not seem to have any distinctive connection to Guadalajara or Jalisco.[113] Some of the tunes may derive from tonadillas.[114]

If the "Jarabe tapatío" did not partly or fully originate in Jalisco, a theory that is by no means proven, it obviously took a strong foothold there. In 1913 a collection was published entitled *Verdadero Jarabe tapatío*, arranged for the piano by José de J. Martínez. It contains roughly the same tunes, with some exceptions, as did once the "Jarabe nacional," but arranged in an order as apparently performed in Jalisco in the early twentieth century.[115] Since 1913 the "Jarabe tapatío" has undergone still more changes. Nowadays the chain of tunes as performed, for example, by trumpet mariachis all over Mexico is completely standardized.

In the nineteenth century, jarabes were adopted by composers of art music for nationalistic purposes. Castellanos gives the following account of this process:

> In order to express their patriotism during the wars of independence, the Mexican composers reverted to arrangements of jarabes. In these movements of intense protest against the Spaniards, the music of the people, suppressed by the colonial authorities, attracted their attention. One of the oldest [art-] jarabes, "puesto para pianoforte por el C. José de Jesús de González Rubio," was composed around 1820. Another jarabe discovered by the author, with the very significant title "Jarabe insurgente" [rebellious jarabe], was composed by Jose Antonio Gómez, called "maestro de los maestros mexicanos." The later "Jarabe nacional" by Tómas León is outstanding, as is the waltz-jarabe by Ancieto Ortega, a title suggesting that jarabe is a species of the Mexican waltz.[116]

In this connection it is interesting to note that Felipe Villanueva, who is best known as a composer of romantic salon music for the piano, borrowed themes from the "Jarabe tapatío" for some of his compositions.[117]

Since 1940 the (revised) "Jarabe tapatío" has been standard in trumpet mariachi groups. It is also included in the repertoire of the Ballet Folklórico de México played on the original instruments, guitars, violins, and harp. As late as the 1920s jarabes were sung and danced in the streets and theatres of Mexico City by Jaliscian groups using these instruments.

The "Jarabe tapatío" became famous internationally through the efforts of Anna Pavlova. On her tour of Mexico in 1918, she recognized the possibility of converting the jarabe into a dance *aux pointes*. Pavlova created a ballet version which she included in her repertoire.[118] Her version was not adopted by other choreographers, but one aspect of it has become traditional in Mexico: the ladies dance on the rim of a large sombrero.[119] In retrospect, the main result of Pavlova's initiative was that the jarabe music became internationally known. At present the most famous tune in the tapatío is the fandango, which gained popularity as the "Mexican Hat Dance."[120]

The term son can be used to characterize the traditional jarabe tunes. Son, in the sense of "air," has also been used in reference to the nationalized jarabe. However, these nationalized jarabes are not always sones in the traditional sense—song dances with intricate polyrhythms and time changes. In fact, some jarabe tunes maintain the son rhythm as it was probably inherited from Spain, nearly unaltered in any way.[121] In any case, the simple triple time, derived from the waltz or jota, seems to be preeminent in the nationalized jarabe of the nineteenth century.[122]

In his *Panorama*, Mendoza includes seventy-two jarabe melodies arranged by meter.[123] This collection reveals that 3/4 and 6/8 time are most common, but 2/4 time may also occur.[124] The majority of the melodies are written in the major key (contrary to Cordero's statement that jarabe melodies are in 2/4 time, tend to be languid, and are written in the minor key).[125] Saldívar confirmed Mendoza's findings. He also stated that jarabes may contain seven parts.[126] Each part is generally composed of three sections with eight measures each; the first and third are purely instrumental, and the middle section is sung.

The *valona* is a chain formation of Spanish origin.[127] In the nineteenth century and even earlier, valonas acted as a kind of Mexican news service, in the same way that corridos did at a later time. They were carried to the people by wandering troubadours, who had the lyrics printed on leaflets which were sold at a low price. Valonas also resemble corridos in that they often describe misfortune, love, and crime. The genre is now declining but survives in certain forms. For example, valonas are performed at fiestas in parts of Jalisco, either independently or incorporated in jarabes.

Jalisco is the center for valonas in Mexico. Valonas of that region tend to begin with an instrumental sinfonía, which is followed by the sung part beginning with a sharp, drawn-out "ay," that finally comes to rest an octave lower after diverse melismata.[128] The basic structure of the valona consists of either sung or recited *plantas* and décimas (metric forms); a planta in the form of a copla followed by four décimas is particularly common.[129] The rhapsodic vocal sections (preferably coplas and décimas) have little accompaniment. They alternate with instrumental sections in 2/4 time, performed by two violins, guitars, and harp. As a coda, the musicians play a lively son in ternary rhythm.

In the region of Tuxcueca, Jalisco, Mendoza found a type of valona whose composition is quite extensive. It consists of a *sinfonía,* a *planta,* two *décimas,* an *arrebol,* two *décimas,* and a *despedida* ("farewell").[130] Mendoza states that the sinfonía may be inserted at several points to provide variation. The melody of the planta and the despedida are identical, always nonrhythmically conceived and modal in character; this melody also serves as the basis of the décimas. The arrebol, on the other hand, is generally in a major key and in a regular rhythm.

2

Mariachi, Norteño, and Marimba Ensembles

The Mariachi

In the preceding chapter I have shown how the son developed in different directions. The huapango, in the form of canciones huapangueadas and commercial meso-huapangos, lost its choreography and regional types of instrumentation. The rhythm, in a relatively standardized version, remained the lowest common denominator of the genre.

The jarabe followed a different path, in that the choreography determined the genre, notwithstanding the new dance steps that were created in the "Jarabe tapatío" on stage. Triple time came to dominate the jarabe, once the waltz, the mazurka, and the jota were introduced into Mexico at the beginning of the nineteenth century.

The son will now be discussed from the viewpoint of a standardized ensemble type, namely the mariachi.[1] To be accurate, there are actually *two* kinds of mariachi band in Mexico. The original mariachi, consisting of string instruments only, belongs to the realm of folk music. String mariachi bands are still to be found in the countryside of central Mexico.[2] Around 1940 a commercial type of mariachi began to develop, primarily in the cities. In these ensembles the original balance of the string instruments was altered by the addition of trumpets.[3] These two kinds of mariachi differ considerably from each other in repertoire and performance style. In the last few decades the folk music mariachi has nearly disappeared, and the mariachi has come to belong almost exclusively to the field of commercial music in Mexico.

The folk mariachi repertoire consists mainly of traditional sones. Sordo Sodi informed me that in parts of central Mexico, especially in the highlands of Jalisco which have long been the homeland of mariachi, there are still string mariachis that only play the traditional melodies of their region. This type of mariachi has become quite rare since the 1940s.[4]

The usual number of musicians in a folk mariachi is five. The conjunto used to consist of two violins, a vihuela, a harp, and a jarana. In the last few decades harps have been largely replaced by bass guitars. The ordinary six-stringed guitar is sometimes used, especially in urbanized areas. Stanford states that "where the introduction has been consolidated, [violins and guitarrones] tend to disappear and the ensemble is reduced to a guitar with a requinto, a smaller six-stringed guitar."[5]

The village of Tecalitlán, from which many famous mariachi musicians come, is reputed to be the center of folk mariachi in Jalisco. The trumpet mariachi has even gained popularity there. A famous commercial group calls itself Mariachi Vargas de Tecalitlán.[6]

The current interpretation of the word mariachi assumes it to be a Spanish rendering of the French *mariage*. It is therefore presumed that the name arose in connection with the wave of French culture that swept over Mexico during the emperor Maximilian's short reign (1864–67). According to this interpretation, the name *mariachi* was given during this period to the Jaliscian harp-violin-vihuela ensembles which used to go from wedding to wedding to play. The musicians were appropriately called *mariacheros*.[7]

J. I. Dávila Garibi suggests that the word "mariachi" stems from an old Cocan expression.[8] The Coca Indians, who lived in Jalisco, are now extinct. Traditionally the mariachi is associated with Cocula, Zacoalco, and some other communities in Jalisco, which were formerly part of the Coca territory.[9] Saldívar further informs me that in the 1870s a Mexican poet designated as "mariache" the stage upon which the dancers and musicians performed jarabes.[10] Saldívar stated that the name was not consistently applied to musical groups playing sones until the present century. This is particularly the case in the states of Michoacán, Jalisco, Guanajuato, Querétaro, and Aguascalientes. In any case, the evidence seems to indicate that the name mariachi (or mariache)[11] dates from a period when harp-violin-vihuela music became widely accepted as *the* festive music of its time, at least in Jalisco and its vicinity.

It may be that folk mariachi ensembles originally were the same as conjuntos de arpa grande. If so, the ensemble arrangement itself is older than the term mariachi, used as a designation of that conjunto. The concept of mariachi may have later influenced the original son repertoire of the violin-vihuela-harp ensembles. This hypothesis is probable, but not yet confirmed. Nevertheless, it is certain that the sones played by conjuntos de arpa grande are not essentially different from sones played by groups called mariachi in regard to instrumentation and style.[12]

It is difficult to trace the exact history of the mariachi during the nineteenth and early twentieth centuries. It may have paralleled that of the jarabe, which was deeply integrated into the musical life of the towns as national music, and then gradually brought back in a renewed form to rural areas.[13] The one important difference is that the mariachi does not seem to have been brought to Mexico City until the 1920s.[14]

The trumpet mariachi is a direct descendant of the harp mariachi. Castañeda states that during the late 1920s a large number of mestizos from all over the country came to Mexico City, which was then alive with a newly aroused nationalism in which music played an important part. At that time some harp mariachis from Jalisco visited the capital.[15]

According to Garrido, it was Emilio Azcárraga Vidaurreta who actually created the trumpet mariachi. Azcárraga was the main initiator and the director of radio station XEW, which opened in Mexico City in 1930. He wanted to broadcast mariachi music played by authentic Jalisco bands, but thought the sound was too thin for reproduction by radio. (The transmission of sound was not very advanced at that time.) He therefore suggested that the melody be carried by a more piercing instrument.[16] A trumpet was added and the harp omitted; the new mariachi ensemble came into being—trumpet (at first only one, later two or three), two or three violins, requinto (an ordinary six-stringed guitar) and guitarrón, with the guitarists also performing as vocalists.[17]

The trumpet mariachi was an immediate success and was widely imitated by the mariachi bands in the capital; new ensembles were formed. The success was such that the trumpet mariachi was soon the country's unofficial national ensemble. Since then the term mariachi is commonly associated only with the trumpet form of ensemble.

Nowadays the composition of the mariachi is completely standardized, except for studio recordings, in which entire string sections may be added or the ensemble supplemented with marimbas, harps, flutes, and saxophones. It was Rubén Fuentes who developed and cultivated the *mariachi sinfónico;* he has had a number of successors.[18]

Trumpet mariachis can be heard everywhere. They play for tourists at fashionable hotels and in squares such as the Plaza Garibaldi in Mexico City, or seated on flower-bedecked boats in the verdant, winding channels of Xochimilco. They are indispensable at the garden parties of the aristocracy and at political banquets. Moreover, many television programs and films overflow with mariachi music, tequila, tears, and national feelings.

Though there is no limit to the repertoire played by these bands, certain melodies never fail to turn up. Popular tunes such as "La negra" and "Guadalajara," and traditional songs such as "Las mañanitas" and "La golondrina" are played again and again. The melody selection seems to be relatively limited, though at times the latest hit songs, Mexican or international, are mingled with indigenous, traditional melodies.

The tourist mariachi acts as a kind of jukebox: offer a coin and listen to the tune of your choice. The different groups sound more or less alike; they use the same figuring in the respective songs and exactly the same performance style. The only variable is the skill of the musicians. Why is it that all trumpet mariachis use precisely the same arrangements, not only in the capital but throughout the country? The reason is probably that the melodies and stylistic elements are learned by ear and passed unchanged in this manner from group to group. The original arrangement may be a stock arrangement or a special one once written by Rubén Fuentes, Gustavo Santiago, or some other composer. Very few mariachi musicians can read music.[19]

The tourist mariachis are only capable of an impersonal repetition in a clichéd manner. Yet interest is kept alive by the characteristic sound, the mixture of the fanfare of trumpets, the scraping of the violins, and the vital plucking of the guitars. The song line, which runs in parallel thirds, is taken up by the guitarists after the instrumental prelude. The voices are vigorous. In terms of rhythm the modern mariachi covers a wide field, from son-like rhythm patterns in fast tunes to the ordinary waltz or flowing bolero in slow songs. As far as repertoire and performance style are concerned, however, there are but few similarities between tourist and folk mariachi.

The trumpet mariachi sound has left its imprint on much of Mexican popular music. Mariachi accompaniment to native canciones rancheras and boleros rancheros is standard. Mariachi ensembles can also bestow a national sound on melodies which were originally not Mexican at all.

At the local level, mariachi groups still fulfill the same functions that they have since the nineteenth century; only the repertoire, the instrumentation, and the terms of employment have changed. The mariachi conjuntos are now attached to trade unions. Mariachis are hired out for an evening, just like marimba and norteño bands, to heighten the gaiety at weddings, birthdays, and other festivities of an official or private nature. There are fixed fees per hour, per song, or per serenade.

An unusual arrangement well worth hearing is created by mariachi orchestras performing at so-called mariachi masses, at which mariachi groups provide the accompaniment for traditional religious songs and hymns. In 1971 Sordo Sodi stated that the mariachi has played this role for some ten years. She emphasized that the mariachi masses were significant in the renewal of the Catholic Church in Mexico. Music in the traditional style is also specially written for these masses. Mariachi masses are performed, for example, every Saturday at 7:00 P.M. in the church of Tlatelolco in Mexico City and every Sunday in the cathedral at Cuernavaca.[20]

The Norteño Band

The norteño groups, which, like mariachis, have their own characteristic instruments and performance styles, have also played a part in the contemporary "national" music. Norteño groups usually consist of three or four instrumentalists who are also the singers. They include a guitarist, an accordionist, a double bass player, and sometimes a performer on the rhythmic spoons. Polka time (2/4), imported from Europe in the early nineteenth century, completely dominates the music played and sung by the norteño bands; polkas are also often played solo on the accordion.

The origin and stronghold of the norteño music is northern Mexico (hence the name).[21] However, norteño groups are heard throughout the country. The style of singing *canciones norteñas* includes extending the final notes of the phrases peculiar to the ranchera. In effect the norteña is most accurately described as a species of ranchera songs.

According to Sordo Sodi, the polka rhythm was most likely associated with canciones norteñas at an early stage. She states that canciones norteñas were at one time accompanied on the vihuela. Beginning in 1850, harp, vihuela, and psaltery were used in the accompaniment of these songs. Around 1890 the jarana and guitar came into use; the accordion appeared still later.

In the 1920s (if not earlier) canciones norteñas became popular in the capital. From there they radiated all over the country. Juan S. Garrido stated in 1971 that the norteño ensemble as it is known today is no more than twenty-five years old. Most commercial norteña songs seem to be of recent composition and many new norteña songs are composed every year. Cornelius Reyna is said to be the foremost norteño singer of Mexico.

The Marimba Band

The marimba is an instrument often used in a commercial context.[22] It resembles a xylophone with tuned keys of cupapé wood and calabash sounding boards. The wooden keys, which are struck by rubber-covered hammers, are arranged like the keyboard of a piano (twelve halftones in each octave).[23] Marimbas vary in size. The marimba is played in many areas of Central America and northern South America, and it is Guatemala's national instrument. In all likelihood the prototype of the instrument was introduced on the American continent by Negro slaves from Africa in the sixteenth or seventeenth century.

The marimba has been played for centuries in the states of Chiapas, Oaxaca, and Tabasco. The rest of the country did not come into contact with the instrument until later. For a long time the repertoire consisted mainly of local melodies. During the nineteenth century the marimba repertoire was enriched by salon waltzes and marches, and later by danzones, boleros, and romantic canciones. In Oaxaca "La sandunga" and "La llorona" became popular marimba pieces. The melodies of Chiapas most often played now are the waltz "Las chiapanecas" and "El rescapetate"; the latter, which combines waltz and Afro-Cuban rhythm, was composed by Rafael de Paz.

The Gómez brothers formed a well-known marimba quartet from Chiapas which played both folk music and classical pieces by such composers as Paganini. This group was one of the first to move into Mexico City in the early 1920s. Its most famous successor was the Brothers Domínguez, who came from San Cristóbal de las Casas in the highlands of Chiapas. The Domínguez brothers played a leading part in the development of popular music in Mexico, not only as performers but also as composers. There were four brothers, Abel, Ernesto, Armando, and the most famous one, Alberto, who wrote such tunes as "Frenesí" and "Perfidia." Like so many other leading musicians in the 1930s, the Domínguez brothers were connected with XEW in Mexico City, the radio station with the country's largest audience.

Before the advent of the "talkies" in the 1920s, the marimba, like the piano, found a place in the cinema. The Domínguez brothers played for silent films, as did other famous marimba bands, such as the Brothers Marín and the Brothers Paniagua. This was the golden age of the marimba.

Even in the 1930s the marimba bands imported to Mexico City from the south consisted by tradition of members of one family; however, they could also be musicians who grew up in the same *barrio* or had some similar close connection. This *hermanos* tradition has been kept alive, especially in Chiapas, but it is on the decline. At a Saint's Day fiesta in San Cristóbal in July 1971 the music was provided by marimba groups of diverse origins; saxophone and trumpet had been added to the marimbas. The repertoire consisted exclusively of commercial music produced in Mexico City.

According to Zeferino Nandayapa, the majority of marimba musicians cannot read music, but learn the melodies by ear. They often pick up songs from the radio or records and rehearse them together. Each of the four musicians in a band has his own part to play in the ensemble. The first marimbist plays the melody, while the other three provide the countermelody, harmony, and bass, respectively. In addition the soloist is expected to improvise with runs and fast tremolos, preferably with four hammers; the other musicians consistently use two.[24]

The distribution of roles is constant in traditional hermanos bands; however, these are becoming rare in Mexico City. Because of the trade unions, groups are now made up of musicians from different places.[25] Nandayapa says that this is reflected in the bands' teamwork. (Nandayapa states that even the marimba band at the Ballet Folklórico de México is not a traditional one.)

There are two main sizes of marimba: the tenor marimba, ranging from two to four-and-one-half octaves, and the marimba grande, comprising six-and-one-half octaves, but intermediate sizes also exist. The largest instrument can by played by four men, the smallest by only one. When a group performs with two instruments, the soloist plays the smaller instrument (*el tiple*), while the other three play the larger one.[26]

Nowadays marimba bands are often enlarged with additional instruments: double bass, drum, saxophone, or others. Furthermore, the marimba often lends its special tremolo flavor to studio orchestras. Carmen Sordo Sodi states that most repertoires are not ensemble-bound. There are melodies intended for specific instruments, for example, "Al son de la marimba" by Abel Domínguez. A son, a canción, or some other type of composition may nevertheless be played by any group of instruments. Different types of ensembles have characteristic performance styles. Played on marimbas, the melodies tend to be fast in tempo, with rapid tremolos. Mariachis, on the other hand, slow down the tempo and use different figurings.

3

The Corrido

The corrido is generally regarded as "very Mexican."[1] It is primarily a literary genre, but can also be defined as a genre blending textual and musical elements.[2]

Two basic types of corrido exist in Mexico, the *romance corrido* and the *corrido mexicano;* they cannot, however, be precisely distinguished from one another. Some confusion also surrounds the use of the terms *corrido* and *romance*.[3] Even in the colonial era they may have been used synonymously.[4] Many books and articles deal with all aspects of the corrido.[5] Others concentrate on the typically Mexican corrido.[6] In this chapter I will trace the historical development of the corrido mexicano, dealing with its predecessor, the romance, as it relates to this process.

The origin of the romance lies in Spanish folklore, as is evidenced by the meter, melody, and range of subjects. The narrative technique and the topics of the romance are reminiscent of the northwestern European ballad, with the distinction that Spanish romances seldom have a refrain. Traditional Spanish romances, such as "La malmaridada," "Delgadina," "Las senas del esposo," "La misa de amor," and "La esposa difunta," are still transmitted orally in Mexico.

The romance tends not to take a strophic form, that is, it does not consist of coplas. Instead it is conceived as being composed of a varying number of related lines, usually with eight syllables per line.[7] The melody phrases are generally repeated at regular intervals, but there are also romances with melodies that change constantly.

An account of the early history of the romance in Spain is not within the scope of this book. It is interesting to note, however, that some romances preserved in Spanish manuscripts date from the Late Middle Ages.[8] Many of these romances (and *villancicos*) were probably elaborations of popular folk songs. They do provide some insight into the modal character of the folk tunes brought to New Spain in the sixteenth century.[9]

Simmons states that no complete, original romance from the sixteenth century has been preserved in Mexico.[10] In fact, very few romances from the colonial period remain whose texts have been preserved in their original printed form. Simmons discounts those romances listed in Mendoza's *Romance y corrido*, stating that it is apparent from their titles that most are learned and literary in nature, and thus not related to the popular tradition that predominated later on.[11]

Only in exceptional cases has the music of romances from the colonial period been preserved in manuscript form. Two early romance corridos, possibly dating from the end of the seventeenth century, exist in a guitar tablature owned by Gabriel Saldívar. Martín de Villegas is named as the composer.[12]

Presumably the melodies written in the romance tradition were altered over the centuries and often replaced by new ones. Durán claims that the roots of the current romance melodies lie no further back than the second half of the eighteenth century. Almost invariably, current melodies do have a major/minor tonality instead of the modality that prevails in fifteenth- and sixteenth-century Spanish manuscripts.[13]

Mendoza analyzes the influence of the Spanish models for the corrido in the following way. The corrido derives its epic form from the romance and *járaca* (a literary genre); preserved in the corrido is their characteristic narrative of heroic feats in battle. Furthermore, the corrido has inherited from the járaca an exaggerated emphasis on manhood (*machismo*). The lyrical corrido derives from coplas, *cantares,* and sentimental *relatos*.[14] Mendoza also lists the most important differences between the Mexican romance and corrido:[15]

> 1) The romance has lines of seven or eight syllables; corridos tend to have eight, but may have up to twenty syllables per line. (This is particularly the case with historical corridos from the state of Guerrero.)[16]
>
> 2) The romance consists mainly of a nonstrophic series of

lines, assonantic, with simple rhymes (*monorrimos*) on lines with an even number; the corrido is strophic, with four or six lines in each verse, and has different types of rhyme.[17]

3) The romance is epic, novelistic, and *morisco*, that is, it deals with fiestas, tournaments, love affairs, and so forth.[18] The corrido expands these themes, becoming a kind of local news service.

4) In musical terms, the romance is "serious," modal, and melodically restrained, while the corrido is "overflowing," lyrical, and of wider melodic range, though it retains the metric and rhythmic characteristics of its Spanish ancestor.[19]

5) The romance usually consists of a dialogue between two principals; in contrast, the corrido is a narrative usually in the first or third person, with the troubadour acting as the (hypothetical) witness of the event described.

Corridos may also contain insertions of dialogue. The same melody is sung to each verse and corridos written after 1910 sometimes have a refrain.

There is good reason to regard copla verses with a rebellious or satirical content as the immediate predecessors of the Mexican corrido. The earliest known Mexican satirical coplas are the *coplas al tapado*.[20] They attack the Spanish rulers, telling of the execution of a colorful figure named Antonio Benavides. According to Sordo Sodi, Inquisition records from the eighteenth century include many coplas ridiculing the Spanish viceroys.

From satirical copla verses spring the fully developed Mexican corrido. In Simmons's view, the evolution of the corrido into a literary genre native to Mexico took place during the late seventeenth and the eighteenth centuries. Unfortunately, this development cannot be traced because the available source material is incomplete.[21]

One of the distinctive features of the Mexican corrido is the manner in which the story is told. As Durán explains: "*El improvisador popular* does not disdain one single detail, nor does he give major importance to the one or the other . . . all elements obtain equal importance."[22] In many cases the *corridista* (corrido singer) begins his performance of a corrido with an opening salutation, and ends with a farewell.[23]

Since Mexican corridos deal with many subjects, the content itself is not relevant as a criterion. The theme of the Revolution may be considered typical, but by no means universal.[24]

In his article "Romances tradicionales de Guerrero," Professor Serrano Martínez writes that there are two main categories of poetry in the state of Guerrero; this holds true for all of Mexico. With Ramon Menéndez-Pidal as his reference, he calls them *el popular* and *el tradicional*.[25] Popular poetry is especially significant, according to Menéndez-Pidal. Even though the poems may be transmitted orally, they have enough of a national basis to be standardized in a single version, without the ideas or their expression undergoing any change. Traditional poetry, on the other hand, is an evolving form.

Serrano Martínez states that the real Mexican corrido is popular poetry which has been freed from the patterns of Spanish poetry and become characteristically Mexican. Romances and corridos in the romance style are considered traditional poetry.

Martínez's statement is confirmed by the current situation in Mexico. Corridos praising national heroes, great events on the battlefield during the Revolution, and related activities are not subject to change, due to their nationalistic origins. On the other hand, corridos that can be linked to the romance español are handed down as folk music, and constantly changed through the process of oral tradition.

Many copla texts from the early nineteenth century are called corridos, but, according to Mendoza, they do not fulfill the criteria of the Mexican corrido.[26] Actually they should be called coplas, since they lack the epic and narrative character of the corrido. However, "real" corridos mexicanos do appear among coplas, and opinions differ as to which corrido preceded the other.

Simmons discerns three stages in the evolution of the Mexican corrido. According to him, the first true corrido that can be identified is the "Corrido de Carlos IV" from the year 1808. It has "cuartelas and consonantial rhyme, which most distinguish the corrido from the Spanish romance." The next stage toward the fully developed corrido is represented by the "Corrido de Leandro Rivera" from 1840. As an example of the third and last stage he mentions "La entrada de Juárez a la ciudad de México" (1867), "which displays the opening salutation, the leave-taking of the singer, the usual dating of the event narrated, all salient characteristics of the fully developed corrido."[27]

Both Carmen Sordo Sodi and Juan S. Garrido designate "El corrido de la pulga" ("The Corrido of the Flea") by Pepe Quevedo as the first real Mexican corrido.[28] Garrido noted that the text of this corrido, which was published in 1821, is more closely akin to a *canción romántica* in form and content, but is nevertheless a corrido.[29] Mendoza states in his anthology that the first examples of real corridos date from the 1820s; in these texts the typical method of character descriptions by the narrator appears as an established form. But, Mendoza adds, the examples are few, perhaps because many texts have disappeared. He also notes that as late as the first half of the century the corrido came only second to *valonas* and *glosas en décima* as the news service of illiterate people, a role it subsequently took over.[30]

During the civil war in the mid-nineteenth century, the corrido developed into a specifically Mexican art form. The course of Mexican history from around 1845 to the present can be traced just by reading extant corrido texts.[31] The religious and legal strife of the Juárez reform period (1855–63) gave rise to corridos, as did the landing of French troops on Mexican territory in 1863, Maximilian's accession to the throne in 1864, and his fall in 1867. But less dramatic corridos were also written. A corrido from 1873 describes the building of the railways. (The railway also inspired waltzes, many of which were published in the newspapers.)[32] Beginning in 1876, songs were sung of the rebels' victories against the hated rule of Porfirio Díaz. The courage and daring of the protagonists are proclaimed in these corridos.

Publishing firms like Casa Wagner y Livien and Imprenta de Murgia (established in 1826) began to publish corrido texts shortly before the mid-nineteenth century, but apparently with reluctance. Juan S. Garrido claims that the very first editors to publish corrido music, Rivera e hijos (about 1850), did not pay the authors; on the contrary, the authors had to pay to have their corridos published. During the Juárez epoch, satirical corrido texts by Guillermo Prieto, Vicente Riva Palacio, A. B. Cuéllar, and others, were also published in newspapers; some of these were, "La orquesta" (1886), "El siglo XIX," "La tos de mi mamá," and "El chinaco."[33]

Antonio Vanegas was the most important publisher of corridos, texts and music, during the late nineteenth century and throughout the Revolution. He started his printing firm in Mexico City in the early 1880s. In addition to recipes, love stories, and the lives of the saints, Vanegas published a large number of corridos, praising the heroes who fought during the age of Juárez and against the rule of Porfirio Díaz. Among these heroes were Macario Romero who, according to legend, was killed for political reasons at the Rancho de Pino Solo in the Pénjamo district where he had gone to meet his fiancee; Valentín Mancera, who spread terror through the haciendas in central Mexico; Nicolás Romero, a soldier who was feared by the French, and many more.

In 1887 the artist José Guadalupe Posada (1852–1913) moved from Aguascalientes, his birthplace, to Mexico City. Posada was a strong advocate of revolutionary views, and he made a significant contribution to the revolutionary trends of the late nineteenth and early twentieth centuries. Before his death in 1913 Posada created no less than twenty-thousand expressive engravings, many of which were illustrations of corrido texts. Posada's career as an illustrator coincided with the golden age of the corrido mexicano. At the time the genre stirred the interest of the entire Mexican people, with the exception of the aristocracy.[34]

By comparing extant melodies printed in the nineteenth century with contemporary corrido tunes, it becomes evident that the corrido style has not changed notably through the years. This does not necessarily apply to performance techniques.[35]

The melodies are generally diatonic, seldom chromatic; they often start with the dominant, and most of them end on the mediant. Each line usually has a melody phrase with eight main notes, one per syllable. If the verse lines diverge from the eight syllable form, as can happen especially in the refrains, the melodies naturally follow suit.

According to Mendoza, the early corrido melodies were monothematic, but at the beginning of the twentieth century polythematic corridos were composed (in other words, corridos using two or more contrasting melodies). Garrido states that Salvador Flores has written polythematic corridos with refrains.

Corridos are often sung in parallel thirds or sixths. When three voices are involved, two of them sing in unison or in parallel octaves.[36] The corrido may assume the rhythms of the polka, march, or waltz. Slow 6/8 time used to predominate. Now 2/4 is used for gay corridos, and waltz time for all others. A gay waltz melody may be combined with a tragic corrido text.[37]

Carlos Chávez considers the corrido a low, "primitive" musical form. "The many four-line verses are all sung with the same monotonous melody, accompanied by tonic-dominant chords on the guitar. If the corrido is to become a dignified musical form, it must be based on the rondo pattern, but with wide variation and freedom."[38] Castañeda holds the opposite opinion, regarding the simplicity of the melody as its strength, indeed, as a deliberate device.[39]

Ever since the independence struggles of the early nineteenth century, the corrido has been very influential in the cultural history of Mexico. The corrido flourished during the Revolution, which originated as a rebellion against the rule of Díaz. During the period from 1910 to 1917, the corrido took a prominent place in the popular music of Mexico.

A number of corridos emerged in connection with the workers' revolt at Río Blanco on January 8, 1907, when some four hundred workers were killed in battles with the Díaz army. This and similar events contributed to Francisco I. Madero's revolt against Díaz in 1910. In the years that followed, every important event became the subject for one or more corridos. The political leaders and the rebels naturally all had their own corridos.[40] (See Example 10.)

The names of some professional corridistas from the revolutionary period were recorded and have been preserved. Carmen Sordo Sodi interviewed the most famous of them all, Samuel M. Lozano, who at one time was Pancho Villa's personal corridista. Sordo Sodi related some interesting facts about the way in which

Example 10. "Corrido de la toma de Ciudad Juárez" (1912)—Mendoza, *El corrido mexicano, antología, introducción y notas*, pp. 27–30

corrido messages were transmitted during the height of the civil war. The military leaders, whether they were members of the central government's forces or one of the rebel armies, employed singers as spies. The singers were expected to go out on reconnaissance missions which were often quite dangerous. These corridistas had the task of infiltrating various enemy camps, where they performed as singers while simultaneously gathering information to report to their own generals, who in turn paid them for what they could deliver. (Very likely, however, some of the singers were double agents.)

Corrido was a term used by the singers themselves. Upon delivering the information, the corridista would ask whether the general (the employer) was prepared to pay for *"de corrido o por parte."* In the former case, the singer charged more, for he would then present all the information he had discovered in improvised verse form. The message itself was called *la bola*.[41] In this respect the corridistas were semiprofessional musicians. The instruments they generally used were the small harp, the guitar or the vihuela, and possibly a bass guitar. They were accustomed to working singly, but since traveling alone was dangerous, occasionally two corridistas would work together.[42]

The corridista was expected to be a good improviser. The melodies he used could be either traditional or new compositions, but they were always based on traditional patterns and intonation.[43]

Professional corridistas (or *trovadores*) are still working in all parts of the country; their repertoires consist exclusively of corridos.[44] Some of them are nationally famous. They travel all over Mexico, performing with their guitars at markets, fiestas, and various other gatherings. They also earn a small income by selling leaflets with the text of their latest "highly topical" corrido. These *trovadores* live by their singing. They often have an enormous repertoire and are skilled in the art of improvisation. (It is generally the text that is improvised, while the melodies are traditional.) There is no shortage of subjects for corridos: murders, accidents of various kinds, political events, and so forth. The singers' repertoire also includes corridos describing the beauty of the places they visit.

There are also corridistas, who work solely on the local level, singing about community events as well as of national affairs. The news on the radio is often the source for the subjects of their corridos, but they supply additional information and details.

Carmen Sordo Sodi described another very special kind of corrido, which was in use between the years 1923 and 1955 in the so-called *misiones culturales,* organized by the Ministry of Education. These missions, which were initiated by José Vasconselos, the Minister of Education under President Alvaro Obregón, were sent to remote areas of Mexico to collect music and dances, and at the same time teach *corridos educativos* (educational corridos), by which the villagers were taught hygiene. Many of the corridos are still sung in farming communities. Most of the songs were written by the missionaries themselves, Manuel M. Ponce, Tata Nacho, Vicente T. Mendoza, Blas Galindo, Alfonso del Río, Angel Salas, and others.[45]

Mendoza believes that the corrido declined after 1930; he claims it has become an artificial product.[46] Here Garrido definitely disagrees. He feels that while the corrido may have lost a certain degree of political influence since the Revolution, it can hardly be considered a dying form. Traditional corridos survive as folk music in various parts of the country, and corridos are successfully produced by a number of composers for the commercial market; Juan S. Garrido is one of these composers.

Garrido states that the modern corrido was introduced into Mexico City in the 1920s by the duet Teté Tapia and Ernesto Rubio. This pair has had many successors, among them the Duo Llera, Trio Garnica-Ascencio, Antonieta Lorca, and Lucha Reyes. These singers perform on radio, television, and in films.

Victor Cordero is the most outstanding exponent of the modern corrido. The incredible popularity of Cordero's corrido, "Juan Charrasqueado," written in the 1940s, is a clear indication that the corrido is very much alive among the Mexican people. Garrido said the fame of this corrido was so great that a man once traveling through Mexico masqueraded as Juan Charrasqueado, even though the character was wholly imaginary. To this day many Mexican women use the word *charrasqueado* to describe obstinate and noisy men, although it actually means "scarred."

In recent decades, corridos, like canciones rancheras, have come to be associated with norteño and mariachi ensembles. The performance styles used in singing corridos and canciones rancheras are closely related.

Various organizations are currently promoting a revival of the corrido tradition. In 1971 SACM arranged a corrido contest for this purpose. Victor Cordero won two prizes at this competition.[47]

Sordo Sodi referred to the tragic events of 1968, when many students were killed by the military, as an example of how nationalism and art can be united in national crises. The Tlatelolco massacres gave rise to a *manifestación popular;* the students used the corrido as a protest form and wrote new texts to traditional corrido melodies. Few new melodies were written, which may be a sign of the symbolic power still held by the traditional corrido melodies in Mexico.

4

The Canción

As a genre the Mexican corrido is relatively homogeneous, while the *canción* reveals an almost total dissolution of that concept.[1] "*Canción*" can designate any type of song, as opposed to an instrumental piece, or it can be used to define specific varieties, such as the *canción romántica mexicana*. In this chapter the term will be applied in the latter, more limited, sense.

The main difference between canciones and corridos is that the canción has a lyrical, often sentimental, quality in the text and melody, while the corrido has an epic or narrative quality. Canciones do occur in copla form, but the verse structure tends to be more varied.[2]

Sordo Sodi states that the lack of source material makes it impossible to assess the age of the canción in Mexico. Some canciones are clearly related to the romance español; canciones have been written in the romance form, but all romances are certainly not canciones.[3]

Sordo Sodi suggests a classification for Mexican canciones on the basis of their function. She distinguishes three main types of canción in Mexico: religious songs, civic songs, and other secular songs. There is of course no clear stylistic delineation between these types and in some instances one canción may belong to more than one group insofar as its function is concerned.

Certain types of Mexican religious songs, primarily *alabados* and *alabanzas*, date back to the sixteenth century. Pious canciones were an important part of Mexico's "popular" music until the Reform movement of the late 1850s achieved separation of church and state; since that time popular music has also been largely secularized. In central Mexico religious tunes are still performed by *concheros*, musicians playing *conchas de amarillo*, which are guitars made of tortoise shells. However, religious canciones no longer belong to the mainstream of Mexican music.

"Civic" refers to those songs that have an outspoken patriotic or official character. The national anthem is of course the primary civic song in Mexico, as it is in other countries. It should be noted that corridos are in no way civic songs; however patriotic they may seem, they are not regarded as official songs.[4]

The canciones that are called secular comprise an enormous field. I will not attempt to cover it completely and will, in fact, deal only with its history during the last 150 years.

Two basic categories of secular canciones existed in the nineteenth century, being based on economic divisions within Mexican society. One group was rooted in the mestizo tradition originating from the rural population; these were mainly "Spanish type" folk songs. The second group consisted of canciones in *bel canto* style, which were sung in the salons of the aristocracy and the middle class.[5]

This classification is affirmed by Mendoza.[6] He distinguishes between two kinds of canción in Mexico. Canciones with a simple structure, possibly with refrains, comprise the first group. These are monothematic melodies composed to copla verses. According to Mendoza, many of these songs, which tend to be about love, may have been sung in Spanish tonadillas in Mexico City during the early nineteenth century. *Canciones epitalámicas*, wedding songs with traditional Spanish character, belong to this group, as do canciones with *versos de aliento entrecortado*.

>   Estando . . . estando amarrado un gallo
>   se me re . . . se me reventó el cordón
>   si será . . . si será mi muerte un rayo
>   o me . . . o me matará un bribón
>   de esos que an . . . de esos que andan a caballo
>   validos . . . validos de la ocasión

This kind of verse is sometimes inserted in jarabes. It may derive from the Basque-Navarre region of Spain, where it frequently occurs in jotas. An abundance of other intricate verse forms of Spanish origin appear in canciones: *ecos, retruécanos* (lines of antithetical verses), and *esdrújulos* (lines of verse with the accent in the antepenultimate).

Thus certain kinds of verse can be traced back to Spain. However, the words are not necessarily of Spanish origin nor is the music. In a review of mestizo folk music, Bruno Nettl discusses the difficulty of tracing the Spanish origins of traditional melodies in Latin America:

> The problem of the origin of Hispanic tunes in Latin American folk music is generally unsolved. But we can say with some certainty that the tunes sung in Latin America are for the most part not simply imports from Spain and Portugal (while the words more frequently are). They are more usually songs either composed in Latin America in the styles brought from Europe centuries ago but so changed by the process of oral tradition that the tunes in Europe that are related to them can no longer be recognized as relatives; or perhaps it is the European tunes that have undergone change.[7]

The second basic type of canción distinguished by Mendoza is the romantic and sentimental Mexican canción (of Italian inspiration).[8] According to Mendoza, the classical form of the romantic canción is characterized by verses of eleven-syllable lines.[9] He outlines its (ideal) textual structure as follows: A A' B B' // C C' B B'.[10] This is balanced by the following thematic melody pattern: A A' B B'// C C B B'.[11]

What Mendoza calls "la canción mexicana romántica y sentimental" was introduced around 1830 into Mexico's middle class and aristocratic circles. Its birth may be directly related to the popularity of the Italian opera at the Coliseo de México beginning in the 1820s. Mendoza further states that Mexican literary romanticism began to emerge at about the same time in books by authors such as Fernando Calderón and Ignacio Rodríguez Galván.[12]

The Italian bel canto style quickly gave rise to romantic canciones in the musical salons. The bel canto style was also transmitted "from the professional opera singers via provincial composers and popular troubadours to the country people."[13] Mendoza asserts that the romantic canción was in its prime from 1850 to 1900. He places special emphasis on the role of the troubadour and composer A. Zúñiga in the development and diffusion of the nineteenth-century canción in Mexico.

To support his theory that the bel canto style extended to the entire population of Mexico, Mendoza cites seven canciones (one of them has an instrumental sinfonia) that were collected at the beginning of the twentieth century in the states of Zacatecas, Puebla, Nuevo León, Jalisco, Hidalgo, and the Federal District.[14] They all have fairly lively melodies with elements of rhythmic formations that are not usually associated with the Spanish style. They lack modal nuances, as they were composed in either the major or minor key.

According to Mendoza, the following qualities can be regarded as Italian rather than Spanish: harmony that is based on the tonic and dominant (in contrast to the Spanish modal nuances); diverse ornamentations of the melody line (mainly mordents); wide intervals; dominant seventh harmonies in cadenzas; triplets figures in the accompaniment; and 4/4 or 12/8 time. Mendoza contrasts these with the specifically Spanish features: eight-syllable lines, 6/8 time, and (Spanish) bolero or *zapateado* rhythms.[15]

A study of the melodies presented by Mendoza clearly indicates that the songs belong to a rather late style. Nevertheless, it is risky to define a specific Italian style on the basis of such loose criteria. The pattern of the music does not have any specific traits in common with Italian bel canto arias.

Both Carmen Sordo Sodi and Juan S. Garrido explicitly denied that the Italian influences in the nineteenth-century canción in Mexico extended beyond the devotees in the big cities. They emphasized that the style of the *canción folklórica* was and continued to be dominated by Spanish influences. The majority of the people simply did not come into direct contact with opera and were exposed to the bel canto style only indirectly, if at all. Thus the concept "romantic and sentimental" cannot be universally applied to the nineteenth-century canción in Mexico. It may accurately describe the bel canto songs in Italian style that were sung in the upper-class salons, but not the folk songs that developed during that time, although they may have been based to an extent on Italian patterns.

The canción played a special part in the age of romanticism, and apparently independence contributed to its growing popularity. Not only were new songs created, but Spanish songs were parodied, often in the spirit of nationalism. Yet also active was the older song tradition that had been brought to Mexico from Spain during the colonial period, handed down by wandering Spanish troubadours, and gradually transformed by native folk singers.

The region of Mexico usually called the Bajío, which includes parts of Michoacán, Jalisco, Querétaro, Aguascalientes, and Guanajuato, was an early center of the canción.[16]

In the mid-nineteenth century, a vigorous type of canción developed in the Bajío and in an area to the south of it. The most distinctive feature of these songs is the rhythm of their melodies, which Mendoza claims derives from the zapateado and jota. (See Examples 11 and 12.)

Example 11. Jaliscian canción—Mendoza, *La canción mexicana: ensayo de clasificación y antología*, pp. 77–79

Example 12. Jaliscian canción—ibid.

Mendoza cites as typical examples "A la orilla de un palomar," "Presciliano Valadez," "Luz eléctrica," and "Golondrina mensajera."[17]

Mendoza notes that traditional canciones are still an integral part of the people's lives in the Bajío. The songs tend to be sung in parallel thirds and/or sixths, according to the Spanish tradition, and accompanied on the guitar or the diatonic harp. They are also included, as are sones, in the repertoires of mariachi and arpa grande ensembles.

In the Bajío, canciones, sones, jarabes, and valonas with instrumental sinfonias and *descansos,* are widely sung and played at birthdays, saints' days, and serenades.[18]

In all parts of Mexico, *mañanitas* are performed at birthday celebrations held early in the morning, thus the name. The traditional birthday song in Mexico is called "Las mañanitas."

Nowadays mariachi bands are often hired to perform mañanitas and *serenatas*, or serenades, which are sung in the evening.

The lake region of Michoacán harbors an enchanting group of canciones, locally known as *pirecuas*. The verses are frequently in the Purépecha (Tarascan) language. According to Concha Michel, an expert on the folklore of Michoacán, these songs are sung mostly by women, in parallel thirds or sixths, accompanied by guitar and jarana.[19]

On their way from Chile to California in the 1850s, a colony of prospectors stopped near the seaside resort of Acapulco. They brought with them Chilean cuecas, which in Guerrero became known as *chilenas*. These songs have survived in the oral tradition of the Guerrero coastlands and have given rise to new songs in the same spirit.[20] One of the special charms of the chilenas lies in the lyrical quality of the texts.[21] The music is akin to the romantic (nineteenth-century) traditions on which much of Mexico's treasure of songs is based. Chilenas are sung to guitar accompaniment in the rhythms and style of the cueca, which closely resemble that of the huapango. Chilenas are also performed by arpa grande orchestras. Agustín Ramírez, who died in 1957, was the outstanding composer of chilenas in the twentieth century.

The Yucatán peninsula, which was until recently isolated from the culture of the rest of the country, is a region with a rare canción tradition. Yucatán has long had cultural bonds by sea with Colombia; through these ties the *bambuco (colombiana)* has taken root in Yucatán. The rhythm of the bambuco, set in 6/8 time by guitars possibly supplemented with a *requinto* (small guitar), is strongly reminiscent of that of the huapango lento. The performance style reveals the *trovador romántico* in the soul of the Yucatecan singer.

The canciones of Yucatán have wonderfully "mild" melancholy tunes, generally written in a minor key. Since Yucatán has always had close cultural contact with neighboring Cuba, the style of the habanera and bolero has also been incorporated into the song tradition of Yucatán. The lyrics have real literary merit, for they have been composed by poets such as Luis Rosas Vega, José Esquivel Pren, Ricardo López Méndez, and others. The texts often deal with the Mayan culture, which is native to Yucatán. Mendoza writes:

In the Bajío the composer is primarily a musician, creating music and text at the same time, in accordance with traditional patterns. On the Yucatán peninsula it is the "true poets" who provide the musicians with texts.[22]

As previously stated, the diffusion of the bel canto melodies was relatively limited. The situation was different with the popular new dances from Paris. The waltz, mazurka, redowa, polka, schottische, and others were rapidly adopted even in remote regions.[23] The waltz rhythm, and to some extent that of the habanera, dominated the late nineteenth-century canción in Mexico.

For obvious reasons the inhabitants of urban areas invariably came into contact more rapidly with the new, influential ideas from Europe. Thus the fashionable dances first arrived in the salons of the aristocracy and the middle class. Some time elapsed before they spread beyond these circles. On the other hand, dances and songs that were integrated into the traditions of the countryside survived there long after they had lost popularity in the cities, where the turnover was much faster.[24]

The diffusion of the nineteenth-century canción in Mexico can thus be traced from the salons of the aristocracy and the middle class (as well as from the opera), to the rural areas. However, the direction of this cycle was sometimes reversed.[25] During periods of civil unrest and growing nationalism, folk music, which may have originated in the upper-class circles, was often reintroduced into the cultural life of the cities.[26] This happened during the Juárez Reform period, when folk songs and dances were performed in the theatres of the capital.[27] In the 1920s nationalist theatrical performances that included folk melodies from all over the country became very popular. During this same period of nationalism, composers with commercial interests—Palmerín, Cárdenas, Ponce, Tata Nacho, and others—derived their inspiration from folk traditions, generally from their own home regions.[28]

Juan S. Garrido defines the entire nineteenth-century canción tradition in Mexico as "Spanish" rather than "Mexican"; according to him, it had no Mexican character at all.[29] Garrido regards the song "Perjura," composed in 1901 by Miguel Lerdo de Tejada, as the first *canción romántica mexicana*.[30] The melody of that song does not appear to be more Mexican than the salon melodies of the nineteenth century. This kind of canción, combining bel canto melos with texts dealing with love in a naïve fashion ("Perjura" is more candid, to be sure), was to be cultivated until about 1950 by a clan of trained composers settled in Mexico City, including Lerdo de Tejada, Alfonso Esparza Oteo, Tata Nacho, and Mario Talavera. (See Example 13.)

The epithet "mexicana," when used in connection with these songs, is not easily clarified. According to Sordo Sodi "mexicana" in this connection may indicate either that the composer is Mexican,

Example 13. "Perjura," canción mexicana by Miguel Lerdo de Tejada—Otto Mayer-Serra, *Música y músicos de Latino-América*

that the song is written in a Mexican style, or that the text concerns a theme of national interest.[31]

Juan S. Garrido defines canción mexicana (with or without the epithet *romántica*) as "a mixture of Spanish influence with a Mexican way of thinking." He further states that around 1910, when the term was created by Manuel M. Ponce, the mestizos sang Spanish and Mexican songs in a style that differed from the Spaniards' way of singing them. There was another "feeling," a new *sentimiento*. According to Garrido, this is not only manifest in the performance style, but also in a kind of Mexican melos type, common in romantic Mexican canciones at the beginning of this century.[32]

I have never succeeded in finding any specifically Mexican melos in these songs. On the other hand, a few texts relate Mexican occurrences (see chapter 9). It is perhaps possible to discern a more specific Mexican flavor in those canciones mexicanas of a more popular vein that spread throughout the country during the Revolution, such as, "La Adelita," "La rielera," "Las cuatro milpas," and "La Valentina." Only a few of the composers of these popular canciones from the revolutionary era are known; it is also difficult to date the tunes. The canciones mexicanas, published with piano accompaniment *á la salon* by Manuel M. Ponce in 1913, were almost certainly sung for decades prior to the Revolution by mestizos in Mexico's rural areas.[33]

During the Revolution, traditional songs were often equipped with newly written texts, loaded with symbolism. Some examples are: "La cucaracha," "Las tres pelonas," "Marchita el alma," and many more.[34] The technique of setting new texts to traditional melodies was not a new practice. Mendoza writes that "La cachucha," a Spanish song presumably brought to Mexico at the beginning of the nineteenth century by seamen from Cádiz, was parodied during the wars of the Reform in the 1850s. The same thing happened with other songs of Spanish origin.[35]

The *canción ranchera* is certainly a kind of song imbued with a lot of "Mexican" spirit, paralleled in this respect only by the corrido. "Canción ranchera" originally referred to peasant songs traditionally sung on haciendas. The genre has had a very interesting development in the last 125 years. As previously noted, country songs were incorporated into theatre performances during the Juárez epoch. However, the original texts dealing with ranch life were discarded, and new texts written by recognized authors were adapted to the tunes, which then often had to be rearranged to fit the new lyrics. A very famous song of this kind written during the 1860s was "El chinaco," the nickname of Juárez's soldiers. This song was performed in the theatre by artists dressed as *charros* (cowboys) or what was called the *chinaco* style; they differ somewhat from the charro dress used today.[36]

During the rule of Porfirio Díaz, the music played at theatre performances and elsewhere in the capital rejected the songs of the common people.[37] Both Sordo Sodi and Garrido emphasize that the revival of the country songs occurred within the framework of the nationalistic theatre in Mexico City which flourished during the Revolution. The songs sung by people living on the haciendas were popularly called *rancheras*. Sordo Sodi says that the word ranchera was not used before 1910 as the name of this song type. The epithet seems to have been invented in the theatre.

The theatre ranchera began as *bocadillos* (interludes) between the acts of the nationalist plays performed on the stages of the capital. Bocadillos might consist of a couple dancing a jarabe or a singer performing some canciones. These songs were described in the program as rancheras. The singer himself might have picked up the song at a *cantina, pulquería,* or some other type of bar where farm workers and various people from the lowest social classes gathered to drink and sing.[38]

The original folk ranchera very soon gave way to new commercially oriented songs, which were imitations of the rural rancheras. The ranchera became an artificial product, viewed as country "style" by the city people. Most of the ranchera singers and songs came from Mexico City.[39]

These urban ranchera songs used to be accompanied by so-called typical orchestras (*conjuntos típicos*), which consisted of instruments such as the psaltery, marimba, and flute. All the musicians were dressed in national costumes. The performance style tended toward the vigorous intonation so typical of the modern corrido and ranchera. Juan S. Garrido mentioned the song "Alborada" by Lauro de Uranga as an example of the ranchera performed in nationalistic plays in Mexico City during the Revolution.[40]

The great triumph of the ranchera occurred in films in the year

1932. Several of the leading ranchera singers, such as Lupe Vélez, Lucha Reyes, Pedro Infante, and Jorge Negrete, went on to become film stars, always appearing with a ranchera song on their lips. Indeed, entire films have been based on ranchera songs; "Allá en el Rancho Grande," "Rayando el sol," and "Pajarillo" were famous films as well as songs. Reliable box office draws such as Pedro Infante and Jorge Negrete appeared in film after film, thus popularizing Mexican ranchera music throughout the Hispanic world. These artists, although now dead, are still among the record stars most in demand. Indeed, the Mexican people have displayed a remarkable devotion to ranchera singers since the 1930s, and many still go on pilgrimages to Pedro Infante's grave.[41] A very characteristic feature of ranchera songs that is also to be found in corridos is the way in which each musical phrase is extended. This "dragging out" of the final notes is actually written out in scores. Another typical aspect of the rancheras was (and is) the straightforward way in which the lyrics relate the message of the songs. The charro costume, taken over from the theatre, is also an important feature.[42]

The contemporary ranchera, including norteña music, may be considered a Mexican equivalent of the country and western songs in the United States, whose history is similar to that of the Mexican ranchera (see Appendix). Both genres were cultivated for many decades in remote areas of the land; both were isolated remnants of songs and styles brought by immigrants from Europe. Mexican rancheras and American country songs began to be popularized nationally in the late 1920s and early 1930s through films and radio. In Mexico the theatre was also an important medium for the diffusion of ranchera songs. The music and singing styles were changed in the process of commercialization.[43]

There are clear stylistic differences between rancheras and country and western songs, particularly in regard to performance techniques; the Mexican artists have a distinctively passionate way of singing. The lyrics of both rancheras and country and western songs often deal with loneliness, betrayed love, and sentimental partings.

Since the 1940s, ranchera songs are generally accompanied by either a trumpet mariachi or a norteño band. While polka time (2/4) prevails in the music played and sung by norteño bands, waltz time, often slow and drawn out, is predominant in the rancheras sung and played by mariachis.[44]

The term ranchera is currently often used in combinations such as *polka ranchera* and *bolero ranchero*. The terms polka and bolero both define certain rhythmic qualities, while ranchera gives a vague indication of the style. Used with bolero, the word ranchero specifies that a mariachi orchestra accompanies the piece, in contrast to the instrumentation of the internationally known bolero. The word may also refer to the nature of the text, the manner of singing, and the charro costume.[45]

5

Modern Dance Rhythms

Mexican folk music is based primarily on Spanish and African models. As shown in Chapter 4, it has also been strongly influenced by the Central European dances that were imported to Latin America (mostly by way of Cuba). These include the eighteenth-century contradance and minuet, the early nineteenth-century waltz, polka, mazurka, and others, the late nineteenth-century Cuban habanera, and various contemporary dances.[1]

In his *Panorama*, Carlos Vega makes a very interesting observation concerning the acceptance of European dances in South America.[2] After the Central European drawing room dances of the eighteenth and nineteenth centuries were adopted in the salons of Buenos Aires, Santiago, Lima, and other big cities, they were "folklorized" in completely different ways in the western and eastern parts of the South American continent (as a result of geographical, social, and purely musical factors not to be discussed here). In the western region, centered in Peru, the contact between the drawing room dances and the preexisting folk music was made in the upper-class salons of the cities. In rural areas the time-honored folk genres (*cuecas* and others) continued to flourish as before.

In the eastern part of the continent, the European dances were integrated into the heritage of folk music; the fashionable dances of Europe were adopted as folk genres in rural areas. The old folk genres vanished almost entirely, although much of their essence was grafted onto country waltzes, polkas, mazurkas, schottisches, habaneras, and tangos.[3]

The musical history of Mexico in the nineteenth century

resembles that of the eastern area. Throughout the country the drawing room dances were incorporated into the folk music. However, the genres of Afro-Spanish origin were also maintained and in fact often enriched by assimilating rhythms and intonations from the fashionable European dances.[4] A number of mestizo genres derived inspiration from the growing nationalism of the nineteenth century, among them the huapango, jarabe, corrido, and canción.[5]

Vega emphasizes that it is very difficult to generalize about the "folklorization process" of Central European dances in Latin American rural areas.[6] Nevertheless, with the support of my informants and Vega's text, I shall endeavor to define the current forms of the dances that were brought to Mexico in the eighteenth, nineteenth, and twentieth centuries.

The contradance is a group dance, or more precisely a square dance, that spread throughout Latin America in the early eighteenth century. Some rural districts of Mexico have preserved contradances. In parts of Nuevo León, for example, contradances such as "Contradanza de Arteaga" and "Lanceros" are still performed on festive occasions. Carmen Sordo Sodi states that the choreography has retained characteristic formations of the Spanish contradance, though often combined with early nineteenth-century dance music such as mazurkas, galops, and polkas.[7]

The mazurka, which flourished in the nineteenth century, is still preserved in some places. In 1944 Vega was able to confirm the existence of some accordion mazurkas in Argentina, as well as in Mexico, long after the mazurka had vanished from the salons of Buenos Aires and Mexico City.[8]

The waltz was most significant in Mexico, since the canción of the late nineteenth century was written almost exclusively in waltz rhythm. When the waltz was introduced into Mexico is not precisely known. However,

> . . . in 1815, an ecclesiastical official reported that the Waltz was becoming widespread. He denounced the Waltz . . . as [a] corrupt importation from degenerate France. All of man's depravity could not invent anything more pernicious, nay, not even Hell itself could spawn a monster more obscene. Only those who have seen the Waltz danced with complete license are in a position to warn of its perils.[9]

Since the nineteenth century many Mexican folk melodies have been based on the waltz rhythm. During the reign of Díaz, the Viennese waltz was very fashionable, especially in the capital. Felipe Villanueva wrote many waltzes in this style for the piano, the "Vals poética" foremost among them.[10]

By far the most famous Viennese-style waltz that was written in Mexico in the late nineteenth century was "Sobre las olas" ("Over the Waves") by Juventino Rosas. "Sobre las olas" became the favorite waltz in Mexico, as well as in Europe where no one would believe that it had been composed by a Mexican.[11] This is probably also the case with other *valsas mexicanas* composed before the Revolution, such as "En alta mar" and "Arpa de oro," salon waltzes by Abundio Martínez from Pachuca, and "Tristes jardines" and "Corazón" by José de Jesús Martínez from Jalisco. These waltzes are still popular in Mexico.[12]

The "Peruvian waltz," a Latin American version of the waltz imbued with syncopation, is also known in Mexico as *vals criollo*. A prominent Mexican exponent of the creole waltz is Alvaro Carillo, who composed "El andariego," and other delicate melodies.

The date that the polka arrived in Mexico is unknown.[13] Sodi thinks it likely that the polka came to Mexico from the United States, perhaps in connection with the Mexican War in 1847. Possibly the polka was not introduced until the reign of Emperor Maximilian (1864–67). During this period, French influences dominated the cultural life of Mexico City, as they did in Porfirio Díaz's time.[14]

The polka gained a foothold in the big cities, but established itself even more firmly in the rural areas. Soldiers, especially those stationed in Tampico and the valley of Puebla, contributed greatly to the diffusion of the polka. Later many revolutionary songs in the polka rhythm were also popularized by the soldiers. The polka has been preserved as a folk music genre in Mexico, especially in the country's northern regions. The dance groups of northern Mexico, particularly those in the state of Chihuahua, have claimed the polka as their rightful genre.[15] The polka style was also integrated into canciones norteñas.

The Mexican polka is patterned exclusively after the traditional European one, that is, gay, lively tunes in 2/4 time. Polkas are usually played by norteño groups, or by a solo accordion. Polka tunes are also frequently performed by trumpet mariachis. An (instrumental) polka very often played is "Jesusita en Chihuahua," a tune sometimes attributed to Quirino F. Mendoza.[16]

The habanera is reputed to have been popularized in Mexico in the mid-nineteenth century by a Spanish zarzuela troupe. This company had picked up the rhythm during a month's stay in Cuba (which was then a Spanish colony).[17] Carlos Vega gives an interesting account of the history of the habanera. He traces its origin to the English contradance, which was assimilated into Spain as *contradanza* or *danza*. It was imported to Cuba in this form around 1825, where it was supplemented with Afro-Cuban rhythms and transformed around 1850 into the habanera. Around 1900 the habanera became a fashionable dance known as *habanera de café*.[18]

The chief characteristic of the Cuban habanera is the *ritmo de hamaca* ("hammock rhythm"), slow or moderately slow 2/4 time. The Cuban habanera is more syncopated than the Mexican, and includes rhythms such as *cinquillo antillano*. In Mexico a habanera rhythm in 6/8 time has also developed, influenced by current mestizo folk music.[19] (See Examples 14, 15, and 16.)

Mid-nineteenth century Cuba also witnessed a "sophisticated" outgrowth of the habanera, namely, the *danza cubana*, also written in moderate 2/4 time. Garrido states that the danza cubana was at first purely instrumental, in the tradition of the habanera, and was sung only later.[20] The danza cubana was created by trained musicians and was also known, appropriately enough, as *danza fina*. Manuel Saumell was among the earliest and most important Cuban composers of danzas finas ("contradanzas") for the piano. He was followed by Ignacio Cervantes, the celebrated Cuban pianist, who between 1875 and 1895 wrote many danzas finas for the piano, which he used to play at his concerts.[21]

The popular music of Mexico, in dance and song form, was strongly influenced by Cuban trends from 1860 to 1900. One of the songs that first made the habanera rhythm popular in Mexico was

Example 14. Habanera rhythm—Mendoza, *Panorama de la música tradicional de México*, p. 102

Example 15. Ciquillo antillano (a); rhythm figures of habanera accompaniment (b), ibid.

Example 16. Five habanera incipits—Mendoza, *Panorama de la música tradicional de México,* p. 102

"La paloma." The composition of this song is attributed to Sebastián Yradier, a Spaniard stationed in Cuba. Whether he wrote it himself or whether it is an arrangement or adaptation of a traditional melody cannot be determined.

"La paloma," which was eventually considered a canción mexicana, and other Cuban songs did much to popularize Cuban popular music in Mexico, and several Mexicans soon began to compose in a similar style. The Cuban danza fina inspired a number of Mexican "serious" composers; many danzas finas and habaneras from the last forty years of the nineteenth century were written for piano by musicians such as Felipe Villanueva, Melesio Morales, Julio Ituarte, Ricardo Castro, Fernando Villalpando, and Jacinto Cuevas.

The habanera, which was also simply called *danza* beginning in about 1870, increasingly took on the form of a canción in the ritmo de hamaca. Even melodies that are presently in no way associated with the habanera rhythm were often considered to be related; for instance, "La sandunga" was issued as "danza habanera" in the late nineteenth century.

The habanera rhythm recurred in several of the Mexican hit songs of the period. From 1870 on Casa Nagel published songs in habanera style by Clemente Aguirre, Genaro Codina, Teofil Pomar, Carlos Curti, and others.[22] Miguel Lerdo de Tejada's famous canción "Perjura," whose score was published in 1901, used the habanera (danza) rhythm. Tata Nacho and Alfonso Esparsa Oteo are among the twentieth-century songwriters who composed canciones mexicanas in the habanera style. Since the 1920s the habanera has been on the decline; only "La paloma" and a few other songs have retained their popularity.[23]

Garrido says that the aristocracy never concerned itself with the habanera. The upper classes always preferred purely European music of Italian or French origin and left the Mexican/Cuban music to the middle and lower classes.[24]

Habanera rhythms paved the way for the *danzón*, a Cuban dance with a rhythm somewhat reminiscent of the rhumba. The danzón became popular in Mexico City at the turn of the century and was widely danced during the heyday of Salón México (a dance-hall in Mexico City) in the 1920s and 1930s.[25] (See Example 17.)

According to Garrido, danzones were originally written for solo piano, but they must have also been played by small groups using

Example 17. Danzón rhythm. The classic danzón form is that of a rondo: ABACADA, with an 8-measure refrain (A) and three episodes of 16, 32, and 32, respectively.

conga drums, one or more wind instruments, piano, and possibly some additional instruments such as the marimba and guitarrón. The danzón never lost its Cuban character, even when lyrics were added. Danzones have declined in popularity, but they are still played "in the old style" at dance halls such as San Angel and California in the capital. Currently the leading danzón orchestra is Acerina y su danzonera.[26]

The foxtrot and the tango were also fashionable dances in the 1920s. The first phonograph records that were imported from the United States included foxtrots, and the dance was also picked up by bands along the Mexican-American border. A large number of foxtrots were written in Mexico in the 1920s. "Mi querido capitán" by José Alfonso Palacio is a well-known example from these early years.

The tango came into fashion somewhat later, in 1922 or 1923. It was introduced into Mexico by composers such as Belisario de Jesús García and Alfonso Esparza Oteo. García's "Tango negro" was sung in Buenos Aires, the stronghold of the tango, by the famous Rosita Quiroga. Esparza Oteo's tango "El sacristán" was also one of the hit tunes of the 1920s in Mexico.

In the beginning the orchestras that played foxtrots and tangos closely imitated the performance styles that prevailed in the countries from which the dances originated. Later the styles became less restricted, particularly in the case of the tango.[27]

In the 1920s Mexico's radio stations played only imported foxtrots, tangos, and danzones. Mexican genres, such as the corrido and the canción ranchera, were ignored. However, the radio did not gain any real importance until 1930, when station XEW was formed.

The Cuban bolero (which is written in 2/4 time, as opposed to the Spanish bolero's 3/4 time) is a very common dance and song form in modern Mexican popular music. Garrido asserts that the first Mexican composers to adopt the bolero (in 1927) were Domingo Casanova from Yucatán and Emilio Pacheco from Campeche (two states in southeastern Mexico, close to Cuba). Countless songs in bolero style were written between 1930 and 1955 by such composers as Agustín Lara.[28]

In Mexico at least two types of bolero currently exist: *bolero romántico* and *bolero ranchero*. The bolero romántico (danced and/or sung) has an international style, closely resembling the music played at large music festivals in Europe and the United States. The bolero ranchero (a song form only), which has been highly popular since around 1955, exhibits distinctively Mexican performance techniques, with a flowing stylized bolero rhythm (or traces of bolero rhythm) in the mariachi accompaniment, and possibly with elements of the norteño sound, produced primarily by the accordion. Boleros performed by trios display no characteristics native to Mexico; they sound exactly the same way in Argentina, Chile, and other Latin American countries. The bolero style is similar in all these countries as well, except for the bolero ranchero, which is restricted to Mexico.

Garrido states that the *beguine* became known in 1935 through Cole Porter's "Begin the Beguine." Since 1942 Mexican composers have adapted the beguine to the bolero, using a slow tempo.[29] Today these two rhythms are indistinguishable as Mexican musicians play them. Currently beguine and bolero may be regarded as *música romántica*, rather than as *música tropical* (a generic name for hot Afro-Cuban dance music). Nevertheless, they may be combined with tropical rhythms, producing hybrids such as the *bolero mambo*.[30] (See Example 18.)

The *rumba*, or rhumba, was imported to Mexico from Cuba in about 1927, and it was followed a few years later by the Cuban *guajira* and *conga* dances; "Uno, dos y tres conga" was a great hit tune in 1936. The *guaracha*, which had been a recognized musical form in Mexico since the late nineteenth century, gained renewed popularity in the 1930s. (See Examples 19 and 20.)

The Brazilian *samba* was introduced into Mexico in 1942 or 1943, but very few Mexican composers have written sambas or *bossanovas;* the latter is a further elaboration on the rather monotonous samba rhythm that was played by dance orchestras in the 1940s and 1950s.[31]

The *mambo*, on the other hand, was extremely popular in

Example 18. Cuban bolero rhythm acclimatized in Mexico. The instruments given here are the typical Cuban ones—information from Sordo Sodi.

| C | F | G | F | C | F |
| I | IV | V | IV | I | IV |

Example 19. Characteristic harmony and rhythm of guajira

Example 20. Conga bass rhythm

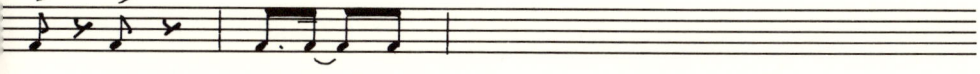

Mexico from the very beginning. A Mexican orchestra conducted by the Cuban musician Dámaso Pérez Prado played the mambo in 1948 for the first time in Mexico.[32] Pérez Prado did not, however, "create" the mambo, as is sometimes thought; according to Garrido, the author was Arsenio Rodríguez, also a native Cuban. Dámaso Pérez Prado makes frequent guest appearances in Mexico, performing the mambo, rhumba, and chachacha with his orchestra, and he is always received with the same enthusiasm. A number of native orchestras play música tropical in approximately the same style.

The march is certainly not a dance, but for the sake of simplicity it will be included among the rhythms genres. In its present form, the military march in Mexico in no way differs from the European one.[33] According to Sordo Sodi, martial music was popularized during the Mexican War in 1846–48, though it must have existed in Mexico before then. Elements of the march rhythm were also infused into canciones. The march was officially established in 1867, when stately military bands were formed. It came into its prime at the turn of the century, when it was regularly performed at bandstands in many Mexican towns.

The national anthem, commissioned in 1854, is a march melody of special significance. The composer was Jaime Nunó, a Spaniard who settled in Mexico, and the text was written by Francisco González Bocanegra from San Luis Potosí. "Mexicanos, al grito de guerra" became extremely popular; it was sung at all nonreligious gatherings as an expression of joy and national solidarity. In 1969 President Gustavo Díaz Ordaz considered it necessary to legally restrict the use of the national anthem.[34]

The *pasodoble* is a type of one-step (though the name means "two-step") that became very popular in the late 1920s, in Latin America as well as in Europe. In Latin America and Spain the pasodoble, played in 2/4 time and closely resembling the march, has long provided the music for *corridas,* the bullfights. These fiery pasodobles, which are performed by brass bands, have also become popular radio music. Agustín Lara and Juan S. Garrido are among the Mexican composers who have written pasodobles in consistently Spanish style.

6
Popular Music Before and After the Revolution

The following chapters deal with the development of urban popular music in Mexico during the past hundred years.[1] Consequently the perspective is somewhat different from that of the preceding chapters. The primary setting for this discussion is Mexico City; I will, however, begin with a brief outline of the cultural and social development of the nation as a whole during the nineteenth century.[2]

The Republic of Mexico has never been homogeneous, either socially or culturally. The country is indeed centrally governed from the capital, but Mexico consists of a number of states (twenty-nine, plus two territories and the Federal District), which in some instances differ considerably from each other in racial groupings, cultural traditions, and economic development.[3] As in all Latin American countries, the social classes are very clearly marked.

After independence was achieved in 1821, efforts toward the cultural and social integration of the country were made. During the liberals' political struggle in the 1850s, which was led by the Zapotecan Indian Benito Juárez, the cultures of the mestizos and Indians gained wider official recognition.[4]

Social tension intensified during the rule of Porfirio Díaz. During his dictatorial rule, Díaz followed a policy that directly favored foreign (primarily North American and British) investments in the country, while the poor population, mainly the farmers and industrial workers, was living in deprived conditions. The native (mestizo and Indian) cultures were again oppressed by the ruling classes.[5]

The devastating changes brought about by the Revolution tore down the traditional social and cultural barriers. But over the years the social divisions have reestablished themselves and are beginning to take on the same structure they had during Don Porfirio's time. The one important difference is that class and racial barriers no longer coincide to the same extent, since the old "Spanish" (*criollo*) upper class was deposed by the Revolution.

Before the country became independent in 1821, the Roman Catholic Church and the viceregal court regulated cultural life in Mexico. After 1821 culture was controlled to an increasing extent by the aristocracy and the rich middle class in the larger towns. Concerts, supported by private individuals, were held regularly, and the attempt was made to start conservatories and musical academies. The present National Conservatory in Mexico City dates back to 1866; in the 1870s it was nationalized and instruction given free of charge.[6]

Performing music in salons and at home seems to have been a widespread practice among the ruling classes. There were a fair number of amateur pianists in the country, many of them women. In the nineteenth century a large quantity of salon music for piano was published, written or arranged by Mexican composers. Mayer-Serra summarized the salon repertoire of the nineteenth century as follows:

> 1) Dance music (polka, mazurka, schottische, waltz, contra dance, quadrille, and so forth)
> 2) Medleys and improvisations on well-known opera and operetta melodies (by Donizetti, Bellini, Verdi, and others)
> 3) Romances, caprices, nocturnes, serenades, idylls
> 4) Exotic piano pieces (Oriental, Moorish, or the like)
> 5) Military marches.[7]

The repertoire also included piano pieces composed for four hands, a form that was very popular in European salons at that time. Other important types of music were medleys and improvisations on *aires nacionales,* in other words, popular folk tunes. Various attempts were also made to write operas that characterized the national spirit.[8]

The concept of nationalism in music is often limited to serious

1 Juventino Rosas, *SACM*

2 Miguel Lerdo de Tejada, *SACM*

3 Macedonio Alcalá, *SACM*

4 Quirino Mendoza, *SACM*

5 Pedro Vargas, *SACM*

6 José Agustín Ramírez, *SACM*

7   Tata Nacho conducting his orquesta típica La Rondalla Mexicana, *SACM*

Ignacio Fernández Esperón "Tata Nacho," *SACM*

9   Juan S. Garrido, *SACM*

10 Agustín Lara, *SACM*

11 Jorge Negrete, *SACM*

12 Pedro Infante, *SACM*

13 Alvaro Carrillo, *SACM*

14 Las Hermanas Huerta, *SACM*

15 Lucha Villa, *SACM*

16 Freddy Fender (see Appendix).
Photo by Nelson Allen.

17 Los Alegres de Terán, a traditional border-area conjunto (see Appendix).
Photo by Nelson Allen © *1975 by Picking Up the Tempo, Inc.*

18 Flaco Jiménez, popular border-sound accordion player (see Appendix).
Photo by Nelson Allen © 1975 by Picking Up the Tempo, Inc.

19. Johnny Rodriguez performing with Texas country musician Willie Nelson (see Appendix). *Photo by Nelson Allen © 1975 by Picking Up the Tempo, Inc.*

20 Doug Sahm (see Appendix). *Photo by Nelson Allen.*

music.⁹ Consequently, the connection between nationalistic art music and folk/popular music is often thought of as a one-way relationship: influences passing from the latter ("inferior") to the former ("refined"). Such a view may go as far as to imply that nationalism cannot be expressed in folk and popular music—an opinion expressed by Luis Sandi.

Sandi's reasoning is correct in that some Mexican serious music does express nationalist trends. Since 1821 serious composers have written rhapsodies and medleys based on folk tunes that convey a national spirit. The trend toward Mexican "national romanticism" in serious music reached its peak between 1910 and 1940. The Mexican composers working during the Revolution and the decades immediately following (Ponce, Chávez, Revueltas, and others) used the music of the mestizos and Indians as the basis of their national romanticism; however, they consistently treated the material of folk origin in a stylized manner, even when authentic instruments were used in performance.¹⁰

Luis Sandi's definition of "musical nationalism" as confined to serious music is far too narrow.¹¹ His own native Mexico offers good evidence of folk and popular music that has functioned primarily as a nationalist expression. The revolutionary corridos, for instance, were imbued with as much nationalistic spirit as were the "learned" works by Ponce and Chávez.¹² The same applies to many of the canciones that were sung during the Revolution. Whether or not these canciones borrowed their intonations from an earlier period is not relevant to this matter. Stylistic qualities are not necessarily related to certain specific functions, for they can assume different roles in different contexts and time periods. Indeed, the prerevolutionary canciones were given (wholly or partially) new texts to conform to the new situation.

During Díaz's regime two main types of popular nationalistic music were evident: the mestizo folk music, which was somewhat rebellious in spirit (huapangos, jarabes, corridos, canciones, rancheras, mariachi ensemble music), and an institutionalized kind of "nationalist" popular music that had no connection with the liberation movement.¹³ On the contrary, this kind of nationalist music received government support during Porfirio Díaz's time.¹⁴

Foremost in this latter category are *orquestas típicas*. The first of these "typical orchestras" was formed in 1884 and consisted exclusively of teachers and students from the National Conservatory in Mexico City. Consequently, all the members of the group had professional musical training. The repertoire consisted of arrangements of the popular dance music of the time: habaneras, pasodobles, mazurkas, polkas, waltzes, and overtures by Franz von Suppé and others.[15]

The nationalistic aspect of the orquestas típicas manifested itself in the choice of instruments and in the charro costumes worn by the musicians, which were similar to those worn by mariachi musicians today. As previously mentioned, these orchestras received government support, for the officials were well aware that this was an excellent way of promoting Mexican culture abroad. Indeed, the Conservatory's orchestra made a highly publicized tour of the United States.[16]

The ensembles consisted of flute, marimba, psaltery, violins, guitars, and guitarrón (bass guitar), all common instruments in the dance orchestras of the time. The leader of the first típica, Carlos Curti, was a skillful marimba player; he was responsible for a number of special arrangements in which the marimba played a leading part.[17]

A second orquesta típica was formed in 1896 by Juan Torre Blanca. This conjunto toured Germany with the specific purpose of spreading knowledge of Mexican music and instruments. The music played by the orchestra may well have been familiar to the Germans, but the sound was foreign and exotic. Instruments such as the marimba, psaltery, and guitarrón were not common in nineteenth-century Europe. The national costumes also contributed to the success of the tour.[18]

The official típicas derived from a tradition that was firmly rooted in the mestizo culture, both urban and rural. Otto Mayer-Serra cites the experience of Ignacio Altamirano, a music lover who in the mid-nineteenth century heard a small orchestra from Huamantla that consisted of a psaltery, guitar, violin, double bass, clarinet, cornet á piston, and flute perform the tune "El torito."[19] Garrido referred to an eye-witness account from 1855 that described a similar kind of orchestra, consisting of relatively the same instruments that later formed the core of the orquesta típica.[20] In all likelihood, such orchestras (though their composition varied) provided dance music throughout the nineteenth century. For the most part these conjuntos remained in the urban areas, but they occasionally performed at haciendas and at village fiestas in the valley of Mexico. Their repertoire was derived to some extent from that of the upper-class salons.

Prior to the Revolution, dance orchestras often consisted of flute, violin, guitar or bandolón (a kind of mandolin), and perhaps a cello.[21] They were gradually replaced by dance bands dominated either by Cuban rhythm instruments or a North American brass section. The repertoire also changed radically in the early 1920s.

However, the earlier type of orchestra survived in the form of official orquestas típicas. Many típicas came into existence during the twentieth century. The orquesta típica formed by Miguel Lerdo de Tejada in 1901 was of particular importance. The following year this orchestra was invited to perform at the Pan-American exhibition in Buffalo, New York.[22] Tejada's orchestra soon became one of the leading entertainment groups in the capital. From 1905 on Tejada and his ensemble played at restaurants in Mexico City, and the orchestra also inaugurated the first nightclub act at the Restaurant Sylvain. In effect, Tejada's orquesta típica was the equivalent of modern mariachi ensembles, some of whom naturally prefer to play at the most expensive clubs, providing a "Mexican atmosphere" for wealthy patrons.

In 1913 Tejada was commissioned by the government to form a large típica, including both instruments and singers, to play on Sundays and at festivities in Chapultepec park in the capital. This Banda Típica de los Cuerpos Rurales was a huge success throughout the Revolution.[23]

During the 1920s Tejada led several orquestas típicas. In 1928–29 he toured the United States and many Latin American countries with a "típica de tipo de concierto" (Garrido's words), with which a number of the leading singers of the time were associated: Talavera, Llera, Vargas, Arvizú, Cornejo, and others.[24] When he returned to Mexico, Tejada was appointed the director of La Orquesta Típica de Policía (later known as Orquesta Miguel Lerdo de Tejada); this orchestra, consisting of seventy-two members, played at several international festivals.[25]

Orquestas típicas displayed great vitality, and new ensembles were formed in succession, both in and beyond Mexico City, with government support. The instruments remained the same, but the repertoire gradually changed.

During a visit to Mérida, Yucatán (Christmas 1972), I had an opportunity to hear the thirty musicians of Orquesta Típica Yucalpetén performing in the main square. The occasion was official; they were celebrating the anniversary of the regional administration. The orchestra began with two numbers sung in unison by three of its own troubadors. The first song was "Mestiza de mi tierra," by Pepe Domínguez of Mérida. This melody, set in fast triple time, is strongly influenced by the jarana style, which is traditional in Yucatán. In the second number the orchestra accompanied a series of singers performing hit tunes dating from the 1930s to the present. All the songs were Mexican, and a surprising number of them (more than half) were written by composers from Yucatán. The bolero rhythm prevailed, but some waltzes were also included in the program. The orchestra, seated on a temporary, improvised stage, created a striking visual impression; all the musicians were wearing the Yucatecan regional costume, the men entirely in white, the women in white dresses with touches of color. The average age of the musicians was fairly advanced, and the same can be said of their musical skill. The arrangements, which were professionally performed, did not deteriorate into sophisticated clichés. The flutes in particular enlivened the music with flowing cascades. Unfortunately, the two psalteries could not make themselves heard despite vigorous efforts by their players.

Along with the orquestas típicas, another type of popular nationalistic music flourished during the Revolution. The corrido can be placed in this category. The corrido was not in itself a new genre in Mexico, but it was more than ever directly associated with political events in the country. Soon every significant event, and every leader, was immortalized in one or more corridos, which passed from mouth to mouth and camp to camp.

The music was accorded official recognition during the Revolution.[26] Gabriel Saldívar, who lived through this chaotic period, had a great deal to say on this subject. According to him, great emphasis was placed on the formation of military choirs. Every regiment had a choir, and there were more than a thousand regiments in Mexico. These military choirs, led by *orfeones* (choir leaders), sang corridos and revolutionary canciones, but also traditional songs native to the region from which they came. Since the regiments crossed the country from one extreme to the other, these military choirs made an essential contribution to the diffusion of regional music in Mexico.

The country must have resounded with choral singing! Not only did every regiment have its own choir, but there were also at least as many choirs attached to industries and factories. Saldívar stated that it was compulsory for businesses with more than fifty employees to form a choir. Choral singing was taught in the schools, too. Saldívar recalled that as late as 1923 in his hometown of San Victoria, Tamaulipas, musicians from Yucatán and Guerrero taught choral arrangements of bambucos and chilenas in the schools.

Nationalism found manifold expression in music. Manuel M. Ponce and Manuel Castro Padilla published collections of canciones mexicanas arranged for piano during the first years of the Revolution (1913 and 1914). Padilla had picked up songs on his journeys around the country; "Santo Señor de Chalma" is one of the songs he published, arranged for piano. Although Ponce did not undertake any exploratory journeys through Mexico, he certainly knew a large number of songs from his native Aguascalientes. He published the songs "La Adelita," "La Valentina," and "Marchita el alma," among others. (These songs were not composed by Ponce himself.) In both Padilla's and Ponce's editions the songs are arranged in the romantic nineteenth-century salon style, especially in regard to the treatment of harmony.[27]

Many of the canciones of the revolutionary era became legendary and spread throughout the land. Melodies that had been popular in the nineteenth century were often used, but extensive efforts were made to mock the song's original texts so that the content was more savage and related to current events, as was the case with "La cucaracha."[28]

Canciones and corridos singing the praises of the Mexican heroes Pancho Villa and Emiliano Zapata were unbelievably popular. Pancho Villa's favorite song was "Las tres pelonas." Legend has it that Villa, who was feared for his violent temper, needed only to lift three fingers for one of the bands that followed his troops to play this tune in order to calm him.[29]

Naturally, a wealth of legends has grown up around the songs that flourished during the Revolution. Hugo de Grial cites the myths associated with some of the most popular canciones from the Revolution, for example, "La Adelita." Opinion is greatly divided as to the origin of this song. It has been claimed by at least seven states on the basis of as many legends. Other versions say that the song was composed during the Revolution. Among these is one lively story which states that a captain named Elíaz Cortázar Ramírez wrote the canción about his love affair with a girl called Adelita. Elíaz sang the song while sitting beside the campfire with his unit, and it soon spread to soldiers stationed throughout northern Mexico. Ramírez was later killed in action, and the song came to symbolize his last farewell to his beloved. According to another version, the verses were written (probably to a traditional melody) by a soldier named Antonio del Río Armento and dedicated to a fourteen-year-old girl in the Red Cross, Adelita Velarde Pérez, who cared for him when he was wounded. The origin of this song will probably never be known. Between 1915–20 it was one of the most popular songs in Mexico, spread by Pancho Villa's soldiers and sung throughout the land, almost as a hymn.[30]

The popular music of Mexico was oriented along traditional social lines until the Revolution. In his interesting article on music during the Mexican Revolution, Daniel Castañeda writes that Mexico had no música popular common to all social classes until the 1920s. Before then the country possessed two kinds of música popular, one based on the European tradition and cultivated by the upper classes, primarily in the towns (this tradition is often referred to as criollo), and the other derived from the Indians and mestizos, the lower classes, who lived in the big-city slums and the rural areas. While the nineteenth century witnessed the diffusion of Central European dances from the capital to the countryside and their assimilation by the mestizos, the social divisions were nevertheless very sharply drawn. What is now known as folk music served as popular music for the mestizos, while the city dwellers had the type of popular music that was (and still is) closely associated with the salon and the ballroom. Unlike the popular music of today, however, this music was limited in terms of its function in the society as a whole.[31]

In the capital, the nationalistic trends in music took hold at a fairly late stage. Several years after the outbreak of the Revolution, the music being written and played was hardly different from that of Porfirio Díaz's time.[32] But in the closing phase of the Revolution, when the members of the former ruling classes were dead or had fled the country, and no new upper class had yet become established, the social divisions in popular music disappeared. Modern dance music, romantic canciones, and mestizo folk music existed harmoniously and were diffused through all levels of society, especially in the towns.[33]

By this time a large number of ensembles and singers from various parts of Mexico were arriving in the capital in search of work. Naturally, they brought a great deal of folk music with them. Around 1920, folk singers performing canciones and corridos, accompanying themselves on the guitar, could be heard on almost every street corner.

This influx of folk music reached its peak between 1920 and 1930. In his article Castañeda lists various kinds of regional ensembles and cancioneros who played and sang in the streets and marketplaces of the capital:[34]

1) Mariachis from Cocula, Jalisco
2) Troubadors from Yucatán
3) Musicians and dancers performing jarabes and sandungas
4) Orquestas típicas, consisting of violin, harp, psaltery, and bandolón
5) Soldiers from the Yaqui region performing "La danza del Pascola"[35]
6) Troubadors from Tamaulipas and Veracruz with guitars and violins
7) Bandas jarochas from Veracruz playing huapangos
8) Cancioneros típicos from Oaxaca singing songs by José López Alavez, Samuel Mondragón, and others
9) Mariachi orchestras from Guerrero playing chilenas, gustos, sones, and malagueñas on violins, vihuelas, guitars, harps, and drums
10) Singers from Michoacán and orquestas típicas from the lake district (near Morelia) presenting sones (canciones) isleños of a sentimental and romantic nature
11) Dance groups, both Indian and mestizo, from all parts of Mexico

12) Marimba groups from Chiapas and Oaxaca (not included in Castañeda's list).

Many of these folk musicians had an opportunity to perform at the theatre. The nationalism that pervaded Mexico City during the 1920s was expressed in the theatrical shows that were staged at the leading theatres in the capital, the Teatro Principal and the Teatro Lírico.[36]

The performance of native music during intermissions between the acts of Spanish comedies was already an established practice at the turn of the nineteenth century. Singers (whether or not they were cast in the current show) appeared singing traditional and newly written songs. The theatres had also developed the custom of entertaining the audience with stories and songs after the play ended (so-called *fines de fiesta*, which were already popular in *tonadillas*).

In the 1920s these traditions reestablished themselves in theatrical productions dealing with the Revolution. Songs with national overtones (often with ranchera type texts) were written and sung by artists such as Lauro de Urango, Felipe Llera, and Don Eduardo Vigil y Robles. The audience often requested the favorite revolutionary songs.[37]

The plays were usually set in Revolution times. The plot was, of course, highly romanticized. Magnificent heroes and lovers acting out their lives in the shadow of war were popular themes. The most interesting aspect of these plays is that they generally incorporated folk music from those areas of the country in which the action of the play was set. For example, "La sandunga" was popularized in a play set in Oaxaca.[38] For many people in the audience, this was undoubtedly their first contact with this melody that was to become so well known. The musicians were from Oaxaca, too; the marimba naturally provided part of the accompaniment. Both musicians and actors wore regional costumes.

Polkas norteñas were played to convey the spirit of northern states. One of the great polkas of the early 1920s was called "La norteña," written by Eduardo Vigil y Robles expressly for a play set in northern Mexico.

One of the most popular dance numbers on the 1920s stage was the "Jarabe tapatío," which included tunes from the "Jarabe oficial" that had been performed in the theatre during the Juárez period some sixty years earlier.[39]

A veritable Latin America fever broke out in Europe in the years following 1910. The tango made a tremendous impact on Paris, and from there it conquered Europe and the United States. For many this was a kind of igniting spark. During its Revolution, Mexico in particular was highly romanticized by the Europeans. Celebrities were also attracted to Mexico by generous contracts.[40]

Among these guest artists was Maria Conesa, the Spanish singer, who toured Mexico in 1908-9. Like other celebrities, she adopted a Mexican canción to take with her on her tours. The canción mexicana that she chose was "La princesa china" by Federico Ruiz; the text clearly reflects the exotic image projected by China.

Other great artists who performed in Mexico in the 1920s were Tito Ruffo, Miguel Fleta, and Tito Schipa. Tito Ruffo, the Italian baritone, was one of the greatest singers of his time. His recording of Miguel Lerdo de Tejada's canción "Perjura," made in New York in 1919, was largely responsible for its international success. Miguel Fleta, the Spanish tenor, included Vigil y Robles's canción "Adiós trigueña" in his repertoire.

Several Mexican stars also gained national fame during this period. Esperanza Iris from the southern state of Tabasco was one of them. According to Garrido, Iris, who sang in operettas and zarzuelas, introduced Franz Lehar's operettas into Mexico. She was one of the performers who concluded her performances with a fin de fiesta, entertaining the audience with stories and songs. Mimi Derba was another stage favorite of the time. She sang canciones mexicanas, and performed in operettas and zarzuelas.

According to Garrido, the wave of nationalism in the theatre began to subside around 1930. However, aspects of this popular form were maintained, primarily through the efforts of a producer and actor named Roberto Soto, an ardent patriot who was very enthusiastic about all things Mexican. Up until 1950 Soto made certain that the theatres in the capital included big Mexican hits in their repertoires. He produced and acted in many shows that were written in the national spirit (*revistas del teatro*), which were filled with Mexican music. "Rayando el sol" and "Mexico a través de los siglos" were among Soto's greatest shows.[41]

But on the whole, the nationalism of revolutionary times began to decline after the 1920s; the sense of political commitment among the people diminished, and the country's leaders became more conservative. The one exception was President Lázaro Cárdenas, a Marxist who was president from 1934 to 1940. Thereafter, the conservatives returned to power. Sordo Sodi feels that Mexican popular music has since then lost touch with nationalism, and that it has not been a factor in the development of the nationalist feeling that is currently alive in Mexico. It appears that the trumpet mariachi, which began to develop in 1940, possesses just as little "real" nationalistic significance as the orquestas típicas.[42]

7
Composers and Musicians Up to the 1940s

One of the most striking patterns in the development of music in Mexico during the last hundred years lies in the life histories of the musicians. At some point in their lives, many of the composers and performers felt compelled to move from their hometowns to Mexico City. In certain instances, they moved in order to study at the National Conservatory, but in most cases the motivation was purely financial. Rural areas offered few opportunities for musicians to survive on a professional level, so they had to go to the capital to earn a living.

In their new environment, most of the musicians adjusted to the demands of the entertainment business, which dictated that their music conform to the fashions of the period. Nevertheless, there were some composers who based their music on the traditional styles they had brought from home.

The life of Juventino Rosas illustrates the career of a successful musician during the Díaz dictatorship.[1] Rosas was born on January 25, 1868, in the village of Santa Cruz in Guanajuato. His father, who was a soldier and a musician (he played the harp), gave Juventino and his older brother, Miguel, their first music lessons. Miguel specialized on the guitar, while Juventino studied the violin. The idea was that the brothers and their father would support the family by forming a trio to play at dances and other festivities in the district. But, since the possibility of earning a living as musicians in the rural areas was very unlikely, the family decided to try their luck in Mexico City. In 1875 they moved to a poor district in the capital; Juventino was then seven years old and could already play "aires" and canzonettas on his violin.[2]

The family lived in impoverished circumstances in Mexico City. Nevertheless, they struggled along by playing music in the streets, supplementing their income with occasional jobs. When his father died, Juventino joined the opera company that accompanied the great singer Angela Peralta on her tours through Mexico. Juventino, who showed great talent as a violinist, was later admitted to the National Conservatory (where tuition was free). However, he only studied there for a short time.[3]

Grial states that in 1885 Juventino and a friend of his who played the bandolón were offered an opportunity to perform at a concert given in the Teatro Nacional which Porfirio Díaz was to attend. (The concert was in honor of the anniversary of the Battle of Puebla in 1863.) Rosas gave a memorable performance of "La sonámbula," and from then on was offered engagements with better trained, privately owned salon orchestras. He acquired patrons, and the magnificent salons were open to him.

In 1891 Rosas dedicated his newly written waltz, "Sobre las olas," to one of his benefactors, Señora Calizta Gutiérrez de Alfaro. The style of the composition is that of a genuine Viennese waltz, which was then in fashion in the salons of the capital. Shortly after this, Juventino was persuaded to sell his waltz to the Casa Wagner for a mere seventeen pesos. "Sobre las olas" soon became a hit unparalleled in the history of Mexican music. Casa Wagner made a fortune from the tune that totaled more than 100,000 pesos. The waltz was soon a hit in Europe too, where it was known as "Über die Wellen." Juventino Rosas died in 1894 at the age of twenty-six, while he was on a tour of Cuba. This waltz was issued with lyrics as a pop tune in the United States during the late 1940s under the title, "The Loveliest Night of the Year."

The next international hit of Mexican origin was the romantic song "Estrellita" ("Little Star"), by Manuel M. Ponce, published in 1912. Ponce was one of the great composers of art music in Mexico, yet, like many of his contemporaries, he also wrote music in a lighter vein. Even today "Estrellita" is included in the repertoire of many nightclub musicians all over the world. Otto Mayer-Serra describes the style that influenced Manuel M. Ponce's canción in the following way:

The first Mexican song to become internationally known in this century, Ponce's "Estrellita," owes much to its model, Schumann's "Traumerei," as its equivalent in the last century, Juventino Rosas's "Sobre las olas" did to Waldteufel and Johann Strauss. This is to say, from the very outset of commercial production, the music of the popular composers, as also concert music, faced the dilemma between cosmopolitanism and nationalism.[4]

A survey of Mexican popular music before 1930 reveals how frequently "serious" composers also wrote music in the lighter vein (songs and dance music). Felipe Villanueva and Ernesto Elorduy, two composers active in Díaz's time, are good examples. Even in 1910 it was still relatively rare for composers to devote themselves exclusively to "serious" or to "popular" music.

Some composers, instrumentalists, and singers who began their musical careers by studying at the National Conservatory were later forced by financial problems to abandon their plans to work as concert performers or opera singers. Mario Talavera, Pedro Vargas, Felipe Llera, and Jorge Negrete were all singers who began in opera but turned to singing popular songs when this proved more profitable. Musicians performing serious music have never found a large market in Mexico.

With the advent of radio and sound film after 1930, there were still many composers, trained at the conservatory, who wrote both serious and popular music, for example Mario Lavista (film music) and Mario Curi. However, it became increasingly customary for musicians and composers to specialize in one field or the other.

Miguel Lerdo de Tejada (1869–1941) can be described as the first musician in Mexico who was totally committed to popular music.[5] He was a pioneer in a number of ways. He was the first Mexican to introduce his own melodies with his own orchestra (an orquesta típica).[6] He was Mexico's first cinema pianist (1907), the first to play popular music at restaurants, and to make recordings.[7] Tejada was audience oriented. He was always alert to the latest styles, and was among the first musicians in Mexico to write fox trots and tangos in the early 1920s. The bulk of his production, however, consisted of canciones mexicanas, whose music reveals an unmistakably romantic flavor ("Perjura," "México bello," and other songs).

A great many composers followed Tejada's example, creating canciones mexicanas in the same romantic spirit.[8] Among Miguel Lerdo de Tejada's closest friends was Mario Talavera (1885–1951), an opera singer who became a canción artist. He also composed songs for himself which he sang with panache. His greatest successes included "China" and "Flor de Mayo."[9]

Marcos A. Jiménez (1882–1944) was born in Michoacán, but at the age of twenty-five he moved to the capital where he wrote several zarzuelas. However, he is best known for his canción "Adiós Mariquita linda," which also served as the theme of a film with the same name.[10]

Maria Grever was never a Mexican citizen. She is said to have been born on a steamer in the middle of the Atlantic Ocean when her parents were on their way to Spain, where they intended to settle. Maria Grever spent her entire life (1884–1951) in Spain, France (where she studied under Debussy), and the United States. From time to time she visited Mexico, which she always considered her real homeland, but she never resided there. During her visits to Mexico, she worked with Miguel Lerdo de Tejada and other prominent composers, who certainly inspired her with their canciones romanticas mexicanas. However, it is equally accurate to attribute her compositional style to Spanish influences. (Some doubt exists about whether it is at all possible to distinguish national styles in popular romantic music, which was, and still is, an international phenomenon.) Among the several hundred songs written by Maria Grever are "Tipitín," "Bésame," "Júrame," and "Muñequita linda."[11]

Alfonso Esparza Oteo (1887–1950) was one of the central figures in Mexican musical life. As a child he studied the piano; Grial recounts a concert given by the twelve-year-old boy in his hometown of Aguascalientes for which he played Beethoven sonatas. Oteo actively participated in the Revolution under Francisco Villa's command, and then made his way to Mexico City, where he joined forces with Lerdo Tejada, Tata Nacho, and Talavera. In 1927 these four formed the group Los Cuatro Ases de la Canción, and after Lerdo de Tejada's death in 1941 the other three became the famous Trio Veneno.

Esparza Oteo was appointed the director of Columbia Records (New York, 1927) and Discos Brunswick (Mexico, 1929), and also held the same position at some radio stations, including XEB. He led La Orquesta Típica Presidencial in the early 1920s and was head of the folklore division of the Instituto de Bellas Artes (the position now occupied by Carmen Sordo Sodi). In 1939 he was active in the founding of the composers' union, El Sindicato de Compositores, which in 1948 became SACM. Esparza Oteo wrote some 150 canciones románticas. The best known among them is "Un viejo amor."[12]

The real name of Tata Nacho (1894–1968) was Ignacio Fernández Esperón (the nickname remained with him from childhood and was his pseudonym throughout his life). Tata Nacho grew up in a middle-class home in the town of Oaxaca. He was already writing canciones mexicanas when he entered the artistic circles in the capital. During 1923–24 he had an opportunity to study harmony and composition under Edgar Varèse in New York; it was hardly possible to acquire such specialized training in Mexico at that time.

Tata Nacho returned to Mexico in 1927 and was immediately offered a position as *investigador de música folklórica* in the *misiones culturales* that José Vasconselos, Minister of Education to President Obregón, had founded in 1923. Tata Nacho was in good company in this job. The other "missionaries" included Manuel M. Ponce, Angel Salas, Vicente T. Mendoza, and Blas Galindo. Their research produced a number of papers and official records, mostly by Vicente Mendoza, who published many of his results in Mexican musical journals such as *Nuestra Música*.[13] Mendoza was the only researcher who had ethnographic training. All the others obtained their positions solely on the basis of their reputations as composers, and their ability to read and write down music.[14]

Tata Nacho did not continue his work as a researcher for long. In 1929 he was sent with a group of intellectuals to a large Ibero-American Exhibition in Seville. From there he went to Paris, where he stayed until 1937, studying with Paul de Flem and Edgar Varèse. On his return to Mexico, Tata Nacho became one of the country's leading cultural personalities. In 1939 (together with Oteo and others) he was involved in the formation of the composers' union. He was also very active in films and radio. In 1947 he joined station XEW, for which he directed a very popular program of Mexican music entitled "Asi es mi tierra" ("This Is My Country"). Some years later Nacho also became leader of the Orquesta Típica de la Ciudad de México. He concluded his career by becoming president of SACM in 1963.[15] Tata Nacho wrote a number of serious pieces, but he is remembered by most people for canciones such as "La borrachita," "Adiós mi chaparrita," and "Nunca, nunca, nunca."[16]

The canción mexicana was often played on station XEW during the golden age of radio (1930–55).[17] During this time these canciones, which originated from an exclusive circle of musicians in Mexico City, were extended to a wider audience. The leading performers were Mario Talavera, Pedro Vargas, María Cornejo, Felipa Llera, and Mario Arvizú.

Around 1955, when television and American rock and roll music became popular simultaneously, the Mexican canción practically disappeared from XEW. Nowadays the genre has been banished to a few "memorial programs" on radio and television

In a previous section I discussed the influx of folk music into Mexico City during the 1920s. During this period many soloists, duets, and larger groups also began to promote *música folklórica* on a commercial basis in the capital and elsewhere. The first commercial folk music group was formed in Tampico, Tamaulipas, in 1922.[18] The quintet called itself El Grupo de los Trovadores Tamaulipecos. They sang regional folk songs with new arrangements. The three Flores Brothers were part of the group.[19]

Among the most successful trovadores to emerge from the revival of folk music in the 1920s were Lorenzo Barcelata from Veracruz and Agustín Ramírez from Guerrero. Both performed *música típica* from their respective hometowns, Barcelata singing huapangos and Ramírez chilenas.[20] They increased their repertoires by writing original songs in the traditional styles. Agustín Ramírez, who died in 1957, is actually the greatest twentieth-century composer (in terms of both quality and quantity) of chilenas.[21] His name is held in high esteem in Guerrero. There is even a corrido dedicated to him, "El corrido de Agustín Ramírez" (by W. F. Armenta), which tells of his life and work. He was a legend even in his lifetime.

Guty Cárdenas, Ricardo Palmerín, and Pepe Domínguez, all from Yucatán, are other composers who commercialized the folk music of their native region through new songs written in the traditional style. *Bambuco* is the style most commonly associated with Yucatán. Raúl Hellmer suggests that the bambuco or, as it is also called, *colombiana*, existed on the Yucatán peninsula in the nineteenth century.[22] Garrido, on the other hand, states categorically that the bambuco style was introduced into Yucatán in 1916 by visiting musicians from Colombia. He also claims that Ricardo Palmerín (1899–1944) was the first Mexican to write a bambuco. Because of these contradictory statements, the safest conclusion is that the bambuco style may have existed in Yucatán before 1916, but that Palmerín was the first to use it commercially.

Palmerín's best known canción, "Peregrina," is in fact an habanera. Like many other songs, it is connected with a romantic legend. "Peregrina" was allegedly dedicated to an American journalist who visited Mérida in the last years of the Revolution and fell in love with Carrillo Puerto, a socialist leader. Her love was requited, and Puerto commissioned a song from Palmerín, begging Alma Reed (the journalist) to stay in Mérida forever, or at least to return often. Palmerín accepted the commission, and the song "Peregrina" ("Pilgrim") was the result. According to Hugo de Grial, who related this story, "Peregrina" was first sung for Alma Reed in 1918 at a political meeting held under the full moon at the Mayan ruins at Chichén-Itzá.[23]

Palmerín was famous in Mérida, but he made little money from his songs. On the advice of a friend, he traveled the thousand miles to Mexico City with his family, hoping to improve his financial situation. Unfortunately, he did not succeed and ended his days in poverty.[24]

Guty Cárdenas (1905–32) acquired great fame during his short lifetime, both as a composer and a singer. He is still widely remembered in Mexico, primarily, of course, on the Yucatán peninsula. Cárdenas began by writing canciones in the "romantic" style typical of the period; his early compositions were often based on the bambuco rhythm. Later he turned to creating more authentic folk renditions. In songs such as "Yucalpetén" and "Caminate del Mayab" he successfully utilized a melos type derived from the Indian music of Yucatán. Fortunately, Guty Cárdenas, who was an excellent singer and guitar player, recorded a considerable number of his songs before he died.[25]

Pepe Domínguez (?–1950) derived some of his inspiration from the mestizo folk dance jarana. Most of his compositions, however, tend toward a later Afro-Cuban style (música tropical); consequently, he was very popular in Cuba and visited Havana on several occasions.[26]

Before the advent of radio, no standard medium for the

promotion of new music existed. A number of composers subsisted by playing for silent films, and naturally they tried to introduce the cinema audiences to their own works. Few were as fortunate as Lerdo de Tejada, who had his own orchestra. It was indeed always possible to have songs published and issued as sheet music, but this seldom helped unless the songs were channeled to the right people. Composers could pay personal visits to the conductors of the military bands that played marches, traditional melodies, and the latest hits in the parks and other public places in the big towns each Sunday. The outdoor concerts given in the Alameda Park in Mexico City by La Banda de Policía (the police band), led by Velino M. Preza, were attended by huge crowds. To persuade this or some other military band to include his tune in their repertoire was a composer's dream.[27]

In the 1920s the market for music in Mexico City was on the whole very open, less selective and rigid than it became when radio took over. The theatre that had grown up in the wake of the Revolution was a focal point. French couplets were set in a Mexican frame of reference and sung in cabarets. In fact, several composers began their careers by "moonlighting" as cabaret and nightclub musicians.[28]

The salons provided a center for a great deal of music and dance. On April 20, 1920, a club opened on Veracruz Street in Mexico City, El Salón México, which was the leading dance hall in the capital for several decades. There were five other big dance halls (*salones*) in Mexico City in 1920, but none could match the popularity of the Salón México.

People from all levels of society frequented the Salón México. The clientele included many working-class people, as well as more affluent types. The women who patronized this salon were for the most part prostitutes. Like many cabarets and restaurants in the capital, Salón México was open all night. The atmosphere was lively, and there were violent brawls at times.[29]

El Salón México owed much of its popularity to the orchestras that played there. Modern Afro-Cuban dance music, danzones in particular, was predominant. The orchestras hired did include native musicians, although the rhythm sections generally consisted of Cuban musicians. Tiburcio Hernández, "Babuco," a drummer from Cuba, was actually present at the inauguration of Salón México. The salon later engaged Conejo Valente, "Acerina," also a

Cuban, who is still working as a drummer and is the leader of a well-known danzón orchestra in Mexico City.[30] But danzones were not the only dances played at the Salón México; tangos, fox trots, waltzes, polkas, and pasodobles were also very popular.[31]

Toward the end of the nationalistic period, the music business came under commercial control for the first time. At the beginning of the 1930s, the radio, film, and record industries quickly became the leading distributors of music. A standard selection of tunes became available throughout the country. For the first time, composers specializing in popular music began to gain nationwide recognition.[32] Agustín Lara (1900–70), composer and performer, emerged as the outstanding exponent of this new age.[33]

Musical experts in Mexico have a tendency to speak and write disparagingly of Lara. There is, for example, a disapproving tone in Mayer-Serra's *The Present State of Music in Mexico*.[34] Lara is often described as the musician who completely abandoned Mexican forms and committed himself to cosmopolitan styles.

This statement calls for some modification. As previously noted, music of varying national origins gained popularity in Mexico between 1900 and 1930: the bambuco from Colombia, the danzón and bolero from Cuba, the fox trot from the United States, the tango from Argentina, and others. The danzón, fox trot, and tango were accepted in their original forms. The bambuco and the bolero, on the other hand, were modified (as the habanera had been previously) to conform to the native canción tradition.[35] The bambuco was of limited importance, but the bolero style dominated Mexican popular music for twenty years (1930 to 1950).

The danzón, fox trot, and tango were danced throughout the 1920s.[36] According to an unconfirmed item in an article written on the occasion of Agustín Lara's death, 80 percent of the music played on the radio before 1930 consisted of tangos.[37] Thus the country was ready for Agustín Lara; his appearance as a composer at the end of the 1920s was timely. The intriguing thing is that so much public interest was focused on a single musician.

Lara was a typical self-taught musician (apart from a few piano lessons as a child). He describes himself as follows:

> I should not be judged as a musician since I am a self-taught, instinctive lyricist. I play the piano by a miracle which can only be attributed to divine power. I was born with a soul to

create music and with the ability to express it although no one taught me how. This is the truth.[38]

Agustín Lara was a typical product of his age in other respects as well. He was enormously productive; his work comprises over five hundred songs. He immediately adopted the new styles that were sweeping the country. Lara joined station XEW and had his own program, "La hora azul" ("The Blue Hour"), which attracted large audiences. Much of the music he presented on this show was his own. Every week at least one new Lara melody was broadcast by XEW.

Agustín Lara also proved to be a great target for gossip columns; his many love affairs and wives (he dedicated hits to all of them) almost constituted a serial in the press. Lara was an idol.

That Lara totally abandoned the Mexican canción is not entirely true. Certainly most of his compositions were tangos, boleros, and danzones ("Mujer," "Enamorada," "Solamente una vez," and others), but he also wrote songs that have always been regarded as very "Mexican."[39] These tunes include the waltz-canción "Farolito," one of his earliest published works (1927).

Before Lara's time, composers rarely wrote songs for a specific performer, unless the composer was a performer himself as in the case of Guty Cárdenas and Mario Talavera. Lara, however, introduced this practice. At the beginning of his career, his favorite artists were Juan Arvizú, Toña la Negra, and Ana María Fernández; later on there were several others. Since Agustín Lara, this type of association between composers and their favorite performers has become a standard practice. To name one example, José Luis Caballero was an important interpreter of Gabriel Ruiz's songs in the 1940s.

Agustín Lara attained a high degree of international fame. A Hispanophile, he wrote that he regarded himself to be as much a Spaniard as a Mexican.[40] Lara dedicated some of his most famous songs to Spanish towns; his bestseller, "Granada," is one of them. Lara was made an honorary Spanish citizen on a visit to Spain in 1965–66.

Lara was financially successful as a composer during his lifetime. According to SACM's statistics, his songs were much more frequently played than those of any other Mexican composer, both in Mexico and in other countries. He was not only famous as a composer, but also as a conductor, pianist, and "singer." P. H. Apel described Lara as an artist and composer in the following terms:

> Composer of some 600 songs—melancholy songs of love, of whispered reproach and moaning despair; his soft piano playing in a darkened room with a single soft light shining on his pinched face has been the most irresistible thing in Mexican entertainment.[41]

Many of Agustín Lara's works were boleros in the Pan-American style of his time. A tremendous number of composers followed his example. All the established orchestras and soloists included at least one bolero in their repertoire. This was particularly true of musical trios, which consist of three singers with their own guitar accompaniment. A number of trios were formed in the late 1920s. The leading group in this and many other respects was the incomparably famous Trio los Panchos. During the thirty years of its continuing popularity, this group has made some forty long-playing records. The Trio los Panchos can honestly be called outstanding promoters of Mexican popular music. They have performed on television and in nightclubs throughout the world.

The group took its present name in 1944 when the musicians appeared at elegant hotels in New York. Alfredo Gil and Chucho Navarro (who began working together in 1939) have been permanent members of the trio; the third member has changed five times since 1944.[42]

Like other trios, Los Panchos started with a repertoire of typically Mexican genres (huapango, ranchera), but soon shifted to singing boleros. Los Panchos set the style in their repertoire and performance techniques for other trios in Mexico and throughout Latin America.[43]

In 1945 Los Panchos made a change in their instrumentation which also became standard for other trios. One of the three Spanish guitars was replaced by a six-stringed requinto. The requinto, which is smaller than an ordinary guitar and tuned a fourth higher, effectively enriched the sound with its lighter and more piercing tone. The requinto is especially suitable for runs and other ornamental stylings.

The most famous Mexican trios besides Los Panchos are: Los Hermanos Martínez Gil (1928), Trio Tariácuri (1933), Los Calaveras (1938), Los Diamantes (1951), and Los Tres Ases (1954).[44]

The style varies little from one group to another, although in the 1960s a number of trios converted their repertoire and performance techniques to a more *balada* (pop) form of music (Los Diamantes, for example).

The duo Garnicia-Ascencio, who appeared just after 1930, and perhaps to a greater extent, Las Hermanas Aguila, were prominent duets; in Mexico most duets, and actually the best ones, consist of women singers. Over the last thirty years the Aguila Sisters have made dozens of records of boleros and canciones mexicanas.

Beginning in the 1930s, dance bands also adopted boleros. In fact, the softer Cuban dances, the *romántica tropical,* reached the height of their popularity during that period. The guaracha and guajira dances, as they were performed in the 1930s, definitely belong to this category.

The danzón is one of the Cuban dances that has retained its style relatively intact through the decades.[45] Its counterpart is the bolero, which has been a divided, changing genre for some twenty years. On one hand, the bolero merged with the ranchera style; boleros rancheros are simply ranchera songs with a slight tendency toward bolero rhythm revealed in the mariachi accompaniment. The bolero romántico followed a different route and became international in style; it bears a strong resemblance to the type of songs that are heard at music festivals in the United States and Europe. Roberto Cantoral, Armando Manzanero, and Antonio Muñóz are prominent exponents of this form.

Both the bolero ranchero and bolero romántico are on the fringes of the genre, but the bolero as a genre is obviously dissolving. The rhythmically accented Cuban type of bolero, such as those written by Lara and his contemporaries, is seldom heard on the radio nowadays. The bolero ranchero and bolero romántico, on the other hand, are very popular and frequently played.

During the twenties, the sound of the dance orchestras was revolutionized. The delicate string arrangements of romantic music were replaced by a sharper, "hotter" sound in which brass instruments played a leading role: trumpet, saxophone, bassoon, and combos consisting of piano, drum, and double bass (often supplemented with banjo or guitar). The accordion and marimba were also often used. The violins did not completely vanish, of course, and they still provide the basis of *la música romántica.*

Among those who adopted tropical rhythms—the danzón,

mambo, rhumba, and chachacha—the orchestras of Carlos Campos and Dámaso Pérez Prado are the two most highly respected ones in Mexico. The Cuban-born Prado resides in Mexico and is a citizen of that country; he has frequently toured Mexico with orchestras consisting solely of Mexican musicians.

Carlos Campos began his career as a pianist with danzón orchestras such as Jaramillo y sus Diablos at the end of the 1930s and at El Salón México in the early 1940s. Danzones still provide the basis of Campos's repertoire, which also includes chachacha and mambo. Carlos Campos's orchestra consists primarily of five saxophones, a few trumpets, and a rhythm section. Campos takes pride in never allowing his arrangements to be divested of their original character. He has stated:

> I believe that one of the reasons why jazz never gained a foothold in Mexico is that it distorts [*desfigura*] the melody right up to the point where it converts to pure rhythm and style.[46]

Traditionally a considerable part of the repertoire in the tropical genre consisted of melodies derived from nineteenth-century opera:

> I am accused of plagiarizing Rossini and other opera composers but my critics forget that there was no limit to arrangements from Rigoletto, La Gioconda, La Traviata and La Bohème during the rise of the danzón in the twenties and thirties. A tradition grew up in this genre; it may be explained by the circumstance that at the time there was hardly any repertoire available, apart from the music of Agustín Lara and Guty Cárdenas. The arrangers used what they could find in other spheres.[47]

Other Mexican dance orchestras imitated North American models. When Juan S. Garrido arrived in Mexico City from his native Chile in 1932, one of the fashionable dance orchestras was called Los Cometas Castañedas and comprised two trumpets, three saxophones, piano, double bass, and drum. The repertoire consisted mostly of American songs, as well as a number of French ones.[48]

Juan S. Garrido formed his band in 1936. According to him, it was the first real "swing" orchestra in Mexico. This orchestra was also important in training swing musicians, some of whom, such as Ramón Marquéz and Juan Arteta, later broke away and formed their own dance bands. Garrido also began to play Mexican songs which had previously been omitted from the repertoires of modern dance bands. He arranged such songs as "Guadalajara" by Pepe Guízar in swing style, with elements of modified huapango rhythm, incorporating some typical Mexican instruments such as the marimba. Garrido's example was followed by Leopoldo Olivares and his orchestra.[49]

During the 1940s Juan S. Garrido's swing orchestra competed for popularity with the orchestras led by Pablo Beltrán Ruiz and Luis Arcaraz. Even today, swing is still highly fashionable among Mexican dance bands. New combinations of instruments have been tried over the years (patterned after the trends in the United States), and the arrangers have been influenced by pop rhythms. Carlos Tirado's orchestra has been particularly active in introducing "new" instrumental sounds. In recent years Ismael Díaz's orchestra has also acquired great popularity in the capital.

8

The Media

Radio

The first radio station in Mexico (CWL) began broadcasting in 1923. Radio developed on a commercial basis from the start, as in the United States.[1] Because of this, the number of radio stations steadily increased. There were also a few "cultural" stations that were not financed by commercials.[2] These included the station belonging to the Secretaría de Educación Pública, which began transmitting in November 1924 through the efforts of José Vasconcelos. This station was purely educational from the beginning, and, according to Sordo Sodi, it contributed to Vasconcelos's national educational projects.[3]

The radio was of no real significance in the 1920s, as there were very few people who were interested in it or could afford to buy radios. (At first listeners had to use ear-phones to pick up the transmissions. Thus they could only listen one at a time.)

During the first years of radio, only American, Argentine, Cuban, and some French music was played. The obvious reason is that the production of Mexican records did not get under way until the late 1920s. With very few exceptions, records were imported from the United States. There were, of course, instances of records made by visiting Mexican artists or by international stars performing Mexican music, but this facet of the recording industry was insignificant compared with all the fox trots and tangos that were produced. In those early years, the Mexican radio stations broadcast almost only recorded music; live programs were not aired to any great extent before 1930. The first station in Mexico to transmit live broadcasts was XEB, which began operating in 1925.[4]

Mexican popular music did not gain recognition on the radio until 1930, when station XEW opened. Juan S. Garrido, who joined the staff of XEW in the mid-thirties, estimates that XEW was then broadcasting 60 percent native popular music. On the other stations, an average 70 to 80 percent of the music was written by foreign composers.[5]

Musicians and composers faced considerable difficulties during the 1920s. The opportunities for them to earn a living were limited. A contract with one of the minor commercial radio stations was highly desirable, although the pay was poor. The relationship between artists and the broadcasting companies can be well illustrated by the career launched by a singing trio, Los Cancioneros del Sur, between 1929 and 1935.[6]

In 1929 XEX, a Mexico City station, held a competition (*concurso*). The people, using ballots available in one of the newspapers published in the capital, were supposed to write down the name of their favorite soloist, duet, trio, and so forth. The most popular ones would win a contract with station XEX. For undiscovered artists, such a competition could mean the difference between success and their continued existence in obscurity. Since then, a considerable number of musicians and singers have become popular through these *concursos de la canción popular*. Nowadays many states have their own annual song competitions, sponsored by radio stations, record companies, and other commercial businesses with vested interests. Naturally, such competitions act as a means of selecting and promoting certain popular trends, especially within folk music.[7]

Los Cancioneros del Sur did not appear to have a good chance in the XEX competition, but they succeeded in winning by a trick; they privately printed a large number of ballots, wrote their name on all of them, and sent them in to XEX. They won, despite the fact that the ink was so fresh it stained the hands of the people counting the votes. Unfortunately, financial difficulties prevented XEX from keeping its end of the bargain. But the trio was referred to another small station, XEFA, located on the Avenida Juárez. They auditioned there and were accepted; Los Cancioneros del Sur were then under contract with XEFA, along with such artists as Chucho Monge and Las Hermanas López.

After a short time with XEFA the trio joined XEB, which was considered Mexico City's leading station at the end of the 1920s. It was owned by La Compañía de Cigarro el Buen Tono. XEB's artistic director was Alfonso Esparza Oteo, and Bernardo San Cristóbal, who later joined XEW, was its manager. The audition was so successful that Los Cancioneros del Sur were asked to give two half-hour live performances that same day during the afternoon, which was prime radio time. They alternated with famous artists such as García Cornejo, Maruca Pérez, María Romero, and the Pepsodent Orchestra conducted by Esparza Oteo. Their fee was fifteen pesos, which was regarded as good pay.

Even at the beginning of the 1930s the radio stations had a small audience, and the sale of radios was very limited. Nevertheless, Emilio Azcárraga Vidaurreta, a farsighted and wealthy man, felt that the time was ripe to invest in a larger radio station than those then broadcasting in Mexico. The station was assigned the call letters XEW. For his inaugural concert, broadcast live, Azcárraga engaged Miguel Lerdo de Tejada and his orchestra, La Típica de la Ciudad de México, as well as Juan Arvizú, Alfonso Ortiz Tirado, La Chacha Aguilar, Los Trovadores Tamaulipecos with Lorenzo Barceleta, and others.

XEW was a great success and soon became Mexico City's leading station. Its golden age lasted until around 1955, when television became popular. XEW had a good reputation with artists, and a contract with the station was regarded as financially rewarding. Agustín Lara was soon under contract, as were Los Hermanos Domínguez and Jorge Negrete.[8] On the other hand, lesser-known artists found it difficult to gain access to this successful station, as its artistic director was very selective. Los Cancioneros del Sur were just barely accepted in 1935, after playing for five years at less well-known radio stations, including that belonging to La Secretaría de Educación Pública. At first the trio had to be content with performing at the worst broadcasting time, namely eight o'clock in the morning. They shared this fate with such artists as Pepe Guízar, who established himself with "Guadalajara" and "El mariachi," songs that are nowadays invariably included in the repertoire of every established trumpet mariachi band.

Raúl Cossío, director of Radio Universidad (owned by the Universidad Nacional Autónoma de México—UNAM) since May 1970, expressed his views on the present state of radio broadcasting.

He deeply deplored the fact that the radio stations in Mexico operate on a commercial basis, as indeed they do throughout Latin America (with the exception of Cuba). Because the medium of radio has never been under government control in Mexico, and the companies are only interested in their profits, the situation has deteriorated greatly.

All the commercial stations are financially dependent on advertisements. Only two stations in Mexico City allow the commercial interests to be subordinate to the quality of the programs they broadcast. Radio Universidad, which was formed in 1940, is in a special position, since it is financed by UNAM and thus not dependent on the income from commercials. A fairly high level of excellence is also attained by XELA, "Buena Música de México." The quality of the programs broadcast by these two stations is manifest both in their content, much of which is classical music, jazz, and folk music (native and foreign), and also in their presentation. Unfortunately, Radio Universidad and XELA, like all stations in Mexico, transmit on low frequencies so that they cannot be picked up outside the capital; it can be difficult to tune in on these stations even in the suburbs.

Radio is a highly competitive business. In the summer of 1971 there were a total of 486 commercial radio stations. The figure has probably risen since then. The distribution of stations among the states was as follows:[9]

Aguascalientes: 4
Campeche: 5
Chiapas: 11
Chihuahua: 33
Coahuila: 30
Colima: 5
Durango: 8
Guanajuato: 23
Guerrero: 12
Hidalgo: 3
Jalisco: 35
Mexico: 5
Michoacán: 25
Morelos: 3
Nayarit: 7
Nuevo León: 20

Oaxaca: 10
Puebla: 11
Querétaro: 5
San Luis Potosí: 13
Sinaloa: 22
Sonora: 35
Tabasco: 7
Tamaulipas: 37
Tlaxcala: 1
Veracruz: 43
Yucatán: 9
Zacatecas: 5
Baja California Norte: 26
Baja California Sur: 2
Quintana Roo: 1
Distrito Federal: 30

The entire system is pointless, Cossío feels, since the various stations (except for the two previously mentioned) offer exactly the same types of programs. They consist exclusively of light music, interspersed with a wide variety of advertisements. The trend is consistent. The only difference is that certain stations concentrate more on Mexican popular music, while others confine themselves to foreign music.

Raúl Cossío was, however, at the time I spoke with him, somewhat optimistic about the situation, believing that the administration of President Luis Echeverría (1970–76) was aware of the problem. Since the end of Díaz Ordaz's term in office, a law has been in effect that requires the radio stations to devote at least 12.5 percent of their total transmission time to "cultural" programs. In reality this measure is unsuccessful, since the stations broadcast the cultural programs during the least expensive transmitting hours, very early in the morning or late at night.[10] The country could certainly benefit from more extensive educational programming. Time should be set aside for broadcasting plays and lectures, a practice that is presently practically nonexistent.[11]

The ownership of radio stations in Mexico is highly profitable because they are tax-exempt. Naturally, the costs of starting a new station are high. Information from SACM shows that the equipment and installation of a new station now costs at least a half-million pesos.[12] Stations are generally owned by corporations (*compañías publicitarias*), each of which has a chain of stations (*cadenas*).[13]

The royalties paid by the stations to SACM, the composers' union, and Asociación Nacional de Artistas (ANDA), the performers' union, are very low.[14] Each of the radio stations plays at least three thousand songs every month, distributed among two hundred to three hundred titles, as popular melodies are broadcast several times a day. More than half the stations pay less then 375 pesos per month per month to SACM, which in turn distributes the royalties for the songs played to composers, songwriters, and arrangers.[15]

Table 1 shows that 118 stations pay from 0 to 249 pesos per month, and the top price paid by any station is 12,125 pesos.[16]

The statistics show that the stations in the Federal District, which includes Mexico City, pay more royalties than most of the others. The fact that SACM passes on some 85 percent of the composers' fees directly to unions in other countries indicates that

TABLE 1
Monthly Royalties Paid by Mexican Radio Stations to SACM

Sum paid (pesos)	Number of Stations	Average Sum	Total Sum
0— 249	118	125	14,750
250— 499	130	375	48,750
500— 749	85	625	53,125
750— 999	37	875	32,375
1,000— 1,249	30	1,125	33,750
1,250— 1,499	17	1,375	23,375
1,500— 1,749	4	1,625	6,500
1,750— 1,999	5	1,875	4,375
2,000— 2,249	7	2,125	14,875
2,250— 2,499	5	2,375	11,875
2,500— 2,749	3	2,625	7,875
2,750— 2,999	6	2,875	17,250
3,000— 3,249	7	3,125	21,875
3,250— 3,499	4	3,375	13,500
3,500— 3,749	1	3,625	3,625
4,500— 4,749	1	4,625	4,625
5,250— 5,499	2	5,375	10,750
5,500— 5,749	1	5,625	5,625
8,000— 8,249	1	8,125	8,125
8,500— 8,749	1	8,625	8,625
12,000—12,249	1	12,125	12,125
	466		362,750

the programs broadcast by these stations in the most urbanized area of Mexico contain a great deal of foreign music.[17]

Nevertheless, SACM receives a large amount of money from countries in which the payment of royalties by radio stations, the recording industry, and others is more rigidly controlled. This is particularly true of countries in which the state controls the media. Table 2 shows payments to and from foreign unions and SACM between 1965 and 1969.[18]

TABLE 2
Money Received from and Distributed to Foreign Unions by SACM 1965-69 (in pesos)

Year	Payments to Foreign Societies	Money Received from Foreign Societies
1965	659,572	1,195,200
1966	699,370	1,133,600
1967	855,322	1,442,400
1968	1,118,997	1,872,800
1969	1,507,457	1,818,400

This table shows that SACM receives more money from abroad than it pays out. Thus the overseas composers' unions lose the most by Mexico's failure to ensure that radio stations pay royalties for all music played.

The radio was SACM's largest source of income until 1969. The recording industry surpassed it in 1970, as shown in Figure 1.[19]

The Record Industry

From the beginning, Eduardo C. Baptista (1897–1971) was the central figure in the Mexican recording industry. Born in Venezuela, he traveled to the United States at the age of fourteen, and worked and studied there for several years, until he settled in Mexico in 1921.[20] In April of that year Baptista and a friend of his opened a shop selling records and phonograph cylinders in Mexico City. At first they were agents for the American Okeh label, which issued fox trots, but they soon began to import tangos and canciones recorded by Carlos Gardel for Odeón in Buenos Aires. The business did not fare well at first; the contract stipulated that they must import a minimum of two thousand copies of each record, and it was difficult to sell so many when only a few people owned record players. The only way to reduce costs was to make their own records in Mexico.

In 1925 Baptista went to New York to buy recording equipment, an acoustic recorder (this was before the days of electronic recording), a cardboard loudspeaker, a rotation mechanism, and all the other necessary items. He returned to Mexico City with his equipment and installed it in a studio in the suburb of Tacubaya. He had a plaster cabin built approximately sixteen feet in diameter, which would hold up to eleven musicians.

The following year the first electric record was made in the United States and new equipment had to be bought to keep pace with the latest developments. Four years elapsed before Baptista was able to begin large-scale industrial production of electric records in Mexico.

The first records made in Mexico were issued under the labels of Olympia, Nacional, Huici, and Artex. In most cases Guillermo Posadas arranged and conducted the recordings, and the singers

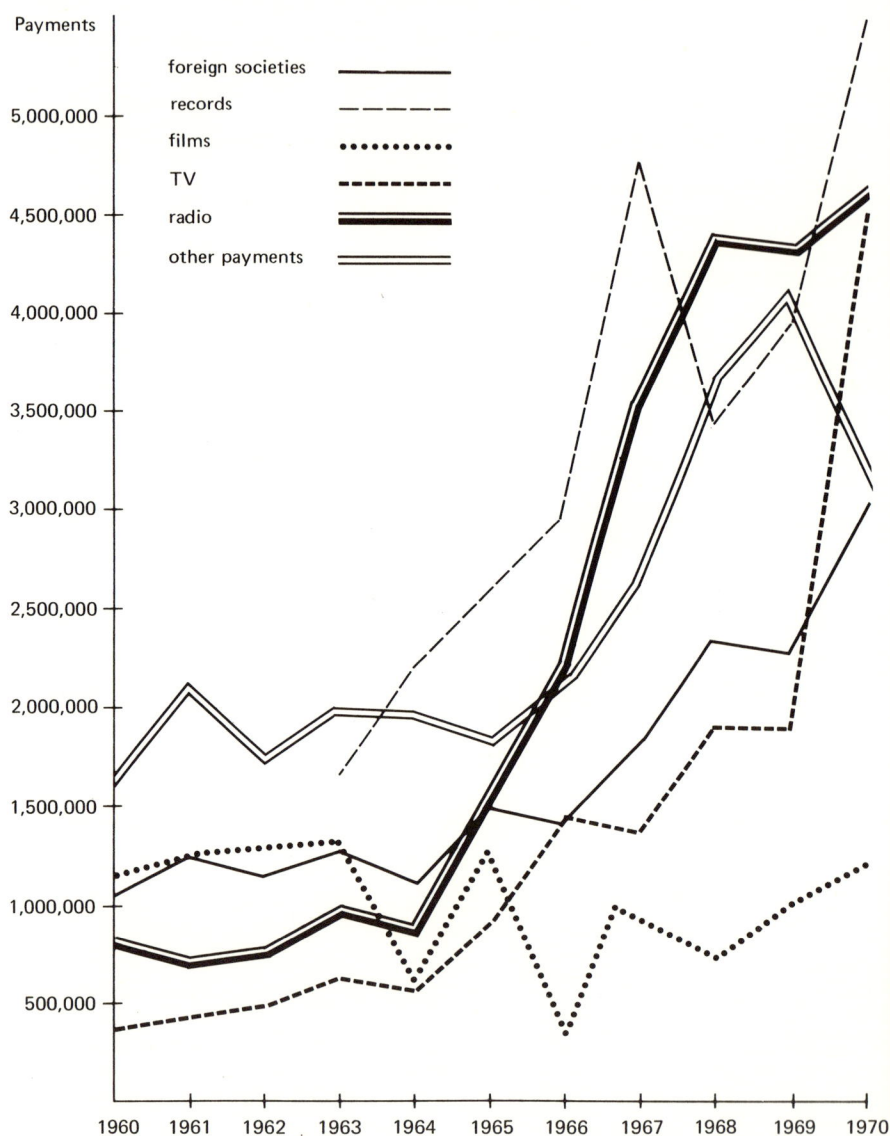

Figure 1. Sources of Payments Received by SACM, 1960–70 (in pesos)

included Salvador García, Guty Cárdenas, Juan Arvizú, Pedro Vargas, Alfonso Ortiz Tirado, and Tito Guízar.

In 1931 Baptista's factory created a new label, Peerless, and shortly after that Eduardo and Gustavo Klinckwort started a company to distribute the Peerless records; this company lasted for fourteen years. Peerless must be regarded as the first label of any importance in Mexico; the records carrying it were sold throughout the country. The artists who recorded for Peerless included Agustín Lara, Toña la Negra, Pedro Infante, and Las Hermanas Aguila.

Eduardo Baptista opened a new factory in 1940. War had already broken out, and raw materials were very scarce. The factory gladly accepted old broken records for reprocessing. Between 1943 and 1947 the record industry in Mexico prospered, due to the large quantity of orders from the United States, but the shortage of raw materials meant that at times the producers could fill only 30 percent of the orders.

Meanwhile, American-owned companies had begun to enter the Mexican market. RCA took the lead by establishing a subsidiary company in Mexico in 1943. Columbia followed suit in 1947. Baptista sold Peerless to Gustavo Klinckwort that same year, but he reentered the market only a few months later by founding Musart, which was administered by Pan Americana de Discos, S.A. (1947). Musart became highly successful. The year after it was founded, its directors signed contracts with Capitol in Hollywood, and some years later with EMI, who had contracts with such stars as Frank Sinatra and Nat King Cole.

This account of the development of the recording industry is seen from Baptista's point of view. Tracing the subtler aspects of ownership and control in this development presents extensive problems. Undoubtedly American-owned companies currently have a great influence on the Mexican record market. The Mexican RCA Victor, which is by far the largest recording company in the country, is indirectly owned by the American company. While Mexican laws prohibit record companies (and businesses in general) to be wholly controlled by foreign capital, the influence exercised by the parent company in the United States is bound to be considerable. The same applies to Mexican Capitol and CBS, with parent companies in the United States. Discos Gamma is operated primarily with Spanish funding.[21] Orfeón, Peerless, and Musart, on the other hand, are entirely Mexican-owned.[22]

Juan S. Garrido estimates that American capital in the Mexican record industry amounts to 50 percent. However, there is no data to support this figure. Besides the large record firms, there are some two hundred small Mexican companies of minor importance.

The big recording companies appear to limit their production to well-known and popular artists. Their policy, in regard to both Mexican and foreign performers, tends to preserve already established tastes. This position was clearly expressed in the statement made by Manuel Villarreal of Columbia in an interview with Otto Mayer-Serra in 1961.

> So far we have planned out recordings on the basis of a "frozen" budget: the artistic director decided that such and such songs should be recorded with such and such performers. . . . But today the industry must be superselective. Every recording should guarantee in advance to sell enough to cover costs. The calculations must be made on estimated sales figures.[23]

In an interview published by *Audiomúsica*, Salvador Suárez, director of Mercado de Discos, Mexico's largest record store, expressed the same view: ". . . the idea is not to limit the production of long-playing records but to be more selective."[24] Suárez believes that all new artists should be tested on singles before they are offered an opportunity to make an album. He states:

> In recent years a whole constellation of ranchera singers has appeared, some of them really good. Yet not one has succeeded in becoming an "artista de base" ["superstar"]. Lola Beltrán continues to hold a place of pride in this genre and she has taken the prize three years running [Mercado de Discos' award, "El Discometro"]. Miguel Aceves Mejía won the same prize in his specialty [ranchera, male vocalist]. Even artists who are now dead, such as Pedro Infante and Jorge Negrete, are still selling very well. . . .[25]

Suárez concludes that the recording companies should limit the number of artists bringing out new albums and concentrate their efforts on releasing old hits that sell reliably well.

The consistent application of such a policy would unquestionably reinforce an already limited system of selecting performers.

Unknown artists would have increased difficulty in gaining recognition. This narrow view may have broadened in recent years, but there is no information to document such a change. And still the same artists dominate the various genres year after year. This is clearly proven by the selection of music on the radio and on records; it is also revealed in the awards that Mercado de Discos gives every year to the best-selling performers in each field. Despite persistent attempts, I was unable to obtain a complete listing of the winners of the Discometro for the past decade. The 1962 listing presented below was published in *Audiomúsica* and is the only complete one this journal has printed. I have noted in parentheses the winners of other years, when such information was available, for the purpose of comparison.[26]

Female Ranchera Singer:	Lola Beltrán (1959–60–61)
Male Ranchera Singer:	Miguel Aceves Mejía (1960–61)
	(D. Zaizar 1959)
Duet:	Las Hermanas Aguila
Ranchera Duet:	Las Hermanas Huerta
Balada Singer:	Enrique Guzmán
Composer (all categories):	Federico Baena
	(Tomás Méndez 1959;
	Rubén Fuentes 1961;
	Tata Nacho 1963)
Orchestra (without vocalist):	Carlos Campos (1959)
Vocal/Instrumental Ensemble:	Sonora Santanera
Male Bolero Singer:	Lucho Gatica
	(Marcos Antonio Muñoz 1961)
Female Bolero Singer:	Olga Guillot
	(Virginia López 1961)
Best Seller (all categories):	Bill Haley
Best New Group:	Los Impala
Songwriter/Singer:	José Alfredo Jiménez
Trio:	Los Panchos (1967)
	(Los Tres Reyes 1959)
Bolero & Ranchera Singer:	Javier Solís (1959–60–66)
Best Seller (deceased):	Pedro Vargas
New Star:	Alvaro Zarmeno

Many of the artists listed have maintained their reputations over a long period of time, for example, Tata Nacho, the Aguila Sisters,

Trio Los Panchos, and Carlos Campos's orchestra. It is not surprising that a special place is reserved for the "Best Seller (deceased)," since the taste of the Mexican public is remarkably conservative, and singers such as Vargas, Infante, and Negrete are still the top sellers. The record companies have invested a great deal of money in reissuing old favorites. (In 1971 RCA released a large collectors' series on its label, Camden.) Often artists who were extremely popular in the 1940s and even earlier have made new recordings of their old hits. Toña la Negra, for example, did this at the beginning of the 1960s.[27]

The special status of the ranchera is revealed by the fact that the list includes both a general category for duets and one for rancheras sung by duets. Note also that a distinction is made between ranchera and bolero-ranchero. José Alfredo Jiménez (d. 1974), still another ranchera singer, appears on the list as the foremost interpreter of his own songs.

Unfortunately, no reliable figures on the total production and sale of records are available. There is an item in *Audiomúsica* to the effect that the ranchera song "Sombras," recorded on a single by Javier Solís in the mid-sixties, sold two hundred thousand copies in one year.[28] However, "Sombras" is not included in SACM's listings of the ten best-selling native melodies between 1963 and 1968. Considering that the potential buyers consist mostly of middle-class city dwellers, particularly the young people, and that they are not likely to buy rancheras, the figure seems highly improbable.

However, record sales did increase tremendously during the 1960s. An article in *Audiomúsica* claims that the sales increased by 12 to 15 percent in 1965–66. The author of the article also mentions that in 1966 the record sales in Mexico brought in 220 million pesos. (No comparable figures are available for later years.)

Single records dominated the market throughout the 1950s. The extended-play record (EP) did not equal the single in sales until 1965.[29] At the same time, the long-playing record (LP), first made in Mexico in 1950, became popular during the 1960s; currently its sales account for a considerable percentage of the total.

The availability of audio equipment, which has always been scarce in Mexico, reportedly increased between 1965 and 1966.[30] The price of record players, tape recorders, amplifiers, loudspeakers, and radios were, and are, far above those in the United

States and Europe. The quality of the equipment sold in Mexico is low compared with that in more highly industrialized countries. (The large recording companies, however, use entirely professional equipment in their studios, imported from the United States).

The *balada*, rock music with overtones of bolero rhythm, accounted for a large percentage of the record sales during the late 1950s and early 1960s. American and English rock music was widely imitated by native performers, with the original texts translated into Spanish. Around 1965 imported original recordings began to compete with these "dubbed" versions.[31]

César Costa and Enrique Guzmán are among the performers who were best known for their imitations of foreign rock and pop singers. Costa became popular at the end of the 1950s through his precise imitations of Paul Anka's songs and performance style. The arrangements were also copied from the original recordings. Guzmán, whose records became hits beginning in 1959 and retained their popularity for some years, also copied American rock and pop songs and their characteristic sound.[32]

In a 1966 article in *Audiomúsica,* Alberto Maravi complained of the lack of independence among Mexican rock and roll and pop groups.[33] He wrote that Mexican groups were still obsessed with imitating foreign styles and sounds. The groups lacked the initiative to create a repertoire of native music, such as was done in Brazil and Argentina.[34] The only new element in Mexico was that Paul Anka, Elvis Presley, and Bill Haley had been superseded by the Beatles and the English and American rock groups that followed in their wake. There was certainly no shortage of Mexican groups in the mid-sixties (Los Johnny Jets, Los Yakis, Los Dominics, Los Hitters, and so forth), but none of them developed a native repertoire. Hit songs such as "Woolly Bully" and "Hang On Sloopy" were freely plagiarized. This trend was changed at the end of the 1960s by the higher quality groups who came mainly from northern Mexico. One of the popular bands in 1968 was called El Muerto de Emiliano Zapata.

The Mexican market was and still is highly dependent on artists who set the style. In 1961 Rubén Fuentes complained about the conformism prevailing among the artists.[35] Only a few of them have developed a personal style, said Fuentes, and his statement holds equally true in the 1970s.

Frequently a Mexican performer is associated with a certain

song or its recording. The record companies actively promote this type of identification by investing a great deal of money in advertising. The standard procedure is that the record companies give large quantities of records to the radio stations.[36] These "gifts" are not always honorable; bribes are quite common. Their interest lies in having the song played as often as possible to acquaint the listeners with it and thus increase record sales. In the United States, this practice is known as "payola."

A successful recording made by a company in Mexico is usually taken up by rival companies. This is a result of the large number of recording companies, which exist despite the fact that the market of potential buyers is relatively limited in comparison with that of many other countries. Heinz Klinckwort (director, Peerless de México) suggested a solution to the problem:

> When an artistic director of a company is confronted with a hit, and believes that he has an artist in his stable [*elenco*], who is able to surpass it, he should make a recording of it; if this is not the case, he should rather refrain from recording it, because it is condemned beforehand.[37]

The big recording companies sign exclusive contracts with artists and orchestras, which means that the artists are bound for a given period of time to record only for the company with whom they are signed. Every recording company has its own group of established artists. In 1961 RCA had 140 artists under contract.[38]

In Mexico few native singers have succeeded in eliciting real enthusiasm from an audience when they perform "live." This applies especially to male and female ranchera singers, who almost invariably overact. There is actually no training nor a real tradition for stage performances.[39] Singers have not proven to be particularly good as film stars, either, but they tend to be more successful on the screen, since the medium can be manipulated to their advantage.

Film Music

Sound films came to Mexico in the early 1930s. Canciones mexicanas and ranchera songs (the latter genre developed and became popular during the 1930s) played a prominent role in sound films when they first appeared. Songs were used partially to take up time; an established performer (somewhat disguised) would appear to sing a canción, either a well-known song or one written for the film. Generally the song was related to the love story that was invariably a part of the plot, but songs with national associations were also popular (such as "Ay, Jalisco no te rajes" by Manuel Esperón).[40]

Yet the filmmakers integrated songs to an even greater extent. The theme song frequently provided the content for the entire film, the plot illustrating the lyrics. Many composers and songwriters realized the opportunity for making a fortune. The most prolific songwriters for films of the 1930s and beyond included Agustín Lara, Manuel Esperón, and Chucho Monge. Monge wrote themes for 176 films, and in 76 of them his songs provided the title of the film in which they were used.[41]

Film music was not only an element loosely incorporated in the plot. The directors also began to coordinate the music to the images in order to emphasize the mood they sought to create. At first the films tended to be overloaded with music, but gradually the directors discovered that silence, too, can be effective in setting the mood. Close cooperation between the director and composer was required. Greater demands were made on the composer's technical abilities. He had to be skillful in creating the instrumentation and able to write down his intentions in musical scores. Thus, "serious" composers with conservatory training usually became the leaders in this field.[42] Silvestre Revueltas proved himself to be one of the greatest composers with his music for *Pescados* (also known as *Redes*) (1935), *Vamos con Pancho Villa* (1936), *El Indio* (1938), *Los de abajo* (1940), and other films.[43]

The most successful composer of film music is unquestionably Mario Lavista (who at one time studied under Revueltas).[44] Lavista was born in 1914 and began writing film music at the age of fourteen. Of the films for which he composed music his favorites include *Los tres huastecos, O tierra* (the music from this film he later arranged as *Tierra muerta*, an orchestral suite), and *Rosenda*. In 1948 his music for *Rosenda* won Lavista the Ariel award, the Mexican equivalent of the American Oscar.

Mario Lavista is one of the three film music composers mentioned in the book *El libro de oro del cine mexicano* (*The Golden Book of Mexican Cinema*). The other two are Francisco Domínguez and Antonio Díaz Conde. Conde is Spanish by birth but acquired Mexican citizenship in the early 1940s. He has participated in many films, such as *Pepita Jiménez, Salón México,* and *Pueblerina.* Francisco Domínguez (born in 1896) spent part of his life collecting folklore material for the archives of the Bellas Artes; he was one of the first composers in Mexico to devote himself to film music.

Mario Lavista stated that Mexican film music does incorporate characteristic features. In many cases the film music composers are inspired by Indian or mestizo folk music. The composers either borrow tunes directly from folk music or write their own themes in a similar style. Authentic folk music is also often used. In 1962 Lavista wrote the music for *Animas Trujano,* directed by Ismael Rodríguez and starring the famous Japanese actor Toshiro Mifune. The setting for this film was among the Indians of Oaxaca and for the accompaniment Lavista used typical Indian instruments such as the huehuetl (drum), the tzeponazli (slit-drum), and the rhythm instrument made of tortoise shell. This film also attracted attention in the United States, where Lavista won a prize for his music.

The Revolution provided a wealth of material for Mexican film makers. The films on this subject for which Lavista wrote the music include *La bandida* and *La cucaracha*. For the latter film Lavista naturally used the song "La cucaracha," but he arranged it for a large orchestra.[45]

It is a common practice to use popular canciones by other composers as the basis for film music. Lavista used tunes by Cuco Sánchez, Gonzalo Curiel, Agustín Lara, and a number of other contemporary popular musicians. Yet he did not make a habit of borrowing music from other composers for his films.

Mexican film producers generally have to work with small budgets, and this has a negative effect on the quality of most of the films.[46] The crew is generally quite pressed for time. Four to five weeks is the usual time span allotted for making a film; six weeks is generous. This, of course, also affects the composers. The work flows in at an unsteady rate. Sometimes they must write a film's music at short notice; then long periods of time elapse without a commission. The pay is meager, so the composers are compelled to take on as much as they can handle. Lavista, who is very productive, writes the music for ten to twelve films per year. In all he has composed the music for some five hundred films.[47]

9

Contemporary Trends

Some Mexican critics tend to exaggerate the importance and international influence of their country's popular music.[1] Juan S. Garrido, Carmen Sordo Sodi, and Juan Herrejón are far more realistic and insightful in their judgments. Juan Herrejón sums up the situation as follows: "We are on the whole underdeveloped and imitators at that."[2]

Indeed, how could it be otherwise? With the United States as an influential neighbor, the mainstream of Mexican (urban) culture has had no space to develop its individuality. With a few outstanding exceptions, the wealth of folk traditions has not reached a larger urban audience. They continue to exist in remote regions, although they are threatened by the tough commercial genres that are played on the radio day and night.[3]

Juan Herrejón suggests that this neglect of native folklore is typical of developing countries.[4] There is a great deal of talk about promoting folklore in official circles in Mexico, but in fact a minimum of effort is made toward that end.[5] This may be attributed to a feeling of inferiority among the Mexicans, who are confronted with the aggressive cultures of more highly industrialized countries. But the most logical explanation is that the executives who control the musical life in Mexico (the managers of recording companies and of the media) are only concerned with financial gains.

Musical styles all over the world are undeniably becoming more uniform; certain genres have acquired a "universal" style. As far as Latin America is concerned, a certain homogeneity has existed in the mestizo folk music for several hundred years owing to the fact that all over the continent this music had common roots and developed under similar social conditions. Diversity in musical and cultural development arose partly because Spanish, African, and Indian elements were interwoven in varying proportions in the different areas.[6]

The popular music of Latin America has acquired its continental styles through a different means. These styles and genres developed much later, and most of them were not finally established until after the advent of the mass media in the 1920s and 1930s. The development was, and is, definitely controlled by commercial factors rather than historical and geographical considerations.

The similarities between the popular music of the various countries have tended to increase. Juan Herrejón made the following statement about this trend: "I believe that the popular music of Latin America has become more or less unified."[7] Today there is a clear conception, both within the continent and outside it, of how the popular music of Latin America "should" sound. The music of Afro-Cuban origin definitely embodies the contemporary American, European, and Japanese view of Latin American popular music: the bolero, rhumba, mambo, samba, tango, and so forth (even though the latter two are not of Caribbean origin).[8]

The prominent feature of the current Latin American style is syncopated rhythm. The sound itself tends to vary considerably. Hot tropical music (mambo, rhumba, and others) often utilizes the sharp sound of brass sections, a feature taken over from jazz. On the other hand, romantic Afro-Cuban dances, such as the bolero and guajira, have never been as tightly set in their arrangements; the same applies to the Brazilian samba and the Argentine tango, at least in Mexico. This is probably because they have not been impressed on the general consciousness by well-known orchestras as, for example, the mambo was; Cuban dance orchestras, such as Pérez Prado's, permanently set this in a style that has remained stable.

Afro-Cuban dance music has been mass-produced for many years in all the Latin American countries and has also been commissioned by others, primarily the United States and the countries of Europe. Latin American genres have therefore acquired international renown. Nevertheless, there are several genres in Latin America with a more limited range. In Mexico this applies above all to corridos and ranchera songs, which seem to be established in that country alone.[9] Otto Mayer-Serra feels that the characteristic Mexican quality is revealed in the performance style.

> Mexicanness consists mainly in the method of interpretation (voices, instruments parts, stamping, clapping, ejaculations etc. + phonetic peculiarities). The atmosphere! . . . the composition of the mariachi band, the special technique of its violins and guitars, its sustained syncopated basses, the piercing sonority of its trumpets (a recent addition) and the way in which the brasses of the village band play slightly off pitch.[10]

One perceives the truth of this statement when one hears foreign versions of Mexican melodies; they sound completely different (unless the artists have made an effort to imitate precisely the Mexican musicians' performance style). On the other hand, even non-Mexican melodies take on a national flavor when they are performed by native musicians, for example, mariachi orchestras. These stylistic features can hardly be recorded in the written melody or arrangement (if indeed there is a score) but are only realized in the performance. Mariachi orchestras—and to some extent norteño groups—usually acquire their repertoire and style by ear, which produces performance techniques that are manifestly different from those of orchestras in other countries.

There is also a specifically Mexican style of singing that is typical of corrido and ranchera artists. The performance of ranchera songs exhibits an inimitable sentimentality, even tearfulness, which seems to be characteristically Mexican.[11] It could be called the "Mexican intonation." This type of singing employs a distinctive lagging drawl, the portamento, at the end of the phrase. The falsetto cries are another popular device, especially in huapango huastecos and rancheras. The women often sing with masculine strength and authority; this applies to música tropical, corridos, and rancheras (singers such as Lucha Reyes, Amalia Mendoza, and Lola Beltrán). Men, on the other hand, are not traditionally accorded this type of emphatic performance style in much of Mexico's folk music.[12]

Distinctively Mexican qualities can thus be discerned in performance styles and techniques. Do the form and structure of the music also reveal certain features characteristic to Mexico? Both José E. Guerrero and Vicente Mendoza have commented on this point.[13] Guerrero mentioned música romántica of Ponce's type, especially its *melodía amplia* which, in his opinion, is most representative of Mexican popular music. Mendoza wrote of the overflowing lyricism of both text and music.

Juan S. Garrido was far less vague in his comments. He was able to cite melodic trends that he feels are typically Mexican. Garrido provided me with a great deal of sheet music that supported his statements. Following is a representative selection of the songs, with Garrido's comments on the specifically Mexican aspects of their style.[14]

"Cocula" is a famous corrido composed by Manuel Esperón, a native of Jalisco. The first half of this corrido is in polka time (2/4), while 3/4 and 6/8 time occur in the second part of the song. The 2/4 melody is typically Mexican, according to Garrido. (See Example 21.)

sung

Example 21. "Cocula" by Manuel Esperón—PHAM

He lays special emphasis on the steeply rising melody line at the beginning, which curves back to the tonic. In the 6/8 section Esperón uses a rhythm common in *sones jaliscienses,* the essence of Coculan folk music. (See Example 22.) This section should be played staccato, recalling the blasts of a trumpet (the accompaniment was primarily intended for trumpet mariachi), and in a fairly

Example 22. "Cocula"

rapid tempo, contrasting with the moderato of the 2/4 section. This is one of many Mexican songs that is a blend of one or more contrasting parts, a characteristic that in all likelihood derives from the country's store of folk music.

Tomás Méndez's ranchera melody, "Gorrioncillo, pecho amarillo," possesses, in Garrido's words, "the characteristic spirit of Mexican music." To emphasize this quality the song should be sung in a moderate tempo. (See Example 23.)

Example 23. "Gorrioncillo, pecho amarillo," canción ranchera by Tomás Méndez—EMMI

This is not in itself a typical ranchera song, but there are some aspects of it that clearly derive from the ranchera, particularly the drawn out closing phrase. The third fall in the sixteenth measure is also typical. The period ends on the tonic, but rancheras ending on the upper third are equally common. Garrido regards the bars that occur in the transition to the nine-measure middle section as particularly Mexican. The melody reaches its climax and the fermata indicates that the singer will make the most of his opportunities. (See Example 24.)

Example 24. "Gorrioncillo, pecho amarillo"

The corrido "Dos rivales" by Manuel Hernández, who is himself a mariachi musician, contains at least two phrases that Garrido describes as inherently Mexican. (See Examples 25 and 26.)

sung

Example 25. "Dos rivales," corrido by Manuel Hernández—PHAM

sung

etc.

Example 26. "Dos rivales"

As a rule, the corrido melodies are constructed of phrases added on in the form of links in a chain. They tend to convey the impression that the melodies can be arbitrarily drawn out in accordance with the requirements of the text. The same pattern is also found in ranchera songs. The thirty-two measure form prevalent in Western music rarely occurs in these songs. Periods of nine or ten measures are not unusual. Sections of rancheras often extend over twenty-six measures, and there may also be a refrain.[15]

In "Dicen que soy mujeriego," another melody by Manuel Esperón, the syncopation in the fourth and fifth measures is typical, as is the ending in thirds. Both these features derive from Mexican folk music. (See Example 27.)

Two typical examples of the ranchera genre are "Hermosísimo lucero" by Cuco Sánchez and "La enorme distancia" by José Alfredo Jiménez. (See Example 28.) The gradual curve of the melody after syncopation breaks up into fourths. (See Example 29.) The phrase has a long ending, the closing notes a second above the tonic.

Example 27. "Dicen que soy mujeriego," canción ranchera by Manuel Esperón—PHAM

Example 28. "Hermosísimo lucero," by Cuco Sánchez—EMMI

Example 29. "La enorme distancia," canción ranchera by José Alfredo Jiménez—EMMI

Some modern huapangos are also included in Garrido's collection; one of them is "El preso numero 9" by Los Hermanos Cantoral. This is a meso-huapango written for trumpet mariachi accompaniment. There is an echo of authentic huapango style both in the dotted figures for the left hand and in the alternations of 3/4 and 6/8 time. (See Example 30.)

Example 30. "El preso número 9," huapango by Los Hermanos Cantoral—PHAM

According to Garrido, the comic song "Pesos sobre pesos" by Salvador Flores Rivera, who writes many canciones of this particular type, may be sung in any tempo without losing its Mexican character. (See Example 31.)

Example 31. "Peso sobre peso," canción by Venturo Romero—PHAM

On the other hand, Garrido claims that the ranchera "El gavilán pollero" only sounds Mexican when it is sung in 4/4 time, despite the 2/4 time specified in the notation. The melody should be sung with a schottische-like rhythm. (See Example 32.)

Garrido's views are those of an individual very sensitive to his country's music, but they are, of course, his personal judgments. In

Example 32. "El gavilán pollero," canción by Venturo Romero—PHAM

making them, he was careful not to assert that the qualities he discussed are exclusively Mexican; indeed, he made no comparisons with other countries.[16]

Certain melodies are universally regarded as characteristically Mexican. This designation is not necessarily derived from their style, their text, their history, or origin. In 1971 Dave Brubeck, the well-known American jazz pianist, played a famous concert in Mexico City. He recorded live a number of tunes that are widely regarded as Mexican: "Cielito lindo," "La paloma," "Sobre las olas," "Bésame mucho," "Allá en el Rancho Grande," "Estrellita," and "La bamba." This is a fairly good cross section of Mexican popular music. The whole range is represented, from "typical Mexican numbers" to foreign tunes that have come to be considered Mexican and Mexican tunes which are not at all Mexican in style, and probably not recognized as Mexican outside the country.

Of course, many typical Mexican songs are not included in Brubeck's record. Among them are "La cucaracha," "La Valentina," "La Adelita," "Adiós Mariquita linda," and "La raspa." This last one was introduced as a dance in European and American dance halls at the end of the 1940s; it was very popular for a short time. The song was generally regarded as very Mexican.[17] Gus Moreno (1910–51), who wrote "La raspa," worked most of his life in Spain. He reinforced the Mexican quality of the song by incorporating measures from the "Mexican Hat Dance" in it.[18]

To the majority of people in other countries, however, Mexican music is not associated with a given artist or tune but with a certain type of orchestra, or rather, a particular "sound." The trumpet mariachi provide the type of music universally (and in some cases exclusively) identified as Mexican. For example, the music of Herb Alpert's Tijuana Brass was based on the trumpet mariachi sound.[19]

There are also other artists in the United States who have combined American and Mexican styles. During his short career (1957–59), Buddy Holly launched the "Tex-Mex" style. In the

United States, certain songs are written in a so-called Mexican spirit, for example, "Juanita Banana" (composed by Howard M. Kenton), "Rosita Tomato," (Howard C. Fox), and "Speedy González" (Kaye D. Hill). These songs present Mexico in caricature.*

The Mexican music that is most popular in other countries is not at all Mexican in style. The three biggest hits are "Bésame mucho" (Consuelo Velázquez), "Cuando calienta el sol" (Rigual Brothers), and "Granada" (Agustín Lara); Lara dedicated this song to the town of Granada in Spain. The music was deliberately written in "Spanish" style. These three lead SACM's statistics on the songs of Mexican origin most often played in other countries. The list is based on live performances by orchestras, and on radio and record sales; it covers a five-year period from the end of 1963 to the end of 1968.[20] (See Figure 2.)

In the same article, SACM published a survey of the Mexican composers who are most frequently played in other countries.[21] (See Figure 3.)

In the summer of 1971 I asked SACM's statistics department for comparable data rating the popularity of composers and songs in Mexico. The information I obtained covers the same period of time as the preceding tables (1963–68). However, these ratings apply only to record sales; no further information was available.[22]

Mexican Composers
1. Agustín Lara
2. Alvaro Carrillo
3. Gonzalo Curiel
4. José Guízar
5. José A. Jiménez
6. Gabriel Ruiz
7. Cuco Sánchez
8. Tomás Méndez
9. Luis Demetrio
10. Armando Manzanero

Mexican Songs
"La media vuelta" (J. A. Jiménez)
"Llegó borracho el borracho" (Jiménez)
"La mentira" (A. Carrillo)

*For a discussion of Mexican influences on American music, see the Appendix, "Border Music of the 1970s in the Southwestern United States."

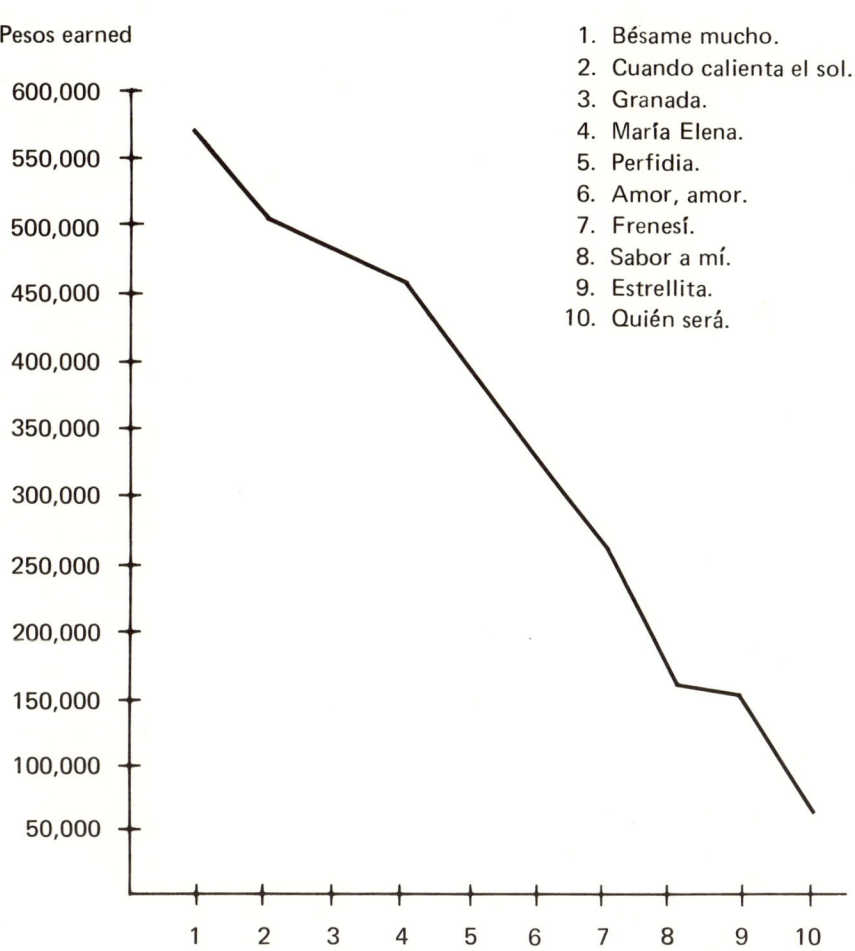

Figure 2. The Ten Mexican Compositions Most Often Played in Foreign Countries between October 1, 1963 and October 1, 1968

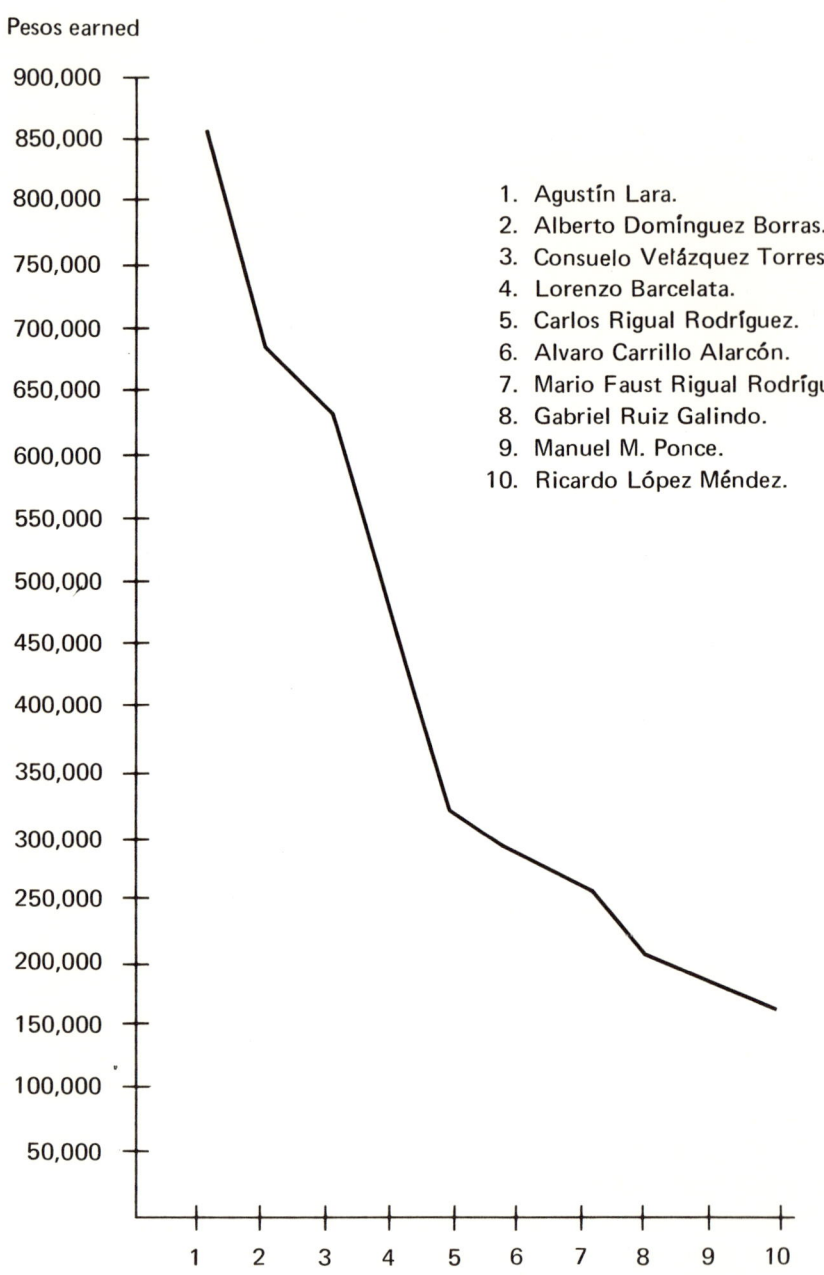

Figure 3. The Ten Mexican Composers Most Often Played in Foreign Countries between October 1, 1963 and October 1, 1968

"Ingratos ojos míos" (B. Villarreal)
"Estoy pensando en tí" (A. Lara)
"Musita" (C. Colorado)
"Reconciliación" (A. Carrillo)
"Mi barquita de madera" (J. Ramírez)
"Entrega total" (A. Pulido)
"Canción de un preso" (F. Valdéz Leal; A. Acuña)

Foreign Composers
1. John Lennon
2. Paul McCartney
3. Rafael Hernández
4. Palito Ortega
5. Leo Dan
6. Dámaso Pérez Prado
7. Bert Russell
8. Jenny Lou Carson
9. Paul Anka
10. Benny Davis/Ted Murry

Foreign Songs
"Despeinada" (P. Ortega)
"Camelia" (P. Ortega)
"Detrás del amor" (B. Davis/T. Murry)
"Como te extraña mi amor" (Leo Dan)
"Es lupe" (B. Russell)
"All You Need is Love" (Lennon/McCartney)
"Celoso" (Jenny Lou Carson)
"Hey Jude" (Lennon/McCartney)
"Palabras" (Gibb/R. B. Mole)
"Norma la de Guadalajara" (Dámaso Pérez Prado)

Comparing the Mexican songs popular in other countries to those that were hits in Mexico during the same time period reveals no overlap at all. Naturally the turnover is faster in the country from which the music originates than elsewhere. However, none of the Mexican songs at the top of the international list were even composed during the five years listed in the charts. Most of them, in fact, date back to 1930–40.[23] They are all composed in styles that closely adhere to international music patterns.

The Mexican songs at the top of the national list are much more recent. All of them were written during or just before 1963–68. Half of the melodies are ranchera songs (numbers 1, 2, 4, 8, and 10), two of them at the top of the list. All the composers on these lists appear to be earning their living by songwriting. Yet this should not obscure the fact that relatively few composers in Mexico can live solely off the royalties from their songs.[24] It is particularly difficult to become successful on the international market where commercial promotion is so important.

Performers and composers of popular music in Mexico generally belong to the middle class. On the other hand, folk musicians in rural areas and street musicians in the cities usually have a lower social status. The street musicians generally earn their living by playing for both tourists and Mexicans. Mariachi orchestras, which are highly respected, are accustomed to playing for a certain fee, seldom less than fifteen pesos per melody (unless they are paid for an entire evening). On the other hand, a large number of street singers (who are often blind) and hurdy-gurdy players accept whatever amount is offered to them.

In the twentieth century a fairly uniform repertoire of street music has emerged in Mexico; the instruments used vary little from one part of the country to another, except in certain rural areas. Marimba, norteño, and mariachi bands flourish throughout Mexico. Their repertoire consists mainly of traditional indigenous melodies. In Cuernavaca, the luxurious resort area some thirty miles south of the capital, I had the opportunity of seeing a list of typical street songs. In the main plaza two ten-year-old boys produced their entire repertoire (about thirty songs) neatly written down on a piece of paper. I was not surprised to find that half the list consisted of canciones and corridos dating back to the Revolution. The rest were film rancheras, traditional huapangos lentos, and canciones such as "Las mañanitas" and "La golondrina."

All marimba and mariachi musicians are members of one of Mexico's trade unions.[25] The commissions negotiated by the unions usually guarantee the musicians a fixed income. But certainly there are many street musicians with no such ties or guarantees. Itinerant singers and "free-lance" performers have to find districts where they can, at best, earn a subsistence for themselves and their families. Originally this also applied to composers and performers of corridos and ranchera songs. But since the beginning of the twentieth century, the most successful ranchera and corrido artists (though they are often brought up in a working-class environment) have achieved middle-class status and moved into rather luxurious urban areas. However, they have retained their rural "touches," including the charro costume; their approach could be considered intrinsically Mexican, as opposed to that of artists working within genres that have an international appeal.

As far as I know, no reliable sociological investigations have been undertaken to determine how the class structure in Mexico affects musical tastes and preferences. The interviews I conducted indicate the following: the indigent living in urban and rural areas prefer to listen to native music, such as corridos and rancheras, while the upper and middle classes, to a certain extent, have lost their native cultural traditions and simply imitate the styles and fashions that stream across the borders, mainly from the United States.

Attempts to ascertain the reasons for these apparent preferences may be misleading.[26] A possible explanation lies in the "simple" musical structure of rancheras and corridos, but stronger emphasis should be placed on the local, somewhat unpolished texts and the "Mexican feeling" in their performance. Another factor to consider is the extent to which the immortal ranchera artists (Negrete, Infante, Jiménez, and others) are glorified in the popular consciousness.

For the present, the safest conclusion may be that a certain gap exists between the long-established native traditions and the current, more international ones. However, the evolution of music in Mexico is an inclusive process, and from it a blending of these diverse elements may provide new forms of indigenous music in the years to come.

APPENDIX
Border Music of the 1970s in the Southwestern United States

Elizabeth H. Heist

Latin-influenced music, including Mexican music, has been heard in various parts of the United States at least since the mid-nineteenth century. Most anthologies of American folksongs include Mexican tunes like "La cucaracha" and "Cielito lindo," and in this century a number of popular melodies by Mexican composers—such as "Perfidia" and "Frenesí" by Alberto Domínguez, and "Granada" and "Solamente una vez" ("You Belong to My Heart") by Agustín Lara—have been successful in the United States. Although several musicians of Mexican ancestry have achieved popularity in different fields in recent years, most have not made music that was especially Mexican. Vicki Carr, a Mexican-American from El Paso, Texas, has recently begun to stress her ethnic origins, but she sings American pop ballads; Carlos Santana, a Mexican-American from California, added a Latin element to rock music of the sixties, but his sound was based primarily on Afro-Cuban beats. Much of this is also true of Trini López. The most Mexican-sounding music of the 1960s was that of Herb Alpert and the Tijuana Brass. Because of the success of his mariachi-influenced recordings and his co-ownership of A&M Records, Alpert is an important figure in the music business, but he himself is not Mexican or of Mexican ancestry.

In the 1970s, however, the music of the Texas-Mexico border region has begun to attract both critical and popular interest. This music is unique among Latin-influenced varieties of North American music in that it grows out of a truly regional culture. It comprises equal parts of Mexican norteño music and American country and western, blues, rhythm and blues, and rock'n'roll. The recent popularity of this kind of music, which I will call border music here although it could also be called Tex-Mex or Chicano, is due in part to the upsurge in ethnic pride among Mexican-Americans in recent years, but its popularity is primarily regional rather than ethnic. The music itself is by no means a product manufactured to sell to an ethnic market; rather it grows out of regional traditions. The traditions of purely Mexican norteño music have been covered in Chapter 2 of this volume; the purpose of this appendix is to survey the American side of contemporary border music—its past, present, and future.

Our survey must begin by glancing at the popular music of Texas in the twentieth century. Texas has one of the richest musical heritages in the United States, equal to that of the southeastern states. Although blues and country music are generally considered to have originated in the Southeast, many pioneering musicians in both fields were Texans. One of the best-known early blues singers, Blind Lemon Jefferson, was from Texas, as is the prolific Lightnin' Hopkins. Many of the West Coast bluesmen of the post-World War II period came out of Texas, among them T-Bone Walker, whose distinctive electric guitar stylings have influenced many of the musicians we will be considering here, among them Doug Sahm.

The "western" half of so-called country and western music is basically Texan in origin. Western swing, one of the most popular varieties of country and western music, originated in Texas in the 1930s; like the border music of today, it combined elements of many separate styles of music. Knocky Parker, piano player with the Light Crust Doughboys, one of the first western swing combos, described the music as "a mixture of Mexican mariachi music from the south with jazz and country strains coming in from the east."[1] Gospel and blues also contributed to the repertoires of Bob Wills and his Texas Playboys and other Texas and Oklahoma western swing orchestras. The original Doughboy combo played fiddle, guitar, and banjo and later added steel guitar, accordion, and piano; the Wills group included brass instruments and drums. Although the popularity of western swing peaked in the 1940s, the influence of Bob Wills is obvious today in any southwestern honky-tonk, where audiences still demand western swing rhythms and Wills compositions like "Faded Love."

Rock'n'roll, the combination of blues and country music that transformed American popular music in the 1950s, numbered many Texans among its greatest performers. Texas's most important rock'n'roll musician, Buddy Holly, has always been associated with the so-called Tex-Mex sound. This term, generally used with no explanation of its meaning, is not really helpful in describing Holly's music or in locating Mexican influences in American popular music. In his excellent study of Holly, Dave Laing describes the main feature of the Tex-Mex style as "barrages of chords, with a powerful 'electric' tone—not merely an acoustic guitar solo amplified, but a unique metallic sound, where each chord echoes into the next."[2] This dense yet open sound indeed resembles that associated with Ritchie Valens, the talented California Mexican-American whose rock'n'roll version of "La bamba" was highly successful in the late fifties, but the sound is also closely related to the electric guitar styles of the black rock'n'rollers Bo Diddley and Chuck Berry, both of whom are midwesterners by birth and bluesmen by tradition. Holly's classic rock'n'roll sound actually bore little relation to geography or regional culture, for Holly was not a traditionalist but an innovator, comparable only to Elvis Presley in stature and influence. Like Presley, he made something completely new out of a remarkable voice and excellent production. As Laing points out, much of his striking guitar sound can also be attributed to his use of the Fender electric guitar; Holly was one of the first rock'n'rollers to use this model.

The Fender guitar is also noteworthy as the namesake of Freddy Fender, the most popular of the border musicians of the seventies. In the choice of a stage name as in many other respects, Fender's career is typical of Texas border music. He discarded his real name so as not to be stereotyped as a "Mexican" in the U.S. market, although he uses his real name as a credit line on Spanish-language songs composed for the Mexican market. He has also recorded under the name of Scotty Wayne, presumably chosen for its "all-American" sound.

Fender's real name is Baldemar Huerta. He was born in 1936 in the border town of San Benito, in southernmost Texas near Brownsville. His parents, agricultural laborers, traveled every summer around the South and Midwest, harvesting crops in Michigan, Ohio, and elsewhere. They spoke no English, and the household radio was tuned only to Mexican border radio stations. Fender grew up with this kind of music and with the music made by his barrio neighbors, "always Mexican music, *rancheros* and *boleros*."³

In the early 1950s, after he had learned English on his travels with the family, Fender would spend evenings in his family's 1947 Chevrolet tuning in Nashville radio stations and listening to country singers and steel guitar players. He was also exposed to the blues when he visited the field camps of black farm workers, where the jukeboxes played records by Muddy Waters, Elmore James, and the great blues shouter Joe Turner. Later, when he joined the Marines, Fender heard records by Elvis Presley and other rockers as well as rhythm and blues artists like Fats Domino and Bobby Bland. All these influences were absorbed in his instrumental and vocal styles, though it should be pointed out that his voice was always distinctively his own, an expressive tenor, even when he sang in a coarse bluesy style.

By 1957, Fender was singing and playing guitar in South Texas bars, though his regular income was still from farm work. His first record was an original composition, "Oh Holy One," in English, backed with a Spanish version of Otis Blackwell's "Don't Be Cruel," an Elvis Presley hit of 1956. With "Wasted Days and Wasted Nights" (1959), a slow, wailing rhythm and blues–styled number composed by Fender and his frequent collaborator Wayne Duncan that has since become a minor classic in the Southwest, he received some national attention and signed with a national label, Imperial. In the course of his career Fender has recorded blues, rock, country, rhythm and blues, and Mexican songs for numerous small Texas labels—Ideal and Norco in San Benito; Duncan and Talent Scout in Harlingen; El Pato, Bego, and ARV in McAllen—and for national labels like Imperial and Argo, a subsidiary of the Chicago label Chess; since 1974 he has recorded for other labels as well (see below).

In 1960 Fender was arrested in Baton Rouge, Louisiana, and convicted of possession of marijuana. He spent two years in Angola Prison in Louisiana and remained in the state even after his release in 1963, performing in New Orleans clubs with local musicians for some five years. During the late sixties, Fender's musical career declined, as he did farm work five days a week and performed only on weekends until in 1974 he became associated with Huey Meaux.

An independent producer based in Houston, Texas, Meaux

records an interesting and varied group of Texas and Louisiana artists on his own labels (currently Starflite and Crazy Cajun) and produces recordings for other labels. He has been instrumental in bringing a number of Texas musicians to national prominence. Unlike most of the American popular music industry, however, Meaux has always stressed quality rather than sheer mass appeal in his recordings, preferring to produce for a relatively small regional audience rather than trying to turn distinctive local styles into mainstream pop. It was Meaux who persuaded Freddy Fender to record "Before the Next Teardrop Falls" and then sold this recording to the national label ABC-Dot. This song's enormous success in 1975 on both pop and country charts has established Fender as an artist of national stature.

Meaux as producer and Fender as singer are two of the three most important figures in border music; the third, whose career is linked to both of theirs, is Doug Sahm, who has been called "his generation's Bob Wills or Buddy Holly."[4] Although Sahm is an Anglo American, his were the first records to bring border music to anything approaching nationwide attention. He grew up in San Antonio, where he absorbed the same mixture of musical influences as Fender did in the deep south of Texas, and made a few recordings on local labels in the early sixties before recording on Huey Meaux's Tribe label in 1964. At this time the American music industry was looking for an answer to the popularity of the Beatles and other British groups. Meaux capitalized on the craze for things British by packaging Sahm in the image of the Beatles and naming his band the Sir Douglas Quintet; although his music as Sir Douglas is identifiably Texan in origin to the educated ear, audiences apparently accepted Sahm as British and made his record "She's About a Mover" a hit in 1965.

After spending some five years in San Francisco, Sahm returned to Texas in 1971, dropped the Sir Douglas name, and recorded *The Return of Doug Saldaña* (according to the liner notes of this album, "Saldaña is a name my friends on the West Side [of San Antonio] gave me many years ago. Being a white boy, but sharing deep things with my Chicano brothers, they decided to call me that."). The same year, Sahm was named "Chicano of the Year" by *Rolling Stone* magazine. *The Return of Doug Saldaña* (Philips PHS 600-353) featured Freddy Fender's "Wasted Days and Wasted

Nights," and Sahm also introduced Fender to the avid popular music audiences of Austin, Texas.

During the 1970s Sahm has remained in Texas, recording with border musicians like keyboard player Augie Meyer and drummer John Pérez (members of the original Sir Douglas Quintet), saxophonist Rocky Morales, and the great accordion player Flaco Jiménez. His other sidemen suggest the increasingly eclectic influences on recent border music; they have included on various sessions the New Orleans pianist Mac Rebennack, who records as Dr. John, soul jazz saxophonist David "Fathead" Newman, white blues keyboard man Barry Goldberg, and New York "folk" musicians David Bromberg and Bob Dylan. As Chet Flippo puts it, Sahm has "an uncanny talent for disappearing into San Antonio's Mexican barrios or the wilds of the Rio Grande Valley and reappearing with a Rocky Morales, Flaco Jiménez, Esteban Jordan, or Freddy Fender."[5] (Like Flaco Jiménez, Esteban Jordan is an accordion player whose style represents a considerable departure from its Mexican roots.) No matter what label he records on, Sahm's records, produced by himself or by Huey Meaux, are inevitably authentic, distinctive Texas-Mexican combinations of soulful country, rock, blues, and rhythm and blues.

Sahm's recordings form an interesting contrast to Fender's in terms of Mexican components. Sahm does not record Mexican songs; most of his recordings are original compositions, while some are standard country and blues numbers. Many of his songs sound thoroughly Mexican, however; an example is "Chicano," a jovial polka composed by Sahm in which Sahm on lead guitar and bajo sexto and Flaco Jiménez on accordion combine with the other sidemen to produce a purely norteño sound. (This cut is on the album *Texas Tornado,* Atlantic SD 7287.) Fender's repertoire is more varied than Sahm's. He records many original compositions in both Spanish and English, Mexican songs—some contemporary and some traditional, like "Allá en el Rancho Grande"—and American songs by other composers, sung sometimes in Spanish, sometimes in English, sometimes both on one song. Unlike Sahm's, his arrangements vary considerably depending on label and producer. On Fender's early records and on those recorded, produced, and distributed by Huey Meaux, he sounds powerful and soulful whether singing Mexican or American material. His successful

ABC-Dot album *Before the Next Teardrop Falls* (DOSD-2020), though produced by Meaux, emphasizes the sweetness of Fender's voice slightly more than his Starflite recordings for Meaux. His Mexican-produced records tend to be less successful in capturing Fender's personal style; although the variety of material included on a single album is striking, the production and arrangements are unimaginative. On the 1974 album *El roble viejo,* made in Mexico and released on the ARV label of McAllen, Texas (ARVLP 1020), the selections range from the title cut, a bilingual version of the American pop hit "Tie a Yellow Ribbon Round the Old Oak Tree," which is pleasant but bland, to an authentically Mexican-style *bolero balada,* "Nuestro juramento." Regardless of its origin, each cut is accompanied with guitar, bass, drums, and organ; the dominance of the organ tends to reduce most of the album to the level of cocktail lounge background music.

The contrast between Sahm's recordings, which are distinctively consistent, and Fender's, most of which have been designed to sell to a specific pop market—sometimes Mexican, sometimes teenage—is due in part to the difference between the power of an Anglo and that of a Chicano vis-à-vis the music industry. As an Anglo with an established reputation, Sahm can afford to be selective. He is relatively able to maintain his artistic independence while making satisfactory business deals with appropriate labels. Fender, on the other hand, as a strictly regional artist and a member of an ethnic minority group, has rarely been in a position to do anything except try to sell himself to whomever he can. Now that he has attained success with a romantic ballad sung in Spanish and English, he is in danger of being exploited in the future as a kind of ethnic commodity because of his potential appeal to so many audiences. Undoubtedly ABC-Dot will produce his future recordings with a view to gaining airplay on as many kinds of radio stations as possible: country, top forty, and easy listening. Fender would do well to look for a more congenial label, such as Atlantic, which has always excelled in rhythm and blues production and provides understanding attention to the styles of most of its artists, including Doug Sahm.

A number of Mexican-American musicians have had careers resembling Fender's in that they have recorded under a variety of Anglo names in whatever styles they thought would sell. Sunny and the Sunliners, a San Antonio vocal group also produced by Huey

Meaux, record for both Chicano and Anglo audiences, fashioning their sound according to the tastes of their audiences. The Sánchez brothers of Albuquerque, New Mexico, all dropped the name Sánchez in the 1950s and 1960s, recording individually on the family-owned Hurricane label as Al Hurricane, Tiny Morrie, and Baby Gaby, singing in a variety of styles. Morrie's older recordings reveal a considerable imitative talent, as many of them are specific copies of the styles of such popular 1950s singers as Fats Domino and Little Richard. Today Morrie's recordings in Spanish under his full name have had success in the Mexican-American market and especially in Mexico.

Another Mexican-American group that has changed its image in recent years is Little Joe and the Latinaires. Based in Temple, Texas, where their leader, Joe Hernández, operates the small Buena Suerte label, the group achieved considerable popularity in Texas and other areas with substantial Mexican-American populations, performing in gold tuxedoes and sequined shirts like the gaudy costumes of black vocal groups in the 1950s. When blacks learned to be proud of their heritage, they stopped costuming themselves in flashy burlesques of white elegance, and Little Joe and the Latinaires similarly decided that their image was too clownish. Now they perform sometimes in flashy clothes as the Latinaires but sometimes in denim as La Familia, with Hernández billing himself as José María DeLeón Hernández. Their music is typical border music growing out of exposure to the usual varieties of local influences. According to Hernández, "Every one of these dudes here in the band has played rock and roll and country—*real* hillbilly country—and has had to play that mariachi junk and has played conjunto."[6] Their lead instruments are guitar and organ (Hernández claims that his was the first local band to use these instruments as leads rather than percussion); back-up instruments are brass. Like other norteño bands, they play polkas, but, as Hernández puts it, they make the polka "heavy." All their music is eclectic; they add brass and organ to polkas and blues guitar to waltzes, occasionally using clarinets and flugelhorns in other dance tempos.

Various kinds of Mexican music are popular in different parts of the United States. While the rich mixed border sound is at its best in South Texas and San Antonio, norteño music is also heard in other Texas cities. In Austin both more traditional conjunto groups like Alfonso Ramos and his Orquesta and the Alegres de Terán and younger, more innovative musicians like Sahm and Flaco Jiménez are popular. The Alegres, a duo playing accordion and bajo sexto, sing corridos in two-part harmony; Jiménez plays eclectic dance music. In Albuquerque numerous Mexican-American musicians are popular, but they perform in more traditionally Mexican or American styles. There are several successful local rock groups, and the single most successful Albuquerque artist, Debbie "La Chicanita" Martínez, performs in a variety of styles, most often with a mariachi band.

Mention must also be made of the country and western singer Johnny Rodríguez. Like Freddy Fender, he is from South Texas (Uvalde) and has attained popularity with bilingual recordings. His songs can generally be classified simply as American country music, however. Because Rodríguez attained success very young—unlike Fender, who is forty years old—he was recorded in Nashville from the very beginning of his career, and his songs are styled in traditional country fashion. The band that accompanies his live performances is made up only of Anglos. Rodríguez's popularity among Mexican-Americans is due more to the fact that he has made bilingual recordings than to any distinctively Mexican style. He has a good tenor voice, very much like Merle Haggard's, and is one of the few Nashville stars young and handsome enough to appeal to a teen-age audience; as a result he has gained many very young fans, both Mexican-American and Anglo, hungry for an idol who can sing country music. His success is more comparable to that of Charlie Pride, the black country singer, than to Freddy Fender's.

By the mid-1970s, border music had attained substantial local success, the beginnings of critical recognition, and limited national circulation. What of its future? To what extent can a distinctively regional style become popular on a national level without losing its distinguishing characteristics? The alternatives are apparently exemplified by Doug Sahm and Freddy Fender: Sahm has never changed his style and has a primarily regional audience; Fender's recent national popularity seems already to be diluting his regional sound, at least on his ABC-Dot album. An artist like Sahm who records in a style popular in only one region of the country is not likely to be promoted heavily by any label, even one like Atlantic that allows him to do what he wants musically; conversely, an artist desirous of enormous national success will be pressured to record in a manner that will appeal to the widest possible audience.

The example of rock'n'roll may provide a clue to the future of this particular regional style. As Charlie Gillett points out, "rock and roll was probably the first music with regional origins to be commercially successful on a nationwide scale."[7] The black blues and rhythm and blues styles that developed into rock'n'roll went through several phases before gaining nationwide acceptance. Before World War II, black artists were completely segregated from white by record companies, who marketed blues records as "race records," "sepia records," and the like. Radio stations did not mix records by black and white artists, as they were assumed to sell to completely separate markets. During the late 1940s and early 1950s, the situation changed gradually; black artists recording in white styles gained airplay on previously all-white radio stations, and white artists began to record exact copies of records by black artists. When disc jockeys like Alan Freed began to mix records by black and white artists in the early years of rock'n'roll, the major record labels finally realized that the opulent white market would buy black styles performed by black musicians and began to change their policies accordingly.

Possibly this pattern of gradual minority group acceptance (originally postulated by sociologist Talcott Parsons as the process of exclusion, assimilation, and inclusion) will hold for border music. Even if it does, however, the older norteño musicians will probably never be recorded by a major, commercial U.S. label. At this writing their recordings are easily available only on the small California folk label Arhoolie.[8] The older generation of southern blues singers rediscovered and rerecorded in the 1950s and 1960s, a comparable group, appeared only on Arhoolie and other small, scholarly and/or insolvent labels. Even the younger generation of bluesmen, those who use electrified instruments, have had little commercial success, perhaps because the blues is a rather restricted musical form. Border music, more eclectic than the blues and more regional than rock'n'roll, will probably not follow the exact precedent of either.

Notes

Preface

1. Dan Malmström, "Om musikinstrument och vokalmusik bland Lacandón-indianerna i Chiapas, Mexico," manuscript (Uppsala, Sweden: Uppsala University, 1968).
2. Görn Holm, "Europeiska stränginstrument hos några mexikanska indianstammar," manuscript (Uppsala, Sweden: Uppsala University, 1970); Claes af Geijerstam, "Some Facts about Flutes and other Wind Instruments among the Mexican Indian Tribes," manuscript (Uppsala, Sweden: Uppsala University, 1969).
3. Locating source material for the folk and popular music of other Latin American countries is equally difficult, with the exception of Argentina, where Carlos Vega conducted extensive research. The German-born musicologist Francisco Curt Lange, director of the Instituto Interamericano de Musicología, based in Montevideo, Uruguay, is another leading scholar of Latin American music. Dr. Isabel Aretz (a former pupil of Carlos Vega) is a famous Venezuelan folk music researcher, as are Carvalho Neto of Brazil and Manuel Danneman of Chile.

Introduction

1. The definition of "classical" music will not be discussed, as it does not apply to this book.
2. This information was provided by Carmen Sordo Sodi in 1971 and 1973.
3. Ibid., 1971.
4. In 1955, at the Seventh Annual Conference of the International Folk Music Council, the following definition of folk music was agreed upon: "Folk music is the product of a musical tradition that evolved through the process of oral transmission. The factors that shape the tradition are 1) continuity, which links the present with the past, 2) variation, which springs from the creative impulse of the individual or group, and 3) selection by the community which determines the form or forms in which the music arrives" (Bruno Nettl, *An Introduction to Folk Music of the United States*, p. 1).
5. K. Kos, "New Dimensions in Folk Music," p. 464.
6. The question of whether newly produced popular music will become folk music in due time is controversial and I shall not discuss it here.
7. For further discussion of the special meanings of the term *folk music* in the United States see Nettl, *An Introduction to Folk Music*.
8. Among nonmusicologists the term *folklórica* is used very frequently indeed. For instance, the corridos of the revolution are often colloquially described as "folklórica." The term may also be used as an equivalent to ethnic music.
9. Bruno Nettl, "Persian Popular Music in 1969," p. 218.
10. This does not apply to the United States. See Bruno Nettl, *An Introduction to Folk Music of the United States*.

11. There are thus at least two criteria for defining popular music: first, its original function, and later the way in which the music is used as it becomes widely known. The same distinction applies to all types of music. In regard to popular music, I emphasize the latter aspect in this book.

12. Carlos Vega, "Mesomusic: an Essay on the Music of the Masses," pp. 1–2.

13. Carlos Chávez, "La música de un pueblo," pp. 638–39. The same view is held by Rubén M. Campos and others.

14. "La música no tiene supervivencias de carácter histórico" (José E. Guerrero).

15. "Que llega por las mayorías . . ." (José E. Guerrero).

16. "Que expresan el sentido del pueblo" . . . "Que escriben para el pueblo" (Luis Sandi). Sandi distinguishes between música popular and música folklórica on the basis of whether or not the composer's name is known.

17. Neither Sandi nor Contreras were prepared to identify música popular as música comercial. Popular music in the widest sense of the word need not, of course, be commercial (and vice versa). Traditional music at fiestas, for example, may act as a kind of local popular music in addition to its possible ritual function. This is quite in line with Contreras's and Sandi's interpretation of "popular."

Chapter 1—The Development of Mexican Genres

1. Carmen Sordo Sodi is of the same opinion.

2. Genre is a concept that can be defined in many different ways. In the context of musicology, a genre usually designates a specific repertoire, texts, and music. These repertoires can be precisely delineated, although the boundaries of individual genres vary. In dealing with Mexican music, I found it practical to extend the scope of the concept "genre," particularly in regard to types of ensemble, as they tend to be closely related to repertoires.

3. Gertrud Kurath and Samuel Martí, *Dances of Anahuac*, p. 142.

4. Robert Stevenson, *Music in Aztec and Inca Territory: Contact and Acculturation Periods*, p. 156.

5. Ibid.; Stevenson writes that 1575 to 1650 was a period of great musical activity, evidenced by the quantity of Church music being composed in Mexico City, Puebla, and Oaxaca. However, lack of musical schools for boys was partly the reason for the decline of neo-Hispanic music in the late seventeenth century.

6. Ibid., p. 231. Stevenson estimates there were some 18,500 Negroes in Mexico in 1580. The number of Spaniards was approximately 15,000. Jacques Soustelle, *La vie quotidenne des Aztéques à la veille de la conquête espagne*, p. 34. He calculates that there were more than one million Indians living in the valley of Mexico around 1500. Magnus Mörner, *Rasblandningen i Latinamerikas historia*, p. 107. He gives the following figures based on research carried out by Woodrow Borah:

Year	Whites (including mestizos)		Indians	
	In New Spain	In Central Mexico	Indians in Central Mexico	
1570	63,000	57,000	4,409,000	(1565)
1646	125,000	114,000	1,500,000	(1650)
1742	565,000	465,000	1,500,000	
1772	784,000	586,000		
1793	1,050,000	780,000	3,700,000	

7. Stevenson, *Music in Aztec and Inca Territory*, p. 233.

8. E. Thomas Stanford, "The Mexican *son*," pp. 66–86. Discussing the derivation of the term *son*, Stanford presumes it originated from peasant models. Gabriel Saldívar (*Historia de*

la música en México, p. 232) writes that the word *son* in Mexico can be traced back to the seventeenth century, when it seems to have been used as a name for songs, especially *picarescos* with obscene texts. Saldívar goes on to say that "the term *son* applied to music alone seems to have been used for the first time in 1766, and it may by then be classified as belonging to the music of the Negroes." Sordo Sodi states that the Negroes brought with them dances such as "El gurumbé," "El paracumbé," "El chacahmbé," "El retambó," "El yeyé," "El bembé," and others. "De estos ritmos se derivan: la guaracha, el bolero, la guajira, el son, el sonecito, y las tonadas" (Sordo Sodi, "La marimba," p. 30). *Sonecito* is the diminutive of son. It seems to denote any kind of tune in the traditional style(s). The word lacks a precise definition. According to Sordo Sodi, it is rarely used nowadays.

9. Stevenson, *Music in Aztec and Inca Territory*, pp. 234–36.

10. Sordo Sodi, "Africa, en los orígenes del 'a-go-go.' "

11. This information was provided in the summer of 1973 by Barbro Cramér, the foremost Swedish expert on flamenco dancing. See also Donn E. Pohren, *The Art of Flamenco*, pp. 39–81; Gilbert Chase, *The Music of Spain*, chapter 15. Recent writings on flamenco include: Ricardo Molina, *Misterios del arte flamenco* (Barcelona: Sagitario, 1967); Ricardo Molina y Antonio Mairena, *Mundo y formas del arte flamenco* (Granada-Sevilla: Librería Al, 1971).

12. The immigrants to Mexico came from all parts of Spain, bringing with them the music of their home districts. The majority came from western Andalusia and Estremadura. See also Mörner, *Rasblandningen i Latinamerikas historia*, pp. 22–25; Jaime Vicens Vives, *Historia social y económica de España y América* (Barcelona, 1957).

13. Frank Harrison, "European Elements in the Music of Two Maya Groups in Chiapas," p. 13; Stevenson, *Music in Aztec and Inca Territory*, pp. 226–30.

14. Ibid.; Pablo Castellanos, *Horizontes de la música precortesiana*.

15. Saldívar also stated that the endings "-nga," "-nge," and "-ngo," as, for example, in "fandango," indicate an African provenience, but these endings could just as well have originated in the Iberian peninsula.

16. Mendoza, *Panorama*, pp. 86–87. He refers to Emilio Cotarelo y Mori, *Colección de entremeses, loas, bailes, jácaras y mojigangas*, vol. 1, pp. 164–273, 233. Chase, *Music of Spain*, p. 268.

17. Carlos Vega, *Panorama de la música popular argentina—con ensayo sobre la ciencia del folklore*, pp. 279–96.

18. Mendoza, *Panorama*, pp. 86–87.

19. Pedro Henríquez Ureña, *La historia de la cultura en la América hispánica*, chapter 3.

20. The word is a diminutive form of *tonada*, which means song.

21. José Subirá, *La tonadilla escénica;* Chase, *Music of Spain*, pp. 128–33.

22. Roger Mindlin, *Die Zarzuela*, pp. 16–17.

23. Mendoza, "Música en el Coliseo de Mexico"; idem, *Panorama*, pp. 108–33; Mayer-Serra, *Música y músicos*, pp. 986–87; Chase, *Music of Spain*, p. 262.

24. Ibid.

25. Mendoza, *Panorama*, p. 58. He states that the only "contemporary" documentation of music derived (indirectly) from the tonadilla is the collection of *24 canciones y jarabes mexicanos*, edited by J. Böhme in Hamburg around 1830. "In it we find, classified as canciones, 'El chui,' 'El guapo,' 'El conejito,' 'La indita,' 'La patera,' two boleras and one caramba, which were part of real tonadillas." Mendoza, "El álbum de *24 canciones y jarabes mexicanos*," pp. 511–41. Mendoza traces remnants of tunes included in Böhme's collection. In the majority of cases Mendoza's "conclusions" are hardly convincing; the parallel may consist of only a few words or lines that are identical or nearly identical. As far as melodies are concerned, only a few (mainly jarabes) can be traced with certainty to nineteenth-century sources.

26. Mendoza, *Panorama*, pp. 58–60.

27. Raúl Hellmer is a collector of Mexican folklore; this information was printed on the cover of the album "Folklore mexicano," vol. 2 (Musart D. 929). It was confirmed by Sordo Sodi in 1973. She mentioned "Cielito lindo," which occurs as a son in several parts of central Mexico. Mendoza's "El álbum de 24 canciones" suggests that the same is true of "La indita."

28. Mendoza, "Música en el Coliseo"; idem, *Panorama*, pp. 58–60.

29. Otto Mayer-Serra, *Panorama de la música mexicana desde la Independencia hasta la actualidad*, pp. 106–107.

30. This information was provided by Sordo Sodi in 1971.

31. Vega, *Panorama de música argentina*, p. 293.

32. Mindlin, *Die Zarzuela*, p. 40; Chase, *Music of Spain*, p. 135.

33. Mayer-Serra, *Panorama de la música mexicana*, p. 115.

34. This information was provided by Juan S. Garrido in 1971.

35. Mindlin, *Die Zarzuela*, pp. 16–17, 39–55; Vega, *Panorama de la música popular argentina*, p. 293. Sainetes already appeared in late eighteenth-century Spain and South America. "Unter einer Zarzuela des género chico versteht man einen Einakter mit Musik und Gesang, von denen an einem Theaterabend regelmässig drei bis vier aufgeführt werden. Er ist heteren, ja sogar übermütig humoristischen inhalts, spielt in der spanischen Gegenwart, und zwar entweder in Madrid selber oder in einer genau umschriebenen Provinz. Er gleicht damit dem Sainete des ausgehenden 18. Jahrhunderts" (Mindlin, *Die Zarzuela*, p. 40.)

36. Otto Mayer-Serra, *The Present State of Music in Mexico*, p. 28.

37. The romance will be further discussed in chapter 3.

38. Bombas are especially popular in the states of Veracruz, Campeche, and Yucatán. Santamaría defines bomba as "copla improvisada, por lo común irónica, intencionada y erótica, que la hace pareja, con relación a algún rival o simplemente galanteándola" (Francisco J. Santamaría, *Diccionario de mejicanismos*). See also Otto Mayer-Serra, *Música y músicos de Latin-América*, vol. 1, pp. 122–23.

39. Vicente T. Mendoza, "La copla musical en México," pp. 189–202; idem, *Panorama de la música tradicional de México*, pp. 50–53.

40. Mendoza, *La décima en México: glosas y valonas*, pp. 39–53.

41. Ibid., pp. 46–47.

42. For an example see Mendoza, *Panorama*, score 188.

43. Mayer-Serra, *Panorama de la música mexicana*, pp. 111–14. Mayer-Serra comments on nineteenth-century huapango dancing and singing in Veracruz; he cites an eyewitness, Antonio García Cubas (about 1870), who explains that the instruments that were used included a harp, a bandola, and a jarana.

44. Gerónimo Baqueiro Fóster, "El huapango," pp. 173–81; Mendoza, *Panorama*, pp. 59–60; Henry Schmidt, "The Huapango: a dithyrambic festival," pp. 147–56; Stanford, "Mexican *son*," pp. 66–68.

45. Francisco Domínguez, Luis Sandi, and Roberto Téllez Girón, *Investigación folklórica en México*, vol. 1, p. 387.

46. For examples see Mendoza, *Panorama*, scores 185 and 186.

47. Emilio Grenet, *Popular Cuban Music*, p. 19; Sordo Sodi, "La Marimba," p. 30. The name *zapateado* seems to be especially flexible in the Isthmus of Tehuantepec in Oaxaca, where almost any kind of traditional instrumental tune, especially those performed by marimbas, may acquire that name.

48. Vicente T. Mendoza, "La canción mexicana: ensayo de clasificación y antología," pp. 77–79; idem, "El folklore y la musicología," p. 122. Referring to a record with marimba music from Tehuantepec, Henrietta Yurchenco writes: "Included in this collection are examples of two basic types of sones (instrumental pieces): one has a well-defined structure divided into contrasting themes with little or no variation, the other consists of a single tune, with variations, some commonly-known, called zapateados, and some freely improvised"

(Yurchenco, "Marimba Music of Tehuantepec," pp. 396–97). See also Mendoza, *Panorama*, score 183.

49. Vega, *Panorama de la música popular argentina*, pp. 260–67.

50. Mendoza, *Panorama*, pp. 12–16. This was confirmed by Sordo Sodi in 1973.

51. Hugo de Grial, *Músicos mexicanos*, p. 272. For further information on the *sandunga* see also Mayer-Serra, *Música y músicos*, pp. 890–91; Mendoza, *Panorama*, pp. 85–86; Alberto Cajigas Langner, *El folklore musical del Istmo de Tehuantepec*.

52. This information was provided by Saldívar in 1971. Pohren, *Art of Flamenco*, p. 80. "Jaleo" is the name of an Andalusian dance; Jerez is a city in Andalusia.

53. Grial, *Músicos mexicanos*, p. 272.

54. I was not able to locate the manuscript referred to by Grial. The opinion put forth here is his own.

55. Mayer-Serra, *Present State of Music*, p. 29.

56. Carlos Vega, *El origen de las danzas folklóricas*, p. 206; Chase, *Music of Spain*, pp. 252–53.

57. Mendoza, *Panorama*, p. 86; Esparanza Pulido, "Música popular de México," p. 13.

58. Besides the pieces discussed here, there are several others of Spanish origin to be found in Mexico. See Mendoza, "La música tradicional española en México," pp. 5–34; idem, *Panorama*.

59. Main sources of information for *son* and *huapango:* Paul Bowles, "On Mexico's Popular Music"; Rubén Campos, *El Folklore y la música mexicana;* Baqueiro Fóster, "El huapango," pp. 174–83; Jean B. Johnson, " 'The huapango,' a Mexican Song Contest"; Mayer-Serra, *Panorama de la música mexicana;* idem, *Música y músicos;* Mendoza, "El álbum de 24 canciones"; idem, "Música en el Coliseo de México"; idem, "La música tradicional española en México"; idem, *Panorama;* Saldívar, *Música en México;* Higinio Vásquez Santa Ana, *Historia de la canción mexicana;* Henry Schmidt, "The huapango," *Hunters and Healers;* Stanford, "Mexican *son*"; interviews with Sordo Sodi, Garrido, Guerrero, and Saldívar.

60. There is no accurate source material regarding the early history of the son.

61. Mendoza, "Música en el Coliseo," pp. 108–33, and *Panorama*, pp. 58–60; Mayer-Serra, *Panorama de música mexicana*.

62. Mendoza, *Panorama*, p. 87, and information provided by Sordo Sodi in 1971. I will only discuss the Mexican son. For information about the Cuban son see: Grenet, *Popular Cuban Music*, p. 36; Mayer-Serra, *Música y músicos*, pp. 931–33.

63. Mendoza, *Panorama*, p. 56.

64. Stanford, "Mexican *son*," pp. 68, 77–80.

65. For an example of the *guajira*, see Grenet, *Popular Cuban Music*, p. 10.

66. Mendoza, *Panorama*, p. 56; Stanford, "Mexican *son*," p. 68.

67. Mendoza, *Panorama*, p. 56. He characterizes "El maracumbé" as the classic son of Jalisco. Hè says it is an adaptation of the Spanish "Paracumbé"; "Paracumbé" was the name of a Spanish theatre dance during the seventeenth century, and it may be that the Jaliscan dance is descended from it. Sordo Sodi puts forward another theory (refer to note 8).

68. Schmidt, "The huapango," *Hunters and Healers;* Stanford, "Mexican *son*," pp. 73–76.

69. Stanford discusses the son as a means of local (regional) identification. "The insistence upon local variants within its geographical area of dissemination, seems to have resulted from the feudal-like political organization" (Stanford, "Mexican *son*," p. 69).

70. Slonimsky somewhat surprisingly asserts that "in colloquial usage the word huapango assumes a generic significance, and is applied to any Mexican dance" (Nicholas Slonimsky, *Music of Latin America*, p. 218).

71. These three interpretations of the word are given by, among others, Schmidt, "The huapango," *Hunters and Healers*, p. 147. On the other hand, Saldívar stated in 1971 that he has carried out extensive research (unpublished) into the name *huapango* and believes that

he can date its first appearance to the beginning of the nineteenth century, 1823. He derives the name from "La canción de la guapa" ("The Song of the Beautiful Girl"). According to Saldívar, the ending "-ngo" indicates an African origin of the word. Whether or not this interpretation is correct, the musical form definitely predates the name.

72. Schmidt, "The huapango," *Hunters and Healers*, p. 156.
73. Ibid., p. 147; Stanford, "Mexican *son*," p. 68.
74. Baqueiro Fóster, "El huapango"; Mendoza, *Panorama*, p. 87; Schmidt, "The huapango," *Hunters and Healers*, p. 150; Stanford, "Mexican *son*," p. 83.
75. Schmidt, "The huapango," *Hunters and Healers*, p. 149; Stanford, "Mexican *son*," pp. 84–85; Sordo Sodi (1971).
76. Baqueiro Fóster, "El huapango," p. 178.
77. Stanford, "Mexican *son*," pp. 68–69. Stanford comments on the possible derivation of the zapateado.
78. Vázquez Santa Ana, *Canción mexicana*.
79. Sordo Sodi provided this information in a letter written on March 18, 1974.
80. Mayer-Serra, *Panorama de música mexicana*, p. 114. He is citing Antonio García Cubas, *Escritos diversos* (Mexico, 1874), pp. 210–17.
81. Information on the huapango huasteco was given to me in January 1973 by Mr. Julio Antonio Coss. For some years Mr. Coss has collected folklore in the Huastec area for the Investigaciones Musicales. Mrs. Sordo Sodi verified the information given by Mr. Coss. See also Stanford, "Mexican *son*," pp. 83–84.
82. Ibid.
83. This information was provided by Sordo Sodi in 1971.
84. This information was provided by Mr. Coss in 1973.
85. Ibid.
86. Pulido, "Música popular de México," p. 12.
87. Stanford, "Mexican *son*," p. 81; interview with Sordo Sodi in 1971.
88. Ibid., pp. 81–82. Note also that *gusto* is a name applied to sones in Guerrero. The chilena appears both as son and as canción in this area. The canción is discussed further in chapter 4.
89. Robert Redfield makes the following observation about the jarana: "[In Mérida] modern dancing has completely replaced the jarana. This means more than a mere change of style. The jarana had a certain amount of religious connotation due to its long association with religious festivities. In fact, it persisted in connection with novenas [religious feasts] after it had ceased to be popular entertainment indulged in for its own sake. Modern dance, on the other hand, is entirely secular" (Robert Redfield, *The Folk Culture of Yucatán*, p. 488).
90. Mayer-Serra, *Música y músicos*, p. 488.
91. For further information on "El butaquito" see Mendoza, "El álbum de 24 canciones."
92. "Authentic" here means sones that are (or were) part of the local or regional traditions that have been orally transmitted.
93. This information was provided by Sordo Sodi in 1973.
94. The possibility also exists of traditional tunes being "stolen" and launched as new compositions. See K. Kos, "New Dimensions in Folk Music."
95. I use the term *meso* in order to distinguish these from the traditional huapangos. The prefix was originally used by Carlos Vega to mean universally popular music. See Vega, "Mesomusic: an essay on the music of the masses," pp. 1–17. The information about the use of huapango huasteco rhythm was provided by Garrido in 1971. He further stated that the name *huapango huasteco* may designate either traditional sones from the Huastec region or the origin of the composer or the group that performed the tunes.
96. This information was derived from an interview with Garrido in 1971.

97. This point was stressed by Luis Sandi in 1971, who stated that the situation has changed rapidly because of the pressure exercised by the mass media.

98. Main sources of information for the *jarabe:* Edith Johnston, *Regional Dances of Mexico;* Mayer-Serra, *Música y músicos;* Mendoza, *Panorama;* Saldívar, *Música en México;* idem, *Monografía sobre el jarabe;* Frances Toor, *A Treasury of Mexican Folkways;* interviews with Sordo Sodi in 1971 and 1973.

99. Mendoza, *Panorama;* in Jalisco valonas are often incorporated in jarabes.

100. Sordo Sodi, 1973; in Michoacán jarabes are also called jarabillos.

101. "[In the] vestido de china . . . red and green predominate . . . , with black and gold ornaments. Very probably this is imitated from the costume of the Andalusian women" (Chase, *Music of Spain,* p. 268).

102. Sordo Sodi, "La Marimba," p. 30.

103. Mendoza, *Panorama,* p. 72.

104. Saldívar, *Música en México,* p. 257; idem, *El jarabe,* pp. 4–5; Mayer-Serra, *Música y músicos,* pp. 517–21; Mendoza, *Panorama,* p. 71. Saldívar's *Música en México* also suggests that the "Jarabe gitano" may have denoted an "African son," such as "El chuchumbé."

105. Mendoza, *Panorama,* pp. 72–73.

106. Don Guillermo Prieto, *Memoria de mis tiempos* (1828), part 1, pp. 108, 347, 349; Mendoza, *Panorama,* pp. 74, 81.

107. Mendoza, "El álbum de 24 canciones."

108. Calderón de la Barca, *La vida en México,* pp. 181, 241, 243; Mendoza, *Panorama,* pp. 74, 80.

109. Mendoza, "El álbum de 24 canciones," p. 518; Mayer-Serra, *Música y músicos,* pp. 110–15. Mayer-Serra refers to García Cubas's book, which was written in the 1870s. Mayer-Serra also gives accounts of the growing popularity of jarabe dancing, especially at wedding parties in the mid-nineteenth century, by citing interesting eyewitnesses.

110. Juan N. Cordero, *Música razonada,* p. 196.

111. Saldívar, *El jarabe,* p. 14; interview with Sordo Sodi in 1971.

112. Ibid.

113. Ibid.

114. This information was provided by Sordo Sodi in 1973.

115. Saldívar, *El jarabe,* pp. 8–9.

116. Pablo Castellanos, "Aspectos del nacionalismo musical mexicano," *Heterofonía* 2 (1968), p. 19; Mayer-Serra, *Panorama de la música mexicana,* pp. 123–26.

117. Ibid., pp. 123–26.

118. Saldívar, *El jarabe,* p. 14; Mayer-Serra, *Música y músicos,* p. 520; interview with Garrido in 1971.

119. Ibid.

120. This information was provided by Sordo Sodi in 1973.

121. Mayer-Serra, *Present State of Music,* p. 29. Jarabe tunes may also be played or sung "outside their context."

122. Slonimsky, *Music of Latin America,* p. 220. To him it is more reminiscent of a mazurka than of a waltz.

123. Mendoza, *Panorama,* pp. 78–79.

124. For examples see: Mendoza, *Panorama,* score 168; Domínguez, Sandi, and Girón, *Investigación folklórica,* vol. 1, pp. 481–82.

125. Cordero, *Música razonada,* p. 190.

126. Saldívar, *El jarabe,* pp. 18–20.

127. Vicente T. Mendoza, *Canciones mexicanas.* Mendoza traces the valona from *polo,* an Andalusian genre, which is mentioned in connection with certain tonadillas in late eighteenth-century Spain.

128. Sordo Sodi stated in 1973 that this characteristic is not to be deduced from Andalusian cante hondo style.
129. Mendoza, *La décima en México,* pp. 638–78; idem, *Panorama,* pp. 90–92; Saldívar, *Música en México,* pp. 244–46.
130. Mendoza, *Panorama,* pp. 90–92.

Chapter 2—Mariachi, Norteño, and Marimba Ensembles

1. Main sources of information for *mariachi* and *norteño* ensembles: Blas Galindo, "El Mariachi," pp. 3–8; Otto Mayer-Serra, *Música y músicos de Latino-América;* Salvador Novo, "Teoría del mariachi"; Francisco J. Santamaría, *Diccionario de mejicanismos;* E. Thomas Stanford, "The Mexican *son*"; interviews with Saldívar in 1971 and Sordo Sodi and Garrido in 1971 and 1973.
2. This information was provided by Sordo Sodi in 1971 and 1973.
3. This information was provided by Sordo Sodi and Garrido in 1971. The date 1940 was given by Garrido in 1973. Stanford, "Mexican *son,*" p. 72; he states that trumpets were added in the 1930s.
4. This information was provided by Sordo Sodi in 1971 and 1973.
5. Stanford, "Mexican *son,*" pp. 80–81; interviews with Garrido and Sordo Sodi in 1971.
6. This information was provided by Sordo Sodi and Garrido in 1971.
7. This information was provided by Saldívar in 1971.
8. Dávila Garibi regards it as improbable that the inhabitants of Cocula and the surrounding countryside would have accepted a French name for their favorite music, as the French were heartily disliked in this region.
9. Santamaría, *Diccionario de mejicanismos;* he derives this information from J. I. Dávila Garibi's *Investigaciones lingüísticas,* vol. 3, pp. 291–93. Stanford, "Mexican *son,*" p. 73; he derives the word from Maria + the diminutive -che.
10. Saldívar did not provide the name of this poet or his poem.
11. Saldívar said the ending "-i" on the word *mariachi* is a recent change, as all nineteenth-century sources give the ending "-e." This spelling remained during the first three decades of the twentieth century. The change to "-i" seems to have originated in Jalisco.
12. Saldívar, 1971; the term *mariachi* is not confined to Jalisco; it occurs also in Guerrero, together with the term *conjunto de arpa grande,* and in some other neighboring states. See also Stanford, "Mexican *son.*"
13. This information was provided by Sordo Sodi in 1971 and 1973.
14. This information was obtained from Santamaría, *Diccionario de mejicanismos,* and confirmed by Garrido in 1973.
15. Daniel Castañeda, "La música y la revolución mexicana," pp. 447–48.
16. This information was provided by Sordo Sodi and Garrido in 1971.
17. Ibid. According to Garrido, the first mariachi orchestra to use a trumpet instead of a harp was led by Silvestre Vargas.
18. Garrido stated in 1971 that Rubén Fuentes has composed in the style of *música folklórica.*
19. There is, of course, a parallel in folk music, where local performance styles tend to dominate, but the trend toward uniformity is never pursued to the degree that it is in the tourist mariachi.
20. This information was provided by Sordo Sodi in 1971 and 1973.
21. This information was provided by Sordo Sodi and Garrido in 1971.
22. Main sources of information for the marimba: Mayer-Serra, *Música y músicos;*

Carmen Sordo Sodi, "La Marimba," pp. 27–30; Henrietta Yurchenco, "Marimba music of Tehuantepec," pp. 396–97; interview with Zeferino Nandayapa, 1971.

23. "Lucas Paniagua seems to have introduced the chromatic keyboard in Mexico around 1895" (Sordo Sodi, "La Marimba," p. 27). Marimbas without chromatic keys are still played in some remote areas. The marimba is also part of the tradition of Indian music, for example, among some tribes in the Chiapas highlands. The Indian village of Venustiano Carranza is famous for the excellent chromatic marimbas that are created and played there.

24. Yurchenco states that the traditional marimba bands in the Tehuantepec area are composed of three instrumentalists. These trios are "rarely heard these days in Tehuantepec" (Yurchenco, "Marimba music," pp. 396–97).

25. My efforts to meet high union officials were unsuccessful. Therefore I cannot provide any statistics on the number of registered marimba and mariachi musicians and orchestras, or data regarding the extent to which musicians transfer between different types of orchestras.

26. Sordo Sodi, "La marimba," p. 27; V. Chonoweth, *The Marimbas of Guatemala* (1964).

Chapter 3—The Corrido

1. Main sources of information for the *corrido:* Gilbert Chase, *The Music of Spain;* Gustavo Durán, "Romance, corrido y plena," pp. 630–39; Juan S. Garrido, "Historia del corrido mexicano" (unpublished manuscript); Celedonio Serrano Martínez, "Romances tradicionales en Guerrero," pp. 7–73; Vicente T. Mendoza, *El romance español y el corrido mexicano;* idem, *El corrido mexicano: antología, introducción y notas;* idem, *Panorama de la música tradicional de México;* Merle E. Simmons, "The Mexican Corrido as a source for interpretive study of Modern Mexico"; interviews with Carmen Sordo Sodi and Juan S. Garrido in 1971 and 1973. (Castañeda's study *El corrido mexicano: su técnica,* published in 1943, unfortunately was not available. This was also the case with some other studies of the romance corrido that were made in the early 1940s. According to Sordo Sodi, this should not detract from the present study in any serious way.)

2. Attempts to limit the corrido to a literary genre immediately results in problems; see Simmons, "Mexican Corrido," p. 10; Mendoza, *Romance y corrido,* p. 118.

3. Mendoza, *Romance y corrido;* idem, *Corrido mexicano;* idem, *Panorama;* traditional romances may be called *corrido, ejemplo, historia,* and *tragedia.* Mexican corridos may also be described according to their content as *romance, historia, narración, ejemplo, tragedia, mañanita, recuerdo, verso,* or *copla.*

4. The expression *corrido* was also used in Spain, especially in Andalusia. Simmons, "Mexican Corrido," p. 20; in his thesis Simmons mentions that the *Diccionario de Autoridades* (1729), p. 617, defines the corrido as being "ligereza y velocidad," (light and fast). The term *corrido* is also used in other Latin American countries as a synonym for *romance español.* Simmons also calls attention to the resemblance between Argentine trovadores of the nineteenth century and their Mexican equivalents.

5. For example, see Mendoza, *Romance y corrido;* idem, *Panorama;* Durán, "Romance, corrido y plena."

6. For example, see Mendoza, *El corrido mexicano;* Garrido, "Historia del corrido mexicano."

7. The division of romances into cuartelas (four-line stanzas) seems to have occurred in the early sixteenth century; it was probably done in colonial Mexico, too (though Durán thinks not). Mendoza, *Panorama,* scores 69 and 72; Mendoza produces some romance corridos in cuartelas. Simmons, "Mexican Corrido"; Simmons considers the cuartelas as one of the salient characteristics of the fully developed Mexican corrido from the mid-nineteenth century on, differentiating it from the *romance español.*

8. These *cancioneros*, which were used at the court of Ferdinand and Isabel, contain romances, villancicos, and other genres taken over from the peasants, in sophisticated three- and four-part settings. The most important of these manuscripts, dating from the end of the fifteenth and the beginning of the sixteenth centuries are: "Cancionero musical de palacio" (A. Barbieri, ed., part 1, 1892, new edition 1947; H. Angles, ed., part 2–3, 1947, 1951); "Cancionero musical de Sevilla," "Cancionero de Segovia," and "Cancionero de Barcelona." Carl-Allan Moberg, *Västerlandets musikhistoria intill 1600*, p. 515; the only collection preserved in contemporary print (Venice, 1556) is kept in the University Library of Uppsala, the so-called Cancionero de Uppsala. W. Apel, ed., *Harvard Dictionary of Music*, p. 736; settings to lute (vihuela) accompaniment are found in the lute books of Narváez, Milán, and Mudarra. Many works have been written on the romance in Spain. Among those concerning the romance in Latin America is one by Ramón Menéndez-Pidal, *Los romances en América* (Buenos Aires: 1939). There are, however, only a few studies in which the music is taken into consideration: Mendoza, *Romance y corrido;* idem, *Panorama;* Durán, "Romance, corrido y plena"; Maria-Ester Grebe, "Modality in Spanish Renaissance vihuela music and archaic Chilean folksongs," pp. 326–43; according to Grebe, modality still prevails in many Chilean romances. This is apparently not the case in Mexico.

9. Durán, "Romance, corrido y plena," p. 633.

10. Ibid.; Simmons, "Mexican Corrido," p. 23. Both authors cite fragments of romances sung by the soldiers of Cortés; these are printed by Bernál Díaz in his *Historia verdadera de la conquista de la Nueva España*, 2 vols. (México, D.F.: Imprenta de J. M. Andrade y F. Escalante, 1867–80).

11. Simmons, "Mexican Corrido," pp. 25, 28; Mendoza, *Romance y corrido*, pp. 183–85.

12. Interview with Saldívar in 1971; the guitar tablature (folio 27) is not transcribed. According to Saldívar, Castañeda reproduced these corrido romances in his *El corrido mexicano*, 1943.

13. Durán, "Romance, corrido y plena," p. 633; Chase, *Music of Spain*, pp. 264–66.

14. Mendoza, *Panorama*, p. 104.

15. Ibid., p. 105.

16. See also Mendoza, *Romance y corrido*.

17. Mendoza, *Panorama*, scores 69 and 72; Simmons, "Mexican Corrido"; Durán, "Romance, corrido y plena."

18. See also Chase, *Music of Spain*, p. 264.

19. The differences and similarities in musical style between Spanish and Mexican romances, and between Mexican romances and corridos, is too complicated to discuss here. There is no authoritative work on the subject to consult, and I have not personally researched the matter. However, I would disagree with Mendoza's judgments made on the basis of the scores presented in his books: romance tunes are generally not modal; corrido tunes are not "overflowing," and they are hardly lyrical. Carmen Sordo Sodi did not agree that the difference between the corrido mexicano and romance is as great as it is often said to be. She even questioned the division of the corrido into two categories, as the terms *romance* and *corrido* seem to be used interchangeably in Mexico (and in many parts of Latin America). There are indeed a number of typical corridos that have the form and content specified by Mendoza and others, but then there are several corridos (romances) that are difficult to assign to one group or the other. This is especially evident in the "folkloristic" tradition still alive in rural areas of Mexico.

20. Mendoza, *Romance y corrido*, p. 126; Simmons, "Mexican Corrido," p. 27; Durán, "Romance, corrido y plena," p. 634; Robert Stevenson, *Music in Aztec and Inca Territory: Contact and Acculturation Periods*, p. 235, n. 172.

21. In his chapter "Geographical Considerations," Simmons discusses the theory that the corrido was born in the interior of northern Mexico: "the principal cultivators of the romance tradition, i.e. the settlers from Andalusia, Estremadura and Asturias, settled in those

regions" (Simmons, "Mexican Corrido"). E. Thomas Stanford ("The Mexican *son*") ascribes the origin of the corrido to the Andalusian jácara with a corrido accompaniment. Stevenson (*Music in Aztec and Inca Territory*, p. 135, n. 172) quotes an early source, the *Reál Academia Española* dictionary, that defines *corrido de la costa* as a "romance ó jácara que se suele acompañar con la guitarra al son del fandango."

22. Durán, "Romance, corrido y plena," p. 635.
23. Simmons, "Mexican Corrido," p. 31.
24. Mendoza, *Panorama*, pp. 105–106. Note also that not nearly all the songs born (or reborn) during the Revolution are corridos, in their meter or narrative style. Nevertheless, revolutionary songs such as "La Adelita," "La Valentina," and "La cucaracha," though they are not corridos in a technical sense, are sometimes considered as such because of their strong revolutionary implication. See also Garrido, "Historia del corrido mexicano," p. 7.
25. Serrano Martínez, "Romances tradicionales," p. 10.
26. Mendoza, "Corrido mexicano," pp. 14–15.
27. Simmons, "Mexican corrido," p. 31.
28. This information was derived from interviews with Sordo Sodi and Garrido in 1971.
29. The music of this corrido-canción is missing.
30. This information was derived from interviews with Sordo Sodi and Garrido in 1971.
31. Simmons devotes the main part of his thesis to a discussion of the value of the corrido texts as an historical source, but I shall not probe into this aspect of them here.
32. This information was derived from an interview with Sordo Sodi in 1971.
33. Ibid.
34. Garrido, "Historia del corrido mexicano," pp. 6–7.
35. This information was derived from an interview with Sordo Sodi in 1971.
36. Durán, "Romance, corrido y plena," p. 636.
37. "Una alegre melodía de vals ligero puede acompañar indiferentemente una relación de hechos triviales o un corrido de los que . . . son llamados tragedias o ejemplos" (Durán, "Romance, corrido y plena," p. 636).
38. García Morillo, *Carlos Chávez, vida y obra* (México, D.F., 1960), p. 84.
39. Carlos Chávez, "La música," *México y la cultura*, pp. 643–45.
40. This information was derived from an interview with Sordo Sodi in 1971.
41. Ibid.
42. Ibid.
43. Certain questions have occurred to me that I cannot answer: Did these corrido singers have any musical training? On what basis was a singer appointed *corridista* to a leader? Did the corrido singers then use the contemporary performance style?
44. Simmons, "Mexican Corrido," p. 13; Mendoza, *El corrido mexicano*, pp. 27–34.
45. See also Garrido, "Historia del corrido mexicano," p. 7.
46. Mendoza, *El corrido mexicano*, pp. 16–17; idem, *Panorama*, p. 105.
47. Garrido, "Historia del corrido mexicano," pp. 9–16; idem, interview; Grial, *Músicos mexicanos*, p. 235.

Chapter 4—The Canción

1. Main sources of information for the *canción:* Daniel Castañeda, "La música y la revolución mexicana, pp. 437–38; Hugo de Grial, *Músicos mexicanos;* Vicente T. Mendoza, *Canciones mexicanas;* idem, *Panorama de la música tradicional de México;* idem, *"La canción mexicana: ensayo de clasificación y antología";* idem, "El folklore y la musicología," pp. 113–23; Concha Michel, *Cantos indígenas de México;* Manuel M. Ponce, *Escritos y composiciones musicales;* Gabriel Saldívar, *Historia de la música en México;* Higinio Vázquez

Santa Ana, *Historia de la canción mexicana;* interviews with Carmen Sordo Sodi and Juan S. Garrido.

2. This information was provided by Garrido in 1971.

3. According to Sordo Sodi, the research conducted thus far at the Colegio de México has concentrated mainly on the structure of the texts. Very little attention has been given to the musical material. Concerning the early canción in Mexico, Saldívar states: "Fué durante los siglos XVI y XVII que la canción mexicana tuvo su gestación, para aparecer como producción propia y característica desde la segunda mitad del siglo XVII, con forma capaz de hacerla distinta de cualquiera otra. . . . En pleno siglo XVII la canción cobra gran fuerza debido a las influencias que recibe, especialmente las españolas, siendo las principales la tonadilla y el bolero" (Saldívar, *Música en México,* pp. 307–308).

4. This information was provided by Sordo Sodi in 1973.

5. Ibid., 1971.

6. Mendoza, *Panorama,* pp. 96–97; idem, *La canción mexicana.* The latter work lists several means of classification.

7. Bruno Nettl, *Folk and Traditional Music of the Western Continents,* p. 193.

8. *Canción romántica* may also serve to designate the purely commercial canción mexicana as it developed in the early 1920s.

9. Mendoza, *La canción mexicana,* pp. 30–35.

10. The majority of "romantic and sentimental" canciones seem to diverge from this pattern.

11. The view expressed by Mendoza is by no means new. See Ponce, *Escritos musicales.* Carlos Chávez echoes Ponce in his statement that the romantic canción consists of two parts and that "la primera se expone la frase francamente melódica, la cual termina en la misma tonalidad en que fué iniciada. La segunda parte está compuesta de dos compases ["measures"] que se repiten para completar la frase musical y, después, el ritornello, característico del final de la primera parte, termina la canción" (Carlos Chávez, "La música," *México y la cultura,* p. 647).

12. Mendoza, *Panorama,* pp. 93–94; see also Vázquez Santa Ana, *Historia.*

13. Ibid.

14. Mendoza, *Panorama,* scores 110–117.

15. Ibid., p. 97.

16. Mendoza, *La canción mexicana,* pp. 30–35.

17. Ibid., pp. 77–79; idem, "El folklore," p. 122.

18. Mendoza, *Panorama,* p. 98.

19. Michel, *Cantos,* pp. 33–47.

20. Vicente T. Mendoza, *El romance español y el corrido mexicano,* pp. 208–209; this information was confirmed by Saldívar and Garrido in 1971. See also Carlos Vega, "Mesomusic: an essay on the music of the masses," pp. 15–16.

21. See Mendoza, "La música de Guerrero," pp. 198–214.

22. Mendoza, *La canción mexicana,* p. 17.

23. Saldívar, *La historia de la música en México,* p. 380; Otto Mayer-Serra, *Panorama de la música mexicana desde la Independencia hasta la actualidad,* pp. 117–19; Mendoza, *Panorama,* p. 14; Carlos Vega, *El origen de las danzas folklóricas;* idem, "Mesomusic," p. 16.

24. This is often referred to in ethnographical literature as "gesunkenes Kulturgut."

25. Vega, *Danzas folklóricas,* pp. 27–35.

26. Vega, "Mesomusic," pp. 14–15; on contradance see also Vega, *Danzas folklóricas,* pp. 83–120.

27. This information was provided by Sordo Sodi in 1973.

28. Ibid., 1971.

29. This information was provided by Garrido in 1971.

30. According to Garrido, "Perjura" was not publicly accepted until around 1912, because the lyrics were offensive to women.

31. Not all songs composed in the "Mexican style" are described as canciones mexicanas. See chapter 3, n. 24.

32. In connection with what he calls "la canción romántica y sentimental," Mendoza states: "The fact that the structure of the romantic canción has developed into something peculiar to our people, especially in Bajío, justifies the designation *Mexican*" (Mendoza, *Canción mexicana*). It is somewhat unclear what exactly Mendoza means when he speaks of the structure. At any rate, no song structure indigenous to Mexico developed during the nineteenth century, according to Sordo Sodi.

33. This information was provided by Garrido in 1971.

34. Castañeda, "La música y la revolución," pp. 437–38.

35. Vicente T. Mendoza, "La cachucha," pp. 289–310; idem, *Panorama;* Castañeda, "La música y la revolución," pp. 437–38.

36. This information was provided by Sordo Sodi in 1973. See also Mayer-Serra, *Panorama de la música mexicana*, p. 115.

37. This information was provided by Sordo Sodi in 1971.

38. This information was provided by Garrido in 1971.

39. This information was provided by Garrido and Juan Herrejón in 1971.

40. This information was provided by Garrido in 1971.

41. Ibid.

42. This information was provided by Sordo Sodi in 1973.

43. For a good account of American country music see Bill C. Malone, *Country Music U.S.A.*, 3rd ed. (Austin: University of Texas Press, 1970). For a short account of the American rural music tradition see Nettl, *Folk and Traditional Music*, p. 201. There is no good source of information for the ranchera tradition in Mexico. The most comprehensive study made so far is included in Mendoza, *Canciones mexicanas*, pp. 51–56. However, Mendoza does not go into the city ranchera at all.

44. Carlos Vega, *Panorama de la música popular argentina*, p. 255; the mazurka has been launched commercially in Argentina as "ranchera."

45. This information was provided by Sordo Sodi in 1971.

Chapter 5—Modern Dance Rhythms

1. Main sources of information: Emilio Grenet, *Popular Cuban Music;* Otto Mayer-Serra, *Panorama de la música mexicana desde la Independencia hasta la actualidad;* Vicente T. Mendoza, *Panorama de la música tradicional de México;* idem, "El tango," pp. 138–54; Carlos Vega, *Panorama de la música popular argentina—con ensayo sobre la ciencia del folklore;* idem, *El origen de las danzas folklóricas;* idem, "Mesomusic: an essay on the music of the masses," pp. 1–17; interviews with Carmen Sordo Sodi and Juan S. Garrido.

2. Vega, *Panorama de la música popular argentina*, pp. 246–47.

3. The tango presents certain problems for scholars since a Spanish (Andalusian) dance named tango existed on the Latin American mainland before the Argentine tango was created at the beginning of the twentieth century. Mendoza and Saldívar distinguish three kinds of tango in Mexico: *tango argentino, tango andaluz,* and *tango africano.* "En México como en Andalucía, el tango es una pieza que se canta y se baila . . . ; desde el principio del siglo XIX se intercaló entre nuestros jarabes" (Mendoza, "El tango," p. 146). In the same article Mendoza also suggests that the habanera, the guaracha, and the Cuban contradanza derive from the Andalusian tango. This is highly questionable, and indeed difficult to prove, because of lack of relevant source material. Carlos Vega has stressed the importance of the

contradance as an ancestor of the Cuban habanera, whereas Mayer-Serra declares: "no será possible aclarar el problema de la prioridad histórica entre diferentes géneros bailables [afro-euro-cubanos]" (Mayer-Serra, *Panorama de la música mexicana*, p. 131). Mendoza's discussion of the tango does not seem authoritative to me, and his definition of tango africano seems unclear indeed. In his statement that the Argentine tango derives from the Andalusian one, however, Mendoza is in agreement with Vega, who states: "La especie en que resplandece ocasionalmente y que da al tango argentino nombre, forma y caracteres, es el tango español; pero en el suburbio bonaerense [Buenos Aires's suburbs], la especie hispánica se introduce en el paterno estrato Oriental . . . y reanimada, enriquecida, conquista París é invade el mundo" (Vega, *Panorama de la música argentina*, pp. 227–28).

4. This information was provided by Sordo Sodi in 1973. See also Vega, "Mesomusic," p. 11.
5. Mayer-Serra, *Panorama de la música mexicana*, p. 115; Mendoza, *Panorama*, pp. 11–15.
6. For an interesting discussion see Vega, *Panorama de la música argentina*, p. 247.
7. This information was provided by Sordo Sodi 1971 and 1973. On the Cuban contradanza see Grenet, *Popular Cuban Music*, pp. 15, 30. On the diffusion process of the contradance see Vega, "Mesomusic," p. 10. On choreography see Vega, *Danzas folklóricas*, pp. 93–120.
8. Vega, *Panorama de la música argentina*, pp. 254–55.
9. Nicholas Slonimsky, *Music of Latin America*, p. 220.
10. Hugo de Grial, *Músicos mexicanos*, p. 38; this information was confirmed by Garrido in 1973.
11. More detailed information in Rosas's life and work is given in chapter 7.
12. This information was provided by Garrido in 1973.
13. Vega, *Panorama de la música argentina*, p. 260. According to Vega, the Argentine rural polka may contain traits from several genres; except for the standard European polka, habaneras, tangos antiguos, milongas, and schottisches are grouped together under the name of polka. There are even polkas in ternary rhythm. (This does not apply to Mexico.)
14. This information was provided by Sordo Sodi in 1971.
15. Ibid.
16. This information was provided by Garrido in 1971.
17. Grenet, *Popular Cuban Music*, pp. 25–26; Mendoza, *Panorama*, p. 100; interview with Garrido in 1971.
18. Vega, "Mesomusic," p. 11.
19. Mendoza, *Panorama*, p. 101. See also the article on the habanera in F. Blume, ed., *Die Musik in Geschichte und Gegenwart*.
20. This information was provided by Garrido, orally, and by letter, in 1973. See also accounts of habanera and contradance in Mayer-Serra, *Panorama de la música mexicana*, pp. 118–19, 129; Grenet, *Popular Cuban Music*, pp. 30–31.
21. Ibid.
22. Ibid.
23. Ibid.
24. Ibid.
25. The earliest mention of the danzón I have seen are the danzones, danzas, y guaraches, which in 1884 were performed in Mexico City by a Compañía de bufos habaneras. Mayer-Serra, *Panorama de la música mexicana*, p. 119. See also Otto Mayer-Serra, *Música y músicos de Latin-América*, pp. 308–309; Grenet, *Popular Cuban Music*, pp. 31–35.
26. This information was provided by Sordo Sodi in 1973.
27. Ibid., 1971.

28. Garrido, interview and letter, 1973; Grenet, *Popular Cuban Music*, pp. 30–31; Mayer-Serra, *Panorama de la música mexicana*, pp. 118–19.

29. This information was provided by Garrido and Dordelly at the Sección de Investigaciones Musicales in 1971.

30. Ibid.

31. Ibid.

32. Ibid.

33. I am disregarding the marches that the Spaniards brought in during the colonial period, which today are played in a relatively "folklorized" manner by village musicians on *chirimía* (shawm) and drum, or by small brass beads.

34. This information was provided by Sordo Sodi in 1973.

Chapter 6—Popular Music Before and After the Revolution

1. Main sources of information: Daniel Castañeda, "La música y la revolución mexicana," pp. 437–38; Otto Mayer-Serra, *Panorama de la música mexicana desde la Independencia hasta la actualidad;* idem, *Música y músicos de Latino-América;* idem, *The Present State of Music in Mexico;* Vicente T. Mendoza, *Panorama de la música tradicional de México; La Sociedad de Autores y Compositores de México: XXV años de la SACM;* interviews with Carmen Sordo Sodi, Juan S. Garrido, Gabriel Saldívar, and Juan Herrejón.

2. For further information on art music refer to Mayer-Serra, *Panorama de la música mexicana;* Robert Stevenson, *Music in Mexico;* Dan Malmström, *Introduction to Twentieth Century Mexican Music*.

3. Birger Möller, *Det tudelade samhället*, p. 130; Magnus Mörner, *Latinamerikas historia*, p. 212. Mexico became culturally more integrated after the Revolution due to the mass media.

4. Indeed a similar reevaluation of the native culture (folklore) always appears to follow in the wake of revolutionary and nationalistic movements in Latin America. This phenomenon could be observed recently in Chile, when Allende's leftist regime was in power.

5. Carlos Chávez discusses the connection between a country's nationalism and its social disintegration: "A country with national unity [con nacionalidad] has no problems with nationalism. The art there is automatically national. In a country in which mutually contrasted groups exist, the lack of national solidarity is expressed in a manifest and exaggerated nationalistic spirit" (Carlos Chávez, "Nacionalismo Musical," *Música, Revista Mexicana* 6 [1930]:8).

6. Malmström, *Introduction to Twentieth Century Mexican Music*, pp. 21–23.

7. Mayer-Serra, *Panorama de la música mexicana*, p. 73.

8. Ibid.; Stevenson, *Music in Mexico;* Malmström, *Introduction to Twentieth Century Mexican Music*.

9. In Mexico, *"nacionalismo"* is inextricably associated with the revolutionary movement of the mestizos. See also Frederic C. Turner, *The Dynamics of Mexican Nationalism* (Chapel Hill: University of North Carolina Press, 1968).

10. The Revolution was more vividly reflected in art and literature, which by their nature project a wholly different level of realism. Immediately after the Revolution, Mexico's three great mural painters, José Clemente Orozco (1886–1949), David Alfaro Siqueiros (1896–1974), and Diego Rivera (1886–1957) began to depict themes from the Revolution in their large mural paintings. Nationalism was also expressed in literature. In his novel *Los de Abajo* (1916), Mariano Azuela describes the Revolution from within and gives a realistic description of how the people experienced its cruelty. See also Malmström, *Introduction to Twentieth Century Mexican Music*, pp. 40–42.

11. Sandi's idea of the connections between nationalistic art music and música popular is indeed an insubstantial one, since art music has received its "national essence" mainly by borrowing melodies, rhythms, instruments, intonations, and so forth from folk and popular music.

12. See Carlos Chávez, "Nacionalismo musical," *Música, Revista Mexicana* 3 (1930):1–3; ibid., 4 (1930):28–32; ibid., 6 (1930):3–7.

13. This conclusion is my own.

14. Porfirio Díaz promoted the institutionalized nationalistic feeling. For example, the centennial of Hidalgo's rebellion against the Spaniards was celebrated in December 1910 with spectacular ceremonies, incorporating national and international elements. Sordo Sodi reports that music played an important part in these celebrations; waltzes and polkas were very popular, but the occasion as a whole gave rise to many satirical corridos (against Díaz).

15. This information was provided by Garrido in 1971. (Unfortunately I have no documentation of his sources.)

16. Ibid.

17. Ibid.

18. Ibid.

19. Mayer-Serra, *Panorama de la música mexicana*, p. 116.

20. This information was provided by Garrido in 1971.

21. This information was provided by Sordo Sodi and Salvador Contreras in 1971.

22. Mayer-Serra, *Música y músicos*, pp. 544–55; Hugo de Grial, *Músicos mexicanos*, pp. 83–85.

23. Ibid.

24. This information was provided by Garrido in 1971.

25. Mayer-Serra, *Música y músicos*, pp. 544–55; Grial, *Músicos mexicanos*, pp. 83–85.

26. As an example of the importance of music in establishing national trends in Mexico around 1918–20, Saldívar mentions Herrera y Ogazón's book, *El nacionalismo musical* (1918), the main part of which is devoted to a discussion of the importance of nationalism in contemporary Mexican art music. That same year Arraoz published a book, *Los orfeones del ejército mexicano* (The Choir Leaders of the Mexican Army). I have not yet seen Arraoz's book.

27. Mayer-Serra believes that Ponce "dió otro paso decisivo hacia una liquidación definitiva de la manera convencional de las estilizaciones folklóricas" (Mayer-Serra, *Panorama de la música mexicana*, p. 148).

28. Castañeda, "La música y la revolución," p. 442.

29. Grial, *Músicos mexicanos*, p. 264.

30. Ibid., pp. 257–59.

31. ". . . era secreto y voces que a nadie adivinaba" (Castañeda, "La música y la revolución").

32. Malmström, *Introduction to Twentieth Century Mexican Music*, pp. 30–34.

33. Castañeda, "La música y la revolución," p. 442.

34. Ibid., pp. 447–48.

35. Yaqui is the name of an Indian tribe in northwestern Mexico. The "pascola" dance and its counterpart, "La danza del venado" (the deer dance), are part of the Yaqui tradition. The music that accompanies the "pascola" dance is probably of European origin, whereas the origin of the music of "danza del venado" is uncertain. See G. Kurath, "The kinetic ecology of Yaqui dance instrumentation," *Ethnomusicology* 2 (1966):28–42.

36. This information was provided by Sordo Sodi and Garrido in 1971.

37. Ibid.

38. This information was provided by Garrido in 1971.

39. Gabriel Saldívar, *Monografía sobre el jarabe*, p. 14; Mayer-Serra, *Música y músicos*, p. 520; interview with Garrido in 1971.

40. This information was provided by Garrido in 1971.
41. Ibid.
42. The following information was provided by Sordo Sodi in 1973. Significantly enough, members of the charro movement of Mexico (*la charrería*) consider the use of charro dresses among mariachi musicians abusive. See Don Carlos del Roncón Gallardo, *El libro del charro mexicano* (Mexico, D.F., 1946).

Chapter 7—Composers and Musicians Up to the 1940s

1. Main sources of information on Rosas's life: Hugo de Grial, *Músicos mexicanos;* Otto Mayer-Serra, *Música y músicos de Latino-América;* interviews with Carmen Sordo Sodi and Juan S. Garrido. Sordo Sodi told me in 1973 that a book devoted entirely to Rosas's life and music was going to be published in Mexico fairly soon.
2. Grial, *Músicos mexicanos,* pp. 38–39.
3. Mayer-Serra, *Música y músicos,* pp. 857–58.
4. Otto Mayer-Serra, *The Present State of Music in Mexico.* The author refers to the "outset of commercial production," but it must be remembered that "Estrellita," like "Sobre las olas," is among the compositions that were sold by their creators to music publishers for a pittance.
5. Mayer-Serra, *Música y músicos,* pp. 549–52; Grial, *Músicos mexicanos,* pp. 82–85.
6. This information was provided by Sordo Sodi in 1973.
7. This information was provided by Garrido in 1971.
8. *Romantic* is used in this context solely as a characteristic stylistic feature. It should not be confused with romanticism as a historical period.
9. Mayer-Serra, *Música y músicos,* p. 948; Grial, *Músicos mexicanos,* p. 127.
10. Mayer-Serra, *Música y músicos,* pp. 523–24; Grial, *Músicos mexicanos,* pp. 114–15.
11. Grial, *Músicos mexicanos,* pp. 123–25.
12. Mayer-Serra, *Música y músicos,* pp. 352–53; Grial, *Músicos mexicanos,* pp. 162–64.
13. There is material available in the files of La Secretaría de Educación Pública in Mexico City.
14. According to Saldívar, Ponce's writings provided the pattern for their method of dealing with folk songs. Rubén M. Campos, who in 1928 published his volume *El folklore y la música mexicana,* was also highly dependent on Ponce; this can most easily be discerned from the piano accompaniment that is forced on the folk tunes.
15. Mayer-Serra, *Música y músicos,* p. 370; Grial, *Músicos mexicanos,* pp. 152–55; Antonio Castro Leal, "La academia de los artes," p. 13A.
16. Grial, *Músicos mexicanos,* p. 156.
17. This information was provided by Sordo Sodi and Garrido in 1971.
18. This information was derived from interviews with Saldívar and Garrido in 1971.
19. This information was provided by Saldívar in 1971.
20. Chilenas are songs or sones in cueca style, whose texts are associated with Guerrero (see chapter 4).
21. This information was provided by Garrido in 1971.
22. This information was taken from commentaries by Raúl Hellmer to "Folklore mexicano," vol. 1 (Musart D. 890). Hellmer states that the bambuco "es producto de la escuela romántica existente en el siglo pasado no solamente en Yucatán, sino también en todo el país" (ibid.). See also Daniel Castañeda, "La música y la revolución mexicana"; Gerónimo Baqueiro Fóster, *La canción popular de Yucatán.*
23. Grial, *Músicos mexicanos,* pp. 142–43. Whether this story is true or not, it clearly illustrates the kind of legend that frequently arose in Mexico during the Revolution.
24. Ibid., pp. 142–43.

25. Ibid., pp. 197–99.
26. Ibid., pp. 195–96.
27. This information was provided by Garrido in 1971.
28. This information was provided by Garrido, Sordo Sodi, and Contreras in 1971.
29. This information was provided by Sordo Sodi and Garrido in 1971.
30. Aaron Copland entitled one of his orchestral pieces *El Salón México* (1936). This work is actually a symphonic suite based on Mexican themes; see also Gilbert Chase, *America's Music: From the Pilgrims to the Present*, pp. 500–501.
31. This information was provided by Garrido in 1971.
32. This was obvious from a questionnaire devised by the Sección de Investigaciones Musicales, including the names of forty-four Mexican composers of popular music.
33. Some sources give his year of birth as 1901; however, the actual year is of minor importance. Main sources of information on Lara: Mayer-Serra, *Música y músicos*, pp. 542–43; idem, *Present State of Music*, pp. 22–23; Luis Sandi, "Agustín Lara y la canción mexicana," pp. 46–49; Agustín Lara, "Con alma de pirata," pp. 50–60; interviews with Sordo Sodi, Herrejón, Sandi, and Garrido in 1971.
34. Otto Mayer-Serra, *The Present State of Music*, pp. 22–23.
35. Sandi, "Agustín Lara," pp. 46–49.
36. These fashionable dances naturally took longer to reach rural areas, and their impact there varied.
37. "Idolo musical," *Visión, Revista Internacional* (August 1954):22–23. The impact of the tango in the 1920s was confirmed by Garrido; but the estimate of 80 percent seems too high.
38. Mayer-Serra, *Música y músicos*, p. 543.
39. For a discussion on Lara's style see Castañeda, *Balance de Agustín Lara*.
40. Lara, "Alma de pirata," p. 57.
41. W. Apel, ed., *Harvard Dictionary of Music*, p. 177.
42. "Los Panchos," *Audiomúsica*, pp. 20–21.
43. This information was provided by Garrido in 1973.
44. "Los Panchos," pp. 20–21.
45. This information was provided by Sordo Sodi and Dordelly at the Sección de Investigaciones Musicales in 1973.
46. "Hasta que se convierte en puro ritmo y estilo" (Otto Mayer-Serra, "Salvador Suárez," p. 14). This description of jazz more accurately depicts bop music, which in the 1940s succeeded swing music in the United States. The bop style was never influential in Mexico.
47. Mayer-Serra, "Carlos Campos," p. 13.
48. This information was provided by Garrido in 1971.
49. Ibid.

Chapter 8—The Media

1. It is not possible at this early stage of research to undertake a detailed analysis of the development and role of the mass media in Mexican society. I shall simply attempt to outline it. My main sources of information were: *La Sociedad de Autores y Compositores de México: XXV años de la SACM* (hereafter cited as *SACM XXV*; the union itself will be cited as SACM); interviews with Juan S. Garrido and Raúl Cossío, the director of Radio Universidad in Mexico City.
2. *SACM XXV*, p. 60.
3. This information was provided by Carmen Sordo Sodi and Juan Garrido in 1971.
4. This information was provided by Garrido in 1971.

5. Ibid.

6. I chose this group since its first contacts with radio are well documented by Domingo Sánchez, "Los Cancioneros del Sur: una época de la canción mexicana," pp. 32–34.

7. According to INBA's files, the most important concursos de música folklórica are: Concurso de Música Folklórica held twice a year at Uruapán, Michoacán, organized by the state government; Concurso Nacional de Huapango (not regularly scheduled); Concurso Nacional de Música Norteña at Ciudad Victoria, Tamaulipas (not regularly scheduled), organized by the state government. Besides concursos there are also song festivals. Every year there is a Festival de la Canción Mexicana Tradicional, organized by la Sección de Música Escolar en los Estados y Territorios (of INBA). There is an annual festival of popular music in Mexico City in April. In August a jazz festival is held. In Mexico City and Guadalajara the country's largest record shop, Mercado de Discos, is very active in this field. See also Krister Malm, "Latinamerikansk musik i stöpsleven," pp. 34–38.

8. This information was provided by Garrido in 1971.

9. The number 486 was given to me at SACM's statistical department. The distribution figures are from *SACM XXV*, p. 63. Table 1 giving the figure 466 dates from 1968–69.

10. This information was provided by Cossío in 1971.

11. The problem of the relationship between the radio and the state is difficult to clarify. It seems that the directors of broadcasting stations try to stay on good terms with the authorities in order to be left undisturbed.

12. *SACM XXV*, pp. 66, 70.

13. Ibid., p. 70. This was confirmed by Garrido in 1973, who said that one of the companies owns approximately 200 stations. It seems likely that commercials appear more frequently on certain stations within the *cadenas* than on others.

14. *SACM XXV*, p. 62; 16.7 percent of the total sum paid by radiodifusoras goes to the Asociación Nacional de Artistas (ANDA) and 83.33 percent to SACM.

15. Ibid., p. 70.

16. Ibid., p. 63. These figures apply to 1968–69.

17. Ibid., p. 77.

18. Ibid., p. 82.

19. Ibid., p. 52.

20. Unless otherwise stated, all the information on the early history of the record industry in Mexico is derived from Otto Mayer-Serra, "Eduardo C. Baptista," pp. 10–12, 17. This source is fairly reliable, as Mayer-Serra obtained all the information firsthand from Mr. Baptista.

21. This information was provided by Sordo Sodi in 1971.

22. This information was provided by Garrido in 1973. *Audiomúsica* 110 (1964); a union among Mexican record producers, La Asociación Mexicana de Productores de Discos (AMPRODIS), was formed in July 1962.

23. Otto Mayer-Serra, "Aires de renovación en 'Discos Columbia,' " p. 9.

24. Otto Mayer-Serra, "Salvador Suárez," pp. 10–12.[a]

25. "Ha logrado desplazar en ventas a una artista ya consagrada" (ibid.).

26. "Los Discometros de 1962," *Audiomúsica* 85 (1962).

27. [Otto Mayer-Serra?], "Hay que devolver la prosperidad a la industria del disco," *Audiomúsica* 30 (1961):9.

28. "Panorama de la música," *Audiomúsica* 175 (1967):9.

29. Ibid.; a single record consists of two songs, an EP of four (45 rpm).

30. Ibid.

31. Ibid.; Alberto Maravi, "Creación e imitación," pp. 9, 27.

32. "Enrique Guzmán," *Audiomúsica* 94 (1963):19–21, 34.

33. Maravi, "Creación e imitación," pp. 9, 27.

34. Roberto Carlos, Palito Ortega, and Leo Dan serve as examples. On Brazil see Gerhard

Béhague, "Bossa and Bossas: Recent Changes in Brazilian Urban Popular Music," pp. 209–33.
35. [Otto Mayer-Serra?], "Hay que devolver la prosperidad a la industria del disco," pp. 11–12. This article consists of interviews with artistic directors at various recording companies.
36. Mayer-Serra, "La industria mexicana del disco," p. 11.
37. Ibid.
38. Ibid.
39. Ibid.; this point is explicitly made by Rubén Fuentes and Heinz Klinckwort in the article.
40. This information was provided by Sordo Sodi, Garrido, and Lavista in 1971.
41. Hugo de Grial, *Músicos mexicanos,* p. 223.
42. This information was provided by Raúl Lavista in 1971.
43. Dan Malmström, *Introduction to Twentieth Century Mexican Music,* p. 60.
44. Sordo Sodi and Garrido agreed completely on this point (1971).
45. This information was provided by Raúl Lavista in 1971.
46. I am referring only to films financed by Mexicans.
47. This information was provided by Raúl Lavista in 1971.

Chapter 9—Contemporary Trends

1. A typical example is José A. Mérida, "Compositores de provincia y del Distrito Federal," pp. 152–55.
2. "Por lo general somos subdesarrollados e imitadores" (Juan Herrejón).
3. I do not have statistics to support this view, but I believe I could discern an improvement between my visits to Mexico in 1968, 1971, and 1973, based on the selection of records available in the shops. Another sign of improvement is that in 1973 the Sección de Investigaciones Musicales seems to have received larger grants for their research work.
4. This theory seems a bit dubious to me. There are examples of the very opposite occurring in certain newly founded African states and elsewhere.
5. Herrejón refers to "valores superficiales."
6. To date, the most comprehensive studies of the musical maps of Latin America have been made by Carlos Vega in his many works; those not listed in the bibliography can be found in any comprehensive musical dictionary.
7. "Yo creo que el sentido latino americano de la música popular es bastante unificado" (Herrejón).
8. This statement represents my personal view based on the research I conducted for this book. No inquiries using questionnaires have been made as yet.
9. However, *ranchera* and *corrido* are used as descriptions of genres in some Latin American countries.
10. Otto Mayer-Serra, *The Present State of Music in Mexico,* p. 29.
11. See also Salvador Novo, *Teoría del mariachi.*
12. This is an interesting phenomenon. Unfortunately, I have no information on social traditions in general and the distribution of roles between the sexes in particular that could clarify this matter. Stanford ("The Mexican *son,*" pp. 66–86) makes some interesting comments on this problem.
13. Interview with José E. Guerrero in 1971; Vicente T. Mendoza, *Panorama de la música tradicional de México,* pp. 108–109.
14. Following is the complete list of sheet music given to me by Garrido:

Composer	Song	Genre
"Cuicho" Cisneros	"Alma de cristal"	canción bolero
V. Cordero	"La flecha"	waltz
V. Cordero	"Gabino Barrera"	corrido
José Angel Espinoza	"El dólar"	canción ranchera
M. Esperón	"Cocula"	corrido
M. Esperón	"Dicen que soy mujeriego"	canción ranchera
M. Esperón	"Alma ranchera"	canción
R. Fuentes	"Los gavilanes"	canción ranchera
M. Hernández	"Dos rivales"	corrido
J. A. Jiménez	"Yo"	canción ranchera
J. A. Jiménez	"La enorme distancia"	canción ranchera
A. Lara	"Aquel amor"	canción mexicana
F. Valdez Leál	"Tú, sólo tú"	canción ranchera
Los Hermanos Cantoral	"El preso numero 9"	huapango
Los Hermanos Cantoral	"El crucifijo de piedra"	huapango
T. Méndez	"Gorrioncillo, pecho amarillo"	canción ranchera
T. Méndez	"Paloma negra"	canción ranchera
T. Méndez	"Puñalada trapera"	canción ranchera
S. Flores Rivera	"Peso sobre peso"	canción cómica
V. Romero	"El gavilán pollero"	canción ranchera
V. Romero	"La burrita"	canción ranchera
C. Sánchez	"Hermosísimo lucero"	canción ranchera
V. Trejo	"Tata Diós"	huapango

15. According to Garrido, the twenty-six-measure ranchera form was created by José Antonio Jiménez.

16. At this stage of research I cannot determine the extent to which the melodies correspond among the Latin American countries and in their relation to Spain.

17. This information was provided by Juan S. Garrido in 1971.

18. Hugo de Grial, *Músicos mexicanos,* p. 213. This information was confirmed by Sordo Sodi.

19. My assumption was confirmed by Garrido and Sordo Sodi.

20. *SACM XXV,* pp. 100–101.

21. Ibid., pp. 98–99.

22. Gómez Barrera (general director of SACM), *Audiomúsica* 80, p. 7; between 1958 and 1963 Agustín Lara earned 93,000 pesos in Mexico, compared with the 850,000 pesos Lara received from foreign countries between 1963 and 1968.

23. SACM, statistics dept., 1971.

24. This information was provided by Tomás Méndez in 1971 and confirmed by Garrido and Sordo Sodi. *SACM XXV,* p. 102; among the 100 leading composers in Mexico (based on their income), the 25 at the top received 47 percent of the total amount of money distributed by SACM between 1963 and 1968.

25. These organizations include: Unión Filharmonica Mexicana; Sindicato Único de Trabajadores de la Música del Distrito Federal (these two accept only musicians from Mexico City); Sindicato Nacional de Trabajadores de la Música (accepts musicians from all over Mexico). Mariachi groups performing in the capital may belong to any of these unions.

26. This information was provided by Sordo Sodi, Garrido, Luis Sandi, and Juan Herrejón. It is assuredly possible to discern social tendencies from preferences for special music genres. It is more difficult to deduce social trends from the internal structure of specific pieces of popular music, or rather to see social relationships reflected in the structure of the music. See also Tibor Kneif, *Musiksoziologie,* p. 21.

Appendix—Border Music of the 1970s in the Southwestern United States

1. Quoted in Bill C. Malone, *Country Music, U.S.A.* (Austin and London: University of Texas Press for the American Folklore Society, 1968), p. 173.
2. Dave Laing, *Buddy Holly* (London: Studio Vista, 1971), p. 71.
3. Freddy Fender, quoted in J. R. Young, "Freddy Fender: El Bebop Kid," *Country Music*, August 1975, p. 61.
4. Chet Flippo, "Texas Rock & Roll Spectacular!," *Phonograph Record*, March 1974, p. 26.
5. Ibid., p. 23.
6. Quoted in Chet Flippo, "Tortilla Flats," *Texas Monthly*, June 1975, p. 30.
7. Charlie Gillett, *The Sound of the City* (New York: 1970; Dell Laurel Edition, 1972), pp. 2–3.
8. Albums available include *Early Corridos Part I* and *Part II*, *Norteño Accordion: the 1930s*, and *Texas-Mexican Border Music: An Introduction*, all on the Arhoolie Folklyric series.

Bibliography

A. Archives and Institutions Consulted

In Mexico City:
  Biblioteca del Conservatorio de Música
  Hemeroteca Nacional de México (periodicals library)
  Mercado de Discos (leading record store)
  Museo Nacional de Antropología (library, recordings, instruments)
  Private collection of Gabriel Saldívar
  Promotora Hispano Americana de Música (the main music publisher)
  Radio Universidad
  RCA de México
  Sección de Investigaciones Musicales del Instituto Nacional de las Bellas Artes (the main source concerning folk and popular music in Mexico; sources include tape recordings, records, sheet music, a library, instruments, and pictures)
  Sociedad de Autores y Compositores de Música (SACM)
  Universidad Nacional Autónoma de México (UNAM), Department of Music
In Europe:
  Ibero-American Institute (Berlin)
  Ibero-American Institute (Goteborg)
  Latin-American Institute (Stockholm)
  Library of the Royal Academy of Music (Stockholm)
  Library of the University of Uppsala

B. Interviews, Mexico City, 1971

Salvador Contreras	(45 minutes):	Mexican music
Raúl Cossío	(30 minutes):	The radio stations
Juan S. Garrido	(3 hours):	History of Mexican popular music
José E. Guerrero	(60 minutes):	Folklore of Mexico
Juan Herrejón	(45 minutes):	Recent trends in Mexican folk and popular music
Raúl Lavista	(60 minutes):	Film music
Tomás Méndez	(30 minutes):	The composer's view
Zeferino Nandayapa	(45 minutes):	Marimba and marimba music
Gabriel Saldívar	(90 minutes):	History of folk and popular music in Mexico
Luis Sandi	(45 minutes):	Mexican music
Carmen Sordo Sodi	(2½ hours):	Mexican music
Consuelo Velázquez	(25 minutes):	The composer's view

The tapes of these interviews have been kept by the author as source material. All interviews have been transcribed, and the transcriptions are filed with the tapes. On a visit to Mexico City in January 1973, I had the opportunity to check details and receive additional information from Carmen Sordo Sodi and Juan S. Garrido. These interviews were not taped.

C. Books and Articles

Aguirre Beltrán, Gonzalo. *La población negra de México, 1519–1810.* México, D.F.: Ediciones Fuentes Cultural, 1946.
———. "Baile de negros." *Heterofonía* 17 (1971):4–10.
Apel, Paul Hermann. *Music of the Americas, North and South.* New York: Vantage Press, 1958.
Apel, W., ed. *Harvard Dictionary of Music.* 2nd ed. Cambridge: Harvard University Press, 1969.
"Aspectos económicos." In *Sociedad de Autores y Compositores de México: XXV años de la SACM.* México, D.F.: SACM, 1971. (Hereafter cited as *SACM XXV*.)
Baqueiro Fóster, Gerónimo. "El huapango." *Revista Musical Mexicana* 8 (1942):174–83.
———. *La canción popular de Yucatán.* México, D.F.: Editorial del Magisterio, 1970.
Behague, Gerhard. "Bossa and Bossas: Recent Changes in Brazilian Urban Popular Music." *Ethnomusicology* 2 (1972):209–33.
Bibliografía histórica mexicana. México, D.F.: El Colegio de México, 1967.
Blom, Eric, ed. *Grove's Dictionary of Music and Musicians.* 5th ed. New York: Grove Press, 1954.
Blume, F., ed. *Die Musik in Geschichte und Gegenwart.* Kassel, Germany: Bärenreiter, 1949–68.
Bowles, Paul. "On Mexico's Popular Music." *Modern Music* 18, no. 4 (1941).
Böhme, J., ed. *24 canciones y jarabes mexicanos (sin autór).* Hamburg, ca. 1830.
Cajigas Lagner, Alberto. *El folklore musical del Istmo de Tehuantepec.* México, D.F., 1961.
Calderón de la Barca, Frances Erskine. *La vida en México.* México, D.F.: Trad. Martínez Sobral, 1920.
Campos, Rubén. *El folklore y la música mexicana.* México, D.F.: Secretaría de Educación Pública, 1928.
———. *Folklore musical de las ciudades.* México, D.F.: Secretaría de Educación Pública, 1930.
———. "La música popular de México." *Revista de Estudios Musicales* 1 (1949):81–91.
———. "Juventino Rosas y la música popular de su época (1880–90)." *Anales del Instituto Nacional de Antropología e Historia* 1 (1939–40):337–53.
Cantric, Robert. "The Blind Man and the Elephant: Scholars on Popular Music." *Ethnomusicology* 2 (1965):100–15.
Castañeda, Daniel. "La música y la revolución mexicana." *Boletín Latin-Americano de Música* 5 (1941):437–38.
———. *Balance de Agustín Lara.* México, D.F.: Ediciones Libres, 1941.
———. *El corrido mexicano, su técnica.* México, D.F.: Editorial "Surco," 1943.
Castellanos, Pablo. "Aspectos del nacionalismo musical mexicano." *Heterofonía* 2 (1968); *Heterofonía* 4 (1969).
———. *Horizontes de la música precortesiana.* Mexico, D.F.: Colegio de México, 1970.
Castro Leal, Antonio. "La academia de los artes." *Excelsior* (Nov. 1969):13A.
Cervantes, Gustavo. "Estudios del mercado de radiodifusión." In *SACM XXV*, pp. 60–80.
Chase, Gilbert. *The Music of Spain.* 2nd ed. New York: Dover Publications, 1959.

―――. *A Guide to the Music of Latin America.* Washington, D.C.: Library of Congress and Pan American Union, 1962.

―――. *America's Music: from the Pilgrims to the Present.* 2nd ed. New York: McGraw-Hill, 1966.

Chávez, Carlos. "Nacionalismo musical." *Música, Revista Mexicana* 3 (1930):28–32; *MRM* 4 (1930):18–22; *MRM* 6 (1930):3–7.

―――. "La creación nacional." *MRM* 6 (1930):3–7.

―――. "La música propia de México." *MRM* 7 (1930):3–7.

―――. "La música." In *México y la cultura,* pp. 601–84. México, D.F., 1946.

Christensen, Dieter. "Musikwissenschaftliche Forschungen in Mexico." In *Das Mexicoproject der Deutschen Forschungsgemeinschaft,* pp. 131–38, Wiesbaden, 1971.

Cordero, Juan N. *Música razonada.* México, D.F.: Oficina de la Secretaría de Fomento, 1897.

Correa de Azevedo, Luiz Heitor. "The Present State and Potential of Music Research in Latin America." In *Perspectives in Musicology,* pp. 149–69, New York: Norton, 1971.

Cortijo, Alahija. *La música popular y los músicos célebres de la América Latina.* Barcelona (no date).

Cosío Villegas, Daniel, ed. *Historia moderna de México.* 7 vols. México, D.F.: Ediciones Fuentes, 1955–66.

Cotarelo y Mori, Emilio. *Colección de entremeses, loas, bailes, jácaras y mojigangas.* 2 vols. Madrid: Bailly-Baillière, 1911.

Crowle, H. A. "An Interpretive Study of the Official Jarabe Tapatío, the National Dance of Old Mexico." Ph.D. dissertation, San Jose State College, California, 1952.

Dahlhaus, Carl, ed. *Studien zur Trivialmusik des 19 Jahrhunderts.* Regensburg, Germany: Gustav Bosse Verlag, 1967.

Domínguez, Francisco; Sandi, Luis; and Téllez Girón, Roberto. *Investigación folklórica en México.* 2 vols. México, D.F.: Secretaría de Educación Pública, 1962–64.

Durán, Gustavo. "Romance, corrido y plena." *Boletín de la Unión Panamericana* (Nov. 1942):630–39.

Economic and Social Progress in Latin America. Washington, D.C.: Inter-American Development Bank (Annual Report), 1962–66–72.

El libro de oro del cine mexicano. Mexico, D.F.: Comisión de Cinematografía, 1949.

"Enrique Guzmán." *Audiomúsica* 94 (1963):19–21, 34.

Fernández, Justino. *Mexican Art.* Feltham, Middlesex, England: The Colour Library of Art, 1967.

Galindo, Blas. "El mariachi." *Boletín del Departamento de Música de la Secretaría de Educación Pública* 1 (1946):3–8.

García Cubas, Antonio. *El libro de mis recuerdos.* Mexico, D.F.: Imprenta de A. García Cubas, 1904.

―――. *Escritos diversos.* México, D.F.: Imprenta de I. Escalante, 1974.

Garrido, Juan S. "Historia del corrido mexicano." Mimeographed. México, D.F., 1971.

Grial, Hugo de [pseud.]. *Músicos mexicanos.* 4th ed. México, D.F.: Editorial Diana, 1971.

Grebe, María-Ester. "Modality in Spanish Renaissance Vihuela Music and Archaic Chilean Folksongs." *Ethnomusicology* 3 (1967):326–43.

Grenet, Emilio. *Popular Cuban Music.* Havana: Carasa y cía, 1939.

Gropp, Arthur E., ed. *A Bibliography of Latin American Bibliographies.* Metuchen, N.J.: Scarecrow Press, 1968.

Handbook of Latin American Studies. vols. 1–13. Cambridge: Harvard University Press. vols. 14–. Gainesville: University of Florida Press. Author index to vols. 1–28 published 1968.

Harrison, Frank. "European Elements in the Music of Two Maya Groups in Chiapas." *Selected Reports* 1, no. 2 (1968). (University of California).

Hanke, Lewis, ed. *The Modern Age.* vol. 2 of *History of Latin American Civilization: Sources and Interpretations.* London: Methuen & Co., 1969.

Henríque Ureña, Pedro. *La historia de la cultura en la América hispánica.* México, D.F.: Fondo de Cultura Económica, 1961.
Herrera Frimont, Celestino. "Breves notas sobre los sones huastecos." Suplemento Dominical de *El Nacional.* México, D.F., 1931.
Hurtado, N. Obregón. *El huapango.* México, D.F.: Secretaría de Educación Pública, 1933.
"Idolo musical." *Visión, Revista Internacional* (Aug. 1, 1954):22–23.
Johnson, Jean B. " 'The huapango,' a Mexican song contest," *California Folklore Quarterly* 1, no. 3 (1942).
Johnson, Marie. *Mexican Folklore.* Evanston, Ill.: Northwestern University Press, 1943.
Johnston, Edith. *Regional Dances of Mexico.* Skokie, Ill.: Dollar Books, 1963.
Kaphan, Iris Selicoff. "Music, Society and Musical Change as Exemplified in Mexico ca. 1900–30: a Study in the Sociology of Music." Ph.D. dissertation, University of California, in progress.
Kneif, Tibor. *Musiksoziologie.* Cologne: Musikverlag Gerig, 1971.
Kos, K. "New dimensions in folk music." *International Review of the Aesthetics and Sociology of Music* 3, no. 1 (1971):461–72.
Kurath, Gertrud, and Martí, Samuel. *Dances of Anahuac.* Chicago: Aldine Publishing Co., 1964.
Lara, Agustín. "Con alma de pirata." *Life en Español* 31, no. 2 (1968):50–60.
Larreba, A. "El cantor popular," *Revista Musical Mexicana* 9 (1942):200–204.
Lissa, Zofia. "Musik und revolution." *International Review of the Aesthetics and Sociology of Music* 5, no. 1 (1974):113–25.
"Los Panchos." *Audiomúsica* 87 (1963):20–21, 34.
Malm, Krister. "Latinamerikansk musik i stöpsleven." *Nutida Musik* 1 (1972–73):34–38.
Malmström, Dan. *Introduction to Twentieth Century Mexican Music.* Sweden: Uppsala University, 1974.
Maravi, Alberto. "Creación é imitación." *Audiomúsica* 165 (1966):9, 27.
Márquez, Los Hermanos. *25 biografías de compositores populares.* Mexico, D.F., 1966.
Mayer-Serra, Otto. *Panorama de la música mexicana desde la Independencia hasta la actualidad.* México, D.F.: Editorial Losana, 1941.
———. *Música y músicos de Latino-América.* 2 vols. México, D.F.: Editorial Atlante, 1947.
———. *The Present State of Music in Mexico.* Washington, D.C.: Pan American Union, 1960.
———. "Carlos Campos." *Audiomúsica* 13 (1960):12–14, 26.
———. "Aires de renovación en 'Discos Columbia.' " *Audiomúsica* 33 (1961):9.
———. "Salvador Suárez." *Audiomúsica* 35 (1961):10–12.
———. "Eduardo C. Baptista." *Audiomúsica* 39 (1961):10–12, 17.
———. "La industria mexicana del disco." *Audiomúsica* 42 (1961).
[Mayer-Serra, Otto?] "Hay que devolver la prosperidad a la industria del disco." *Audiomúsica* 30 (1961):11–12.
McCowell, John H. "The Mexican Corrido: Formula and Theme in a Ballad Tradition." *Journal of American Folklore* 85 (1972):205–20.
Mendoza, Vicente T. *El romance español y el corrido mexicano.* México, D.F.: Universidad Nacional Autónoma de México, 1939.
———. "El álbum de 24 canciones y jarabes mexicanos." *Boletín Latino-Americano de Música* (1941):511–41.
———. "La copla musical en México." *Anuario de la Sociedad Folklórica de México* 5 (1945):189–202.
———. *La décima en México: glosas y valonas.* Buenos Aires: Editorial Losana, 1947.
———. "La décima, sus derivaciones musicales en América." *Nuestra Música* 6 (1947):78–113.
———. "La música de Guerrero." *Nuestra Música* 15 (1947): 198–214.
———. *Canciones mexicanas.* New York: Pan American Union, 1948.

———. "El tango." *Nuestra Música* 18 (1950):138–54.
———. "La cachucha." *Nuestra Música* 20 (1950):289–310.
———. "Música en el Coliseo de México." *Nuestra Música* 26 (1952):108–33.
———. "La música tradicional española en México." *Nuestra Música* 29 (1953):5–34.
———. *El corrido mexicano, antología, introducción y notas*. México, D.F.: Letras Mexicanas, Fondo de Cultura Económica, 1954.
———. *Panorama de la música tradicional de México*. México, D.F.: Imprenta Universitaria, 1956.
———. *La canción mexicana: ensayo de clasificación y antología*. Estudios de folklore, no. 1. México, D.F.: Universidad Nacional Autónoma de México, 1961.
———. "El folklore y la musicología." *Anales del Instituto de Investigaciones Estéticas* 30 (1961):113–23.
Mérida, José A. "Compositores de provincia y del Distrito Federal." In *SACM XXV*, pp. 152–55.
Merriam, Alan P. *The Anthropology of Music*. Evanston, Ill.: Northwestern University Press, 1964.
Michel, Concha. *Cantos indígenas de México*. México, D.F., 1951.
Mindlin, Roger. *Die Zarzuela*. Zurich: Atlante Verlag, 1965.
Mitzelfelt, H. E. *Nationalistic Trends in Contemporary Mexican Music*. Seattle: University of Washington Press, 1945.
Moedano Navarro, Gabriel. "Bibliografía del profesor Vicente T. Mendoza." In *25 estudios de folklore*, pp. 23–27. México, D.F.: Universidad Nacional Autónoma de México, 1971.
Moberg, Carl-Allen. *Västerlandets musikhistoria intill 1600*. Stockholm: Natur och Kultur, 1973.
Möller, Birger. *Det tudelade samhället*. U-länder i omvandling. 2nd ed. Stockholm: Bonniers, 1969.
Mörner, Magnus. *Latinamerikas historia*. Stockholm: Natur och Kultur, 1969.
———. *Rasblandningen i Latinamerikas historia*. Stockholm: Natur och Kultur, 1967.
Mörner, Magnus, ed. *Problem i Modern Historia: Latinamerika*. Lund, Sweden: Studenlitteratur, 1970.
Nettl, Bruno. *An Introduction to Folk Music of the United States*. Detroit: Wayne State University Press, 1960.
———. *Folk and Traditional Music of the Western Continents*. Englewood Cliff, N.J.: Prentice-Hall, 1965.
———. "Persian Popular Music in 1969." *Ethnomusicology* 2 (1972):218–39.
Novo, Salvador. "Teoría del mariachi." Mimeographed. México, D.F.
"Panorama 1964 de la música popular." *Audiomúsica* 126 (1964):9.
"Panorama de la música popular (1965–66)." *Audiomúsica* 151 (1966):8–9.
"Panorama de la música popular (1966–76)." *Audiomúsica* 175 (1967):9, 26.
Pérez Martínez, Hector. *Trayectoria del corrido*. México, D.F., 1935.
Pohren, Donn E. *The Art of Flamenco*. Morón de la Frontera: Society of Spanish Studies, 1962.
Ponce, Manuel M. *Escritos y composiciones musicales*. México, D.F.: Ed. Cultura, 1917.
———. "La canción mexicana." Suplemento de Navidad de *Revista de Revistas*, México, D.F., 1912.
———. *Nuevos escritos musicales*. México, D.F.: Editorial Stylo, 1948.
Prieto, Guillermo. *Memorias de mis tiempos*. 2 vols. México, D.F.: V. d. C. Bouret, 1906.
Pulido, Esperanza. "Música popular de México." *Heterofonía* 36 (1974):12–16.
Redfield, Robert. *The Folk Culture of Yucatán*. Chicago: University of Chicago Press, 1941.
Reitze, Glenn L. "Trovadores mexicanos." *Américas* 22, no. 2 (1970):36–37.
"Renovación de la canción mexicana." *Audiomúsica* 159 (1966):9, 26.

"Reproches amargos dichos con valor civil." *Audiomúsica* 86 (1963):7–8.
Reyes de la Maza, Luis. *El teatro en México entre la reforma y el imperio (1810–1910)*. México, D.F.: Imprenta Universitaria, 1958.
Ríos Toledano, Miguel. *Colección de 30 jarabes, sones principales y más populares aires nacionales de la República Mexicana*. México, D.F., ca. 1884.
Robledo González, Carlos. *Colección de danzas y bailes regionales mexicanos, recopilados y arreglados para piano*. México, D.F. (no date).
Romero, Jesús C. *La música en Zacatecas y los músicos zacatecanos*. México, D.F.: Universidad Nacional Autónoma de México, 1963.
Ruiz Castañeda, María del Carmen, and Vázquez Valle, Irene. "La música popular en la época juarista." *Revista de la Universidad México* 26, no. 11 (1972):5–50.
Ruiz Cavalho de Baqueiro, Eloisa. *Tradiciones, folklore, música y músicos de Campeche*. Campeche: Publicaciones de Gobierno del Estado de Campeche, 1970.
Saldívar, Gabriel. *Historia de la música en México*. México, D.F.: Ed. Cultura, 1934.
———. *Monografía sobre el jarabe*. México, D.F.: Talleres Gráficos de la Nación, 1937.
Sánchez, Domingo. "Los Cancioneros del Sur, una época de la canción mexicana." *Revista SACM* 1 (Jan.-Apr. 1971):32–34.
Sandi, Luis. "Agustín Lara y la canción mexicana." *Música, Revista Mexicana* 9–10 (Dec. 1930-Jan. 1931):46–49.
Santamaría, Francisco J. *Diccionario de mejicanismos*. México, D.F.: Ed. Porrúa, 1959.
Schmidt, Henry. "The Huapango: a Dithyrambic Festival." In *Hunters and Healers: Folklore Types and Topics*, edited by M. Hudson Wilson, pp. 147–56. Austin: University of Texas Press, 1971.
Serrano Martínez, Celedonio. "Romances tradicionales en Guerrero." *Anuario de la Sociedad Folklórica de México* 7 (1951):7–73.
Simmons, Merle Edwin. "The Mexican Corrido as a Source for Interpretive Study of Modern Mexico (1870–1950): with a Consideration of the Origins and Development of the Corrido Tradition," Ph.D. dissertation, University of Michigan, 1951.
Slonimsky, Nicholas. *Music of Latin America*. New York: Thomas Y. Crowell, 1945.
Sociedad de Autores y Compositores de México: XXV años de la SACM. México, D.F.: SACM, 1971.
Social Economic Progress in Latin America. Washington, D.C., 1966.
Social Progress Trust Fund. Washington, D.C., 1962.
Sordo Sodi, María del Carmen. "Africa en los orígenes del 'a go-go.'" *El Sol de México* (newspaper), Sección C, Jan. 21, 1967.
———. "La marimba." *Heterofonía* 22 (Jan.-Feb. 1972):27–30.
Soustelle, Jacques. *La vie quotidenne des Aztèques à la veille de la conquète espagne*. Paris: Librairie Hachette, 1955.
Stanford, E. Thomas. "Vicente T. Mendoza, *Lírica narrativa de México: El corrido*" (book review). *Ethnomusicology* 1 (1966):111–14.
———. "The villancico and the Mexican corrido." *Anales del Instituto Nacional de Antropología é Historia* 23 (1970).
———. "The Mexican son." *Yearbook of the International Folk Music Council* 4 (1972):66–86.
Stark, R. B.; Peane, T.; and Cobos, R. *Music of the Spanish Folk Plays in Mexico*. Santa Fe: Museum of New Mexico Press, 1969.
Statistical Abstract of Latin America. Los Angeles: University of California, Latin American Center, 1955.
Stevenson, Robert. *Music in Mexico*. New York: Thomas Y. Crowell, 1952.
———. *Music in Aztec and Inca Territory: Contact and Acculturation Periods*. Los Angeles: University of California Press, 1968.

Subirá, José. *La tonadilla escénica*. Madrid: Col. "Labor," Sec. V. Música, 1933.
Toor, Frances. *A Treasury of Mexican Folkways*. New York: Crown Publishers, 1947.
Torner, Eduardo M. "La rítmica en la música tradicional española." *Nuestra Música* 9 (1948):551–68.
Vásquez Santa Ana, Higinio. *Canciones, cantares y corridos mexicanos*. 2 vols. México, D.F.: Imprenta de León Sánchez, 1925.
———. *Historia de la canción mexicana*. México, D.F.: Talleres Gráficos de la Nación, 1931.
———. *Fiestas y costumbres mexicanas*. México, D.F.: Ediciones Balas, 1940.
——— and Dávila Garibi, J. I. *El carnaval*. México, D.F.: Talleres Gráficos de la Nación, 1931.
Vega, Carlos. *Panorama de la música popular argentina—con ensayo sobre la ciencia del folklore*. Buenos Aires: Ed. Losana, 1944.
———. *El origen de las danzas folklóricas*. Buenos Aires: Ricordi Americana, 1956.
———. "Mesomusic: an essay on the music of the masses." *Ethnomusicology* 1 (1966):1–17.
Verdadero jarabe tapatío arreglado por J. de J. González Rúbio. México. D.F., 1913.
Yurchenco, Henrietta. "Marimba Music of Tehuantepec." *Ethnomusicology* 2 (1973): 396–97.

Comments on Recordings

The Mexican market abounds with records of native folk and popular music. However, it should be noted that the epithet *folkloric*, which frequently appears on records with Mexican (and Latin American) music, does not necessarily mean that the record contains authentic folk music. In the last few years numerous records have been released that contain Mexican folk music, sones (huapangos) in particular. I would like to recommend those records that have been released by Folkways in the United States, by the National Museum of Anthropology in Mexico City, and by the Instituto Nacional de las Bellas Artes, for example, the series "Folklore Mexicano."

As for popular Mexican music, I would like to recommend the Camden (RCA) series (Cam 1 and so forth). Further information is given in: a) Latin American long-playing records available in the United States in *Interamerican Music Bulletin* 71 (1971); b) H. Yurchenco, "Taping History of Mexico," *American Record Guide* 33 (New York, 1966):4–7, 80–85.

Many books listed in the bibliography contain sheet music. The most important publishers of Mexican popular music are Promotora Hispano Americana de Música (PHAM) and Editorial Mexicana de Música Internacional (EMMI).

Index

A & M records, 138
"A la orilla de un palomar," 63
ABC-Dot records, 142, 144
accordion, 45, 46, 72, 73, 78, 104, 139, 143, 146
Acerina y su danzonera, 77. *See also* Valente, Conejo
Aceves Mejía, Miguel, 116, 117
Acuña, A., 135
"Adiós Mariquita linda," 96, 131
"Adiós mi chaparrita," 98
"Adiós trigueña," 91
African influences, 11–12, 21, 22, 71
Afro-Cuban influences, 12, 25, 99, 124, 138. *See also* Cuban influences
Aguila Sisters, 104, 115, 117
Aguirre, Clemente, 76
Aguirre Beltrán, Gonzalo, 11
"Ahualulco," 4
aires nacionales, 15, 82
"Al son de la marimba," 48
alabados, 59
alabanzas, 59
"Alborada," 68
Alcalá, Macedonio, 7
Alegres de Terán, 146
"All You Need is Love," 135
"Allá en el Rancho Grande," 131, 143
Alpert, Herb, 131, 138
Altamirano, Ignacio, 84
ANDA (Asociación Nacional de Artistas), 111
Animas Trujano (film), 122
Anka, Paul, 119, 135
Apel, P. H., 103
Arcaraz, Luis, 106
Argo records, 141
Arhoolie records, 147
Armenta, W. F., 98
"Arpa de oro," 73
arpa grande, 24, 27, 63, 64
arrebol, 40
Arteta, Juan, 105
Artex records, 113
ARV records, 141, 144

Arvizú, Juan, 85, 102, 109, 115
Arvizú, Mario, 98
"Asi es mi tierra," 97
Asociación Nacional de Artistas (ANDA), 111
Atlantic records, 144, 146
Audiomúsica, 116, 117, 118, 119
"Ay, Jalisco no te rajes," 121
ayayays, 14
Azcárraga Vidaurreta, Emilio, 43, 109

"Babuco," 100
Baena, Federico, 117
bajo sexto, 143, 146
baladas, 119
Ballet Folklórico de México, 3, 26, 38, 48
bambuco, 64, 98–99, 101
Banda de Policía, 100
Banda Típica de los Cuerpos Rurales, 85
bandolón, 85, 89
banjo, 104, 139
Baptista, Eduardo C., 113–15
Barcelata, Lorenzo, 32–33, 98, 109
bass guitar, 144. *See also* guitarrón
bassoon, 104
Beatles, 119, 142
Before the Next Teardrop Falls (album), 144
"Before the Next Teardrop Falls" (song), 142
"Begin the Beguine," 78
Bego records, 141
beguine, 78
bel canto style, 16, 60, 61–62, 65, 66
Bellini, Vincenzo, 82
Beltrán, Lola, 116, 117, 125
Beltrán Ruiz, Pablo, 106
Berry, Chuck, 140
"Bésame," 96
"Bésame mucho," 131, 132
birthday celebrations, 63
Blackwell, Otis, 141
Bland, Bobby, 141
blues, 139, 147
bocadillos, 68

178

Index

Böhme, J., 37
bolero mambo, 78
boleros, 12, 20, 47, 64, 77–78, 79, 101, 103, 104, 119, 124, 141
boleros rancheros, 70, 78, 104, 118
boleros románticos, 78, 104
bombas, 17
border music, 138–147
bossanova, 78
Bretón, Tomás, 16
Bromberg, David, 143
Brubeck, Dave, 131
Buena Suerte records, 145
bullfights, 80

Caballero, José Luis, 102
Calderón, Fernando, 61
Calderón de la Barca, Frances Erskine, 37
"Camelia," 135
"Caminante del Mayab," 99
Campos, Carlos, 105, 117, 118
canario, 13
cañas, 14
"Canción de un preso," 135
Cancioneros del Sur, 108–109
canciones, 59–70, 72, 83, 89
canciones epitalámicas, 60
canciones huapangueadas, 32
canciones mexicanas, 65–67, 91, 95, 96, 98, 120
canciones norteñas, 46. See also norteño bands
canciones rancheras, 67–70. See also rancheras
Cantoral, Roberto, 104
Cantoral Brothers, 130
Capitol records, 115
caprices, 82
Cárdenas, Guty, 7, 65, 98, 99, 102, 105, 115
Cárdenas, Lázaro, 92
Carillo, Alvaro, 73, 132, 135
Carr, Vicki, 138
Carrillo Puerto, 99
Carson, Jenny Lou, 135
Casa Nagel, 76
Casa Wagner y Livien, 53, 94
cascabel, 13
Castañeda, Daniel, 43, 55, 88, 89
Castellanos, Pablo, 38
Castillo, Nicandro, 33
Castro, Ricardo, 76
Castro Padilla, Manuel, 87
Catholic Church, 10, 11, 45, 82
CBS, 115
cello, 85
"Celoso," 135

Cervantes, Ignacio, 74
Chacha Aguilar, La, 109
chachacha, 80, 105
chacona, 14
Chase, Gilbert, 12
Chávez, Carlos, 6, 55, 83
Chess records, 141
"Chicano," 143
chilenas, 64, 89
"Chin chun chan," 16
"China," 96
chinaco style, 68
choirs, 86–87
"Cielito lindo," 27, 32, 131, 138
cinema. See film music
cinquillo antillano, 74, 75
clarinet, 27, 145
"Cocula," 126
Codina, Genaro, 76
colombiana, 98
Colorado, C., 135
Columbia records, 96, 115, 116
Cometas Castañedas, Los, 105
"Como te extraña mi amor," 135
Compañía de Cigarro el Buen Tono, 109
composers, 6, 7–8, 65, 93–103, 132, 134, 135. See also specific names
composers' union. See SACM: Sindicato de Compositores
conchas de amarillo, 60
Conesa, María, 91
conga (dance), 78, 79
conga drums, 77
conjuntos huastecos, 26
conjuntos jarochos, 25
conjuntos típicos, 68
"Contradanza de Arteaga," 72
contradanzas, 13, 71, 72, 74, 82
coplas, 17, 21, 23, 25, 40, 51
coplas al tapado, 51
"Corazón," 73
Cordero, Juan N., 37, 39
Cordero, Victor, 57, 58
Cornejo, García, 85, 109
Cornejo, María, 98
cornet, 27, 84
corridas, 80
"Corrido de Carlos IV," 52
"Corrido de Leandro Rivera," 52
corridos, 39, 49–58, 68, 72, 83, 86, 87, 125, 128, 137
Cortázar Ramírez, Elíaz, 88
Coss, Antonio, 27
Cossío, Raúl, 109–10, 111
Costa, César, 119
country and western music, 69, 139, 145, 146

Crazy Cajun records, 142
"Cuando calienta el sol," 132
Cuatro Ases de la Canción, 96
Cuban influences, 71, 74–76, 77, 78–80, 104. *See also* Afro-Cuban influences
cueca, 33, 64, 71
Cuéllar, A. B., 53
Cuevas, Jacinto, 76
Curi, Mario, 95
Curiel, Gonzalo, 122, 132
Curti, Carlos, 76, 84
CWL (first radio station in Mexico City), 107

Dan, Leo, 135
dances, 11, 12–13, 16, 25–27, 71–80, 82, 89, 104–105. *See also specific dances*
danza cubana, 74
danza fina, 74, 76
"Danza habanera," 76
danzones, 12, 47, 76–77, 100, 101, 104–105
Dávila Garibi, J. I., 42
Davis, Benny, 135
Debussy, Claude, 96
décimas, 17–18, 40, 53
DeLeón Hernández, José María (Joe Hernández), 145
"Delgadina," 49
Demetrio, Luis, 132
Derba, Mimi, 91
despedida, 40
"Despeinada," 135
"Detrás del amor," 135
Díaz, Ismael, 106
Díaz, Porfirio, 53, 54, 55, 68, 73, 81, 83, 89, 94
Díaz Conde, Antonio, 122
Díaz Ordaz, Gustavo, 80, 111
"Dicen que soy mujeriego," 128, 129
Diddley, Bo, 140
"Diós nunca muere," 7
Discometro, 116, 117
Discos Brunswick, 96
Discos Gamma, 115
Dr. John (Mac Rebennack), 143
Domínguez, Abel, 48
Domínguez, Alberto, 47, 138
Domínguez, Francisco, 121, 122
Domínguez, Pepe, 86, 98, 99
Domínguez Brothers, 47, 109
Domino, Fats, 141, 145
Donizetti, Gaetano, 82
"Don't Be Cruel," 141
"Dos rivales," 128
double bass, 45, 48, 84, 104
drums, 10, 27, 48, 77, 89, 104, 122, 139, 144

Duncan, Wayne, 141
Duncan records, 141
Duo Llera, 57
Durán, Gustavo, 50, 51
Dylan, Bob, 143

ecos, 60
"Eine Kleine Nachtmusik," 5
"El aforrado," 37
"El agua nieve," 27
"El ahualulco," 37
"El andariego," 73
"El atole," 37
"El bejuquito," 15, 32
"El burro," 23
"El caimán," 27
"El cascabel," 26
"El chinaco," 53, 68
"El chirripampli," 15
"El corrido de Agustín Ramírez," 98
"El corrido de la pulga," 53
"El costumbre," 27
"El currataco," 23–24
"El distinguido," 23
"El gavilán pollero," 130, 131
"El huateque," 27
El Indio (film), 121
El libro de oro del cine mexicano, 121
"El llorar," 27
"El maracumbé," 24
"El mariachi," 109
"El mosquito," 23
El Muerto de Emiliano Zapata, 119
"El palomo," 37, 38
"El paseo de Ixtacalaco," 14
El Pato records, 141
"El perico," 37
"El preso numero 9," 130
"El rescapetate," 47
El roble viejo (album), 144
"El sacristán," 77
"El siglo XIX," 53
"El siguisirí," 26
"El tapatío," 37
"El torito," 84
"El venado," 23
"El zanganito," 15
Elisondo, José F., 16
Elorduy, Ernesto, 95
EMI records, 115
"En alta mar," 73
"Enamorada," 102
"Entrega total," 135
"Es lupe," 135
Echeverría, Luis, 111
esdrújulos, 61

Esparza Oteo, Alfonso, 66, 76, 77, 96–97, 109
Esperón, Manuel, 121, 126, 128
Esquivel Pren, José, 64
Esteve, Pablo, 13
"Estoy pensando en tí," 135
"Estrellita," 94–95, 131
ethnic music, 1–3
European influences, 10, 12–16, 71, 72, 88. See also Italian influences; Spanish influences

"Faded Love," 139
fandango, 12, 13, 14, 18, 23, 37, 39
"Farolito," 102
Fender, Freddy, 140–42, 143–44, 146
Fender guitar, 140
Fernández, Ana María, 102
Fernández Esperón, Ignacio. See Nacho, Tata
fiestas, 10–11. See also fines de fiesta
film music, 47, 68–69, 95, 120–22
fines de fiesta, 90, 91
Flem, Paul de, 97
Fleta, Miguel, 91
Flippo, Chet, 143
"Flor, blanca flor," 18
"Flor de Mayo," 96
Flores, Salvador, 54
Flores Brothers, 98
Flores Rivera, Salvador, 130
flugelhorn, 145
flute, 10, 27, 44, 68, 84, 85, 86
folk music, 1, 2, 3–4, 8, 9–16, 71–72, 73, 83, 89–90, 98, 122, 125, 126–27, 128
Fox, Howard C., 132
fox trot, 77, 95, 101
Franco, Francisco, 21
Freed, Alan, 147
"Frenesí," 47, 138
Fuentes, Rubén, 44, 117, 119

Gaby, Baby, 145
Galindo, Blas, 97
"Gallo negro," 21
galops, 72
Gante, Pedro de, 10
García, Belisario de Jesús, 77
García, Salvador, 115
García Cubas, Antonio, 26, 37
Gardel, Carlos, 113
Garnicia-Ascencio, 57, 104
Garrido, Juan S., 8, 32, 33, 43, 46, 53, 62, 65, 67, 68, 74, 76, 77, 78, 80, 84, 91, 98–99, 105–106, 108, 116, 123, 126–31
Gatica, Lucho, 117
Gil, Alfredo, 103

Gillett, Charlie, 147
Girón, Téllez, 18
glosas, 17, 53
Goldberg, Barry, 143
"Golondrina mensajera," 63
Gómez, Jose Antonio, 38
Gómez Brothers, 47
Gonzáles Bocanegra, Francisco, 80
González Rubio, C. José de Jesús de, 38
Gorda, Luis G., 16
"Gorrioncillo, pecho amarillo," 127
gospel music, 139
"Granada," 102, 132, 138
Grenet, Emilio, 19
Grever, María, 96
Grial, Hugo de, 20, 87, 94, 96, 99
Grupo de los Trovadores Tamaulipecos, 98, 109
"Guadalajara," 44, 106, 109
guajira, 78, 79, 124
guaracha, 78
"Guayabas," 15
Guerrero, José E., 6–7, 125
Guillot, Olga, 117
guitar, 22, 24, 25, 26, 27, 33, 38, 40, 42, 45, 46, 56, 60, 63, 64, 84, 85, 89, 103, 104, 139, 140, 143, 144, 145
guitarra quinta, 26
guitarrón (bass guitar), 27–28, 42, 43, 56, 77, 84
Guízar, José, 132
Guízar, Pepe, 106, 109, 115
gustos, 89
Gutiérrez de Alfaro, Calizta, 94
Guzmán, Enrique, 117, 119
gypsy music, 22

habaneras, 12, 64, 71, 74–76, 84
Haggard, Merle, 146
Haley, Bill, 117, 119
hammock rhythm (ritmo de hamaca), 74, 76
"Hang On Sloopy," 119
harp, 24, 26, 27, 38, 40, 42, 43, 44, 46, 56, 63, 89
heel dances, 19, 21, 25
Heist, Elizabeth H., 138
Hellmer, Raúl, 15, 98
"Hermosísimo lucero," 128, 129
Hernández, Manuel, 128
Hernández, Rafael, 135
Hernández, Tiburcio, 100
Herrejón, Juan, 8, 123, 124
"Hey Jude," 135
Hill, Kaye D., 132
Holly, Buddy, 131, 140
Hopkins, Lightnin', 139

huapangos, 4, 17, 18, 24–35, 41, 72, 83, 89, 125, 130
huapangos lentos, 32, 64
huapanguera, 27
huehuetl, 122
Huerta, Baldemar. *See* Fender, Freddy
Huerta Sisters, 117
Huici records, 113
Hurricane records, 145

Ideal records, 141
idylls, 82
Imperial records, 141
Imprenta de Murgia, 53
Indian influences, 1–2, 9–11, 15, 22, 81–82, 88, 99, 122
Infante, Pedro, 69, 115, 116, 118, 137
"Ingratos ojos míos," 135
Instituto Nacional de las Bellas Artes, 97
Iris, Esperanza, 91
Italian influences, 61–62
Ituarte, Julio, 76

"Jaleo Andaluz," 20
"Jaleo de Jerez," 20
James, Elmore, 141
"Jarabe de la botella," 36
"Jarabe de manteca," 36
"Jarabe gatuno," 36
"Jarabe insurgente," 38
"Jarabe jalisciense," 36
"Jarabe largo," 36
"Jarabe michoacano," 36
"Jarabe mixteco," 36
"Jarabe nacional," 15, 37–38
"Jarabe oficial," 37, 90–91
"Jarabe pateño," 36
"Jarabe tapatío," 15, 37–39, 41, 90
jarabes, 18, 19, 21, 35–39, 41, 43, 63, 72, 83, 89
Jaramillo y sus Diablos, 105
jarana, 24–25, 26, 27, 42, 46, 64
jarana dances, 21, 29–32
jazz, 105, 124
Jefferson, Blind Lemon, 139
"Jesusita en Chihuahua," 74
Jiménez, Flaco, 143, 146
Jiménez, José Alfredo, 117, 118, 128, 132, 137
Jiménez, Marcos A., 96
Jordan, Esteban, 143
jota, 21, 32, 35, 41, 63
"Juan Charrasqueado," 57
"Juanita Banana," 132
Juárez, Benito, 15, 37, 81
"Júrame," 96

Kenton, Howard M., 132
Klinckwort, Eduardo, 115
Klinckwort, Gustavo, 115
Klinckwort, Heinz, 120
Kos, K., 3

"La Adelita," 67, 87, 88, 131
"La bamba," 4, 15, 26, 32, 131, 140
La bandida (film), 122
"La borrachita," 98
"La cachucha," 67
"La canción mixteca," 17
"La chipacuará," 15
"La chuparosa," 27
La cucaracha (film), 122
"La cucaracha," 4, 67, 87, 122, 131, 138
"La cuera," 32
"La danza de los Quetzales," 10
"La danza de los viejitos," 2–3
"La danza del Pascola," 89
"La danza del volador," 10
"La Diana," 37
"La dolorosa," 16
"La enorme distancia," 128, 129
"La entrada de Juárez a la ciudad de México," 52–53
"La esposa difunta," 49
La Familia, 145
"La golondrina," 44, 136
"La hora azul," 102
"La india frutera," 15
"La indita," 15, 26
"La jarana," 15
"La llorona," 21, 47
"La malagueña," 19, 29–31
"La malmaridada," 49
"La media vuelta," 132
"La mentira," 132
"La misa de amor," 49
"La negra," 44
"La norteña," 90
"La orquesta," 53
"La paloma," 76, 131
"La patera," 14
"La princesa china," 91
"La raspa," 131
"La rielera," 67
"La sandunga," 20–21, 47, 76, 90
"La solterita," 14
"La sonámbula," 94
"La tapatía," 37
"La tos de mi mamá," 53
"La Valentina," 67, 87, 131
"La verbena de la paloma," 16
La vida en México (Calderón de la Barca), 37

Index

Laing, Dave, 140
"Lanceros," 72
Lara, Agustín, 7–8, 80, 101–103, 105, 109, 115, 121, 122, 132, 135, 138
"Las chiapanecas," 47
"Las cuatro milpas," 67
"Las mañanitas," 44, 63, 136
"Las moscas," 23
"Las senas del esposo," 49
"Las tres pelonas," 67, 87
Latinaires, 145
Lavista, Mario, 95, 121, 122
Lehar, Franz, 91
Lennon, John, 135
León, Tómas, 38
Lerdo de Tejada, Miguel, 65, 66, 76, 85, 91, 95–96, 100, 109
Libro de mis recuerdos (García Cubas), 37
Light Crust Doughboys, 139
"Limas," 15
Little Joe and the Latinaires, 145
Little Richard, 145
"Llegó borracho el borracho," 132
Llera, Felipe, 85, 90, 95, 98
López, Trini, 138
López, Virginia, 117
López Alavez, José, 7, 89
López Méndez, Ricardo, 64
López Sisters, 108
Lorca, Antonieta, 57
Los Calaveras, 103
Los de abajo (film), 121
Los Diamantes, 103, 104
Los Dominics, 119
"Los enanos," 37, 38
Los Folkloristas, 3
Los Hitters, 119
Los Impala, 117
Los Johnny Jets, 119
Los Tres Ases, 103
Los tres huastecos, 121
Los Tres Reyes, 117
Los Trovadores Tamaulipecos, 98, 109
Los Yakis, 119
"Loveliest Night of the Year, The," 94
Lozano, Samuel M., 55
"Luz eléctrica," 63

Madero, Francisco I., 55
malagueñas, 13, 14, 18–19, 89
mambo, 78–80, 105, 124
mañanitas, 63–64
Mancera, Valentín, 54
Manzanero, Armando, 104, 132
Maravi, Alberto, 119
marches, 47, 80, 82

"Marchita el alma," 67, 87
mariachi sinfónico, 44
Mariachi Vargas de Tecalitlán, 42
mariachis, 4, 22, 28, 33, 38, 41–45, 57, 63, 64, 69–70, 73, 83, 84, 89, 92, 125, 131, 136
marimba bands, 46–48, 90, 136
marimbas, 33, 44, 46–48, 68, 77, 84, 104, 106
Marín Brothers, 47
Marquéz, Ramón, 105
Martínez, Abundio, 73
Martínez, Debbie "La Chicanita," 146
Martínez, José de J., 38, 73
Maximilian, 37, 42, 53, 73
Mayer-Serra, Otto, 15, 16, 17, 21, 82, 84, 94, 101, 116, 124–25
mazurkas, 16, 41, 65, 71, 72, 82, 84
McCartney, Paul, 135
Meaux, Huey, 141–42, 143, 144–45
melodía amplia, 125
Memoria de mi tiempo (Prieto), 37
Méndez, Tomás, 117, 127, 132
Mendoza, Amalia, 125
Mendoza, Quirino F., 32, 74, 125
Mendoza, Vicente, 9, 12, 13, 14, 18, 22, 23, 36, 39, 50, 53, 54, 60, 61–62, 63, 64–65, 97, 125–26
Menéndez-Pidal, Ramon, 52
Mercado de Discos, 116, 117
"Mestiza de mi tierra," 86
mestizos, 2, 11, 12, 21–22, 60, 72, 81–82, 83, 84, 88, 89, 122, 123
"Mexican Hat Dance," 39, 131
"Mexicanos, al grito de guerra," 80
"Mexico a través de los siglos," 91
"México adorado," 14
"México bello," 95
Meyer, Augie, 143
"Mi barquita de madera," 135
"Mi querido capitán," 77
Michel, Concha, 64
Mifune, Toshiro, 122
Mindlin, Roger, 14
minuets, 16, 71
Misón, Luis, 13
Mole, R. B., 135
Mondragón, Samuel, 89
Monge, Chucho, 108, 121
Morales, Melesio, 15, 76
Morales, Rocky, 143
Moreno, Gus, 131
Morrie, Tiny, 145
Mozart, Wolfgang Amadeus, 5
"Mujer," 102
"Muñequita linda," 96
Muñoz, Antonio, 104
Muñoz, Marcos Antonio, 117

Murguía, M., 37
Murry, Ted, 135
Musart records, 115
música étnica. *See* ethnic music
música folklórica. *See* folk music
música popular. *See* popular music
música popularizada, 7
Música razonada (Cordero), 37
música tradicional, 4
música tropical, 78, 99, 125. *See also* Afro-Cuban influences
"Musita," 135

Nacho, Tata, 57, 65, 66, 76, 96, 97–98, 117
Nacional records, 113
Nandayapa, Zeferino, 47, 48
National Conservatory (Mexico City), 82, 83–84, 93, 94, 95
nationalism, 11, 12, 15–16, 82–84, 86–90, 91–92, 95
Navarro, Chucho, 103
Nebuchadnezzar (Verdi), 5
Negrete, Jorge, 69, 95, 109, 116, 118, 137
Negro influences, 11–12, 15, 22. *See also* African influences; Afro-Cuban influences
Nettl, Bruno, 5, 61
Newman, David "Fathead," 143
nocturnes, 82
Norco records, 141
"Norma la de Guadalajara," 135
norteño bands, 45–46, 57, 69, 73, 125, 136, 145
Nuestra Música, 97
"Nuestro juramento," 144
"Nunca, nunca, nunca," 98
Nunó, Jaime, 80

O tierra (film), 121
Obregón, Alvaro, 57, 97
Odeón records, 113
"Oh Holy One," 141
Okeh records, 113
Olivares, Leopoldo, 106
Olympia records, 113
opera, 16, 61, 82, 95, 105
Orfeón records, 115
organ, 144, 145
Orquesta Miguel Lerdo de Tejada, 85
Orquesta Típica de la Ciudad de México, 97, 109
Orquesta Típica de Policía, 85
Orquesta Típica Presidencial, 97
Orquesta Típica Yucalpetén, 86
orquestas típicas, 83–86, 89, 95
Ortega, Ancieto, 38
Ortega, Palito, 135

Ortiz Tirado, Alfonso, 109, 115
"Over the Waves" ("Sobre las olas"), 73, 94, 95, 131

Paganini, Nicolò, 47
"Palabras," 135
Palacio, José Alfonso, 77
Palmerín, Ricardo, 7, 65, 98, 99
Pan Americana de Discos, S.A., 115
"Pan de jarabe," 36
Paniagua Brothers, 47
Panorama de la música popular argentina (Vega), 13, 71
Panorama de la música tradicional de México (Mendoza), 9, 39
paracumbe, 13
Parker, Knocky, 139
Parsons, Talcott, 147
pasacalle, 14
pasodobles, 80, 84, 101
pavane, 12
Pavlova, Anna, 39
Paz, Rafael de, 47
Peerless de México, 115, 120
Pepita Jiménez (film), 122
Pepsodent Orchestra, 109
Peralta, Angela, 94
"Peregrina," 99
Pérez, John, 143
Pérez, Maruca, 109
Pérez Prado, Dámaso, 80, 124, 135
"Perfidia," 47, 138
"Perjura," 65, 66, 76, 91, 95
Peruvian waltz, 73
Pescados (film), 121. *See also Redes*
"Pesos sobre pesos," 130
peteneras, 12, 13, 14
Phrygian modality, 19, 21
piano, 47, 76, 77, 82, 104, 139
pirecuas, 64
plainsong, 10
plantas, 40
polkas, 16, 46, 65, 71, 72, 73–74, 82, 84, 90, 101, 145
polkas rancheras, 70
Pomar, Teofil, 76
Ponce, Manuel M., 57, 65, 67, 83, 87, 94–95, 97, 125
popular music, 5–8, 95, 108, 124, 125–26
Porter, Cole, 78
Posada, José Guadalupe, 54
Posadas, Guillermo, 113
"Presciliano Valadez," 63
Present State of Music in Mexico, The (Mayer-Serra), 17, 101
Presley, Elvis, 119, 140, 141
Preza, Velino M., 100

Index

Pride, Charlie, 146
Prieto, Guillermo, 37, 53
psaltery, 46, 68, 84, 89
Pueblerina (film), 122
Pulido, A., 135

quadrille, 82
Quevedo, Pepe, 53
Quiroga, Rosita, 77

radio, 43, 77, 95, 107–13, 147
Radio Universidad, 109, 110
Ramírez, Agustín, 64, 98
Ramírez, J., 135
Ramón Ortiz, Máximo, 20
Ramos, Alfonso, 146
rancheras, 68–70, 83, 118, 120, 125, 128, 129, 137, 141
"Rayando el sol," 91
RCA Victor, 115, 120
Rebennack, Mac, 143
"Reconciliación," 135
record industry, 113–20
Redes, 121
redowas, 65
Reed, Alma, 99
religious music, 59–60. *See also* Catholic Church; gospel music
requinto, 24, 42, 43, 64, 103
retruécanos, 60–61
Return of Doug Saldaña, The, 142
revistas del teatro, 91
Revueltas, Silvestre, 83, 121
Reyes, Lucha, 57, 69, 125
Reyna, Cornelius, 46
rhumba, 78, 80, 105, 124
rhythm and blues, 139, 147
Rigual Brothers, 132
Río Armento, Antonio del, 88
Ríos Toledano, Miguel, 37
ritmo de hamaca, 74, 76
Riva Palacio, Vicente, 53
Rivera e hijos, 53
rock and roll, 98, 119, 138, 139–40, 145, 146, 147
Rodríguez, Arsenio, 80
Rodríguez, Ismael, 122
Rodríguez, Johnny, 146
Rodríguez Galván, Ignacio, 61
Rolling Stone, 142
Romance y corrido (Mendoza), 50
romances, 17, 49–51, 82
"Romances tradicionales de Guerrero" (Martínez), 52
Romero, Macario, 54
Romero, María, 109
Romero, Nicolás, 54

Rosas, Juventino, 73, 93–94, 95
Rosas, Miguel, 93
Rosas Vega, Luis, 64
Rosenda (film), 121
"Rosita Tomato," 132
Rossini, Gioacchino Antonio, 105
royalties, 111–13, 114
Rubio, Ernesto, 57
Ruffo, Tito, 91
Ruiz, Federico, 91
Ruiz, Gabriel, 102, 132

SACM, 58, 97, 102, 111–13, 114, 118, 132
Sahm, Doug, 139, 142–43, 144, 146
sainetes, 14, 16
Salas, Angel, 97
Saldívar, Gabriel, 12, 20, 37, 39, 42, 50, 87
Salón México (film), 122
samba, 8, 78, 124
San Cristóbal, Bernardo, 109
Sánchez, Cuco, 122, 128, 132
Sánchez Brothers, 145
Sandi, Luis, 7, 83
sandungas, 20–21, 89
Santana, Carlos, 138
Santanera, Sonora, 117
Santiago, Gustavo, 44
"Santo Señor de Chalma," 87
sarabanda, 12, 14
Saumell, Manuel, 74
saxophone, 33, 44, 47, 48, 104, 105, 143
Schipa, Tito, 91
Schmidt, Henry, 24
schottisches, 16, 65, 71, 82
Schumann, Robert, 95
serenades, 64, 82
"Serenata huasteca," 32
Serrano, José, 16
Serrano Martínez, Celedonio, 52
sesquialtera rhythm, 23
"She's About a Mover," 142
Simmons, Merle Edwin, 51, 52
Sindicato de Compositores, 97
sinfonía, 23, 37, 40, 63
Sir Douglas Quintet, 142, 143
"Sobre las olas," 73, 94, 95, 131
"Solamente una vez," 102, 138
Solís, Javier, 117, 118
"Sombras," 118
sones, 8, 22–35, 39, 41, 63, 89
Sordo Sodi, María del Carmen, 8, 11, 15, 22, 26, 32, 42, 46, 48, 53, 55–56, 57, 58, 59, 66, 68, 72, 73, 80, 92, 97, 107, 123
Soto, Roberto, 91
Spanish influences, 9–10, 12–22, 27, 36, 49–51, 60–61, 62–63, 67, 71, 96
"Speedy González," 132

Stanford, E. Thomas, 23, 28, 42
Starflite records, 142, 144
steel guitar, 139
Stevenson, Robert, 11
Strauss, Johann, 95
Suárez, Salvador, 116
Sunny and the Sunliners, 144–45
Suppé, Franz von, 84
swing, 105–106. See also western swing

Talavera, Mario, 66, 85, 95, 96, 98, 102
Talent Scout records, 141
tango, 14, 20, 71, 77, 91, 95, 101, 124
"Tango negro," 77
"Tata Dios," 33, 34
television, 98
Tex-Mex style, 131, 139, 140
Texas, 139–47
Texas Playboys, 139
Texas Tornado, 143
theatre music, 13–16, 68, 90–91. See also tonadillas escénicas
"Tie a Yellow Ribbon Round the Old Oak Tree," 144
Tierra muerta (orchestral suite), 121
Tijuana Brass, 131, 138
"Tilingo lingo," 4
típicas, 83–86, 89
"Tipitín," 96
Tirado, Carlos, 106
tonadillas escénicas, 13–15, 22, 32, 60, 90
Toña la Negra, 102, 115
Torre Blanca, Juan, 84
traditional music, 4
"Traicionera," 32
"Traumerei," 95
Trejo, Valeriano, 33
tribal music, 1–3
Tribe records, 142
Trio Garnica-Ascencio, 57, 104
Trio los Panchos, 103, 117, 118
Trio Tariácuri, 103
Trio Veneno, 96
"Tristes jardines," 73
trumpet, 10, 27, 33, 38, 41, 43, 47, 104, 105
trumpet mariachis. See mariachis
Turner, Joe, 141
tzeponazli, 122

"Un viejo amor," 97
Universidad Nacional Autónoma de México (UNAM), 109, 110
"Uno, dos y tres conga," 78
Uranga, Lauro de, 68, 90

Valdéz Leal, F., 135

Valens, Ritchie, 140
Valente, Conejo, 100–101
valonas, 17, 39–40, 53, 63
"Vals poética," 73
Vamos con Pancho Villa (film), 121
Vanegas, Antonio, 53–54
vaquería, 13
Varèse, Edgar, 97
Vargas, Pedro, 85, 95, 98, 115, 117, 118
Vasconcelos, José, 57, 97, 107
Vásquez Santa Ana, Higinio, 25
Vega, Carlos, 6, 13, 16, 71, 72
Velarde Pérez, Adelita, 88
Velázquez, Consuelo, 132
Vélez, Lupe, 69
Verdadero Jarabe tapatío (Martínez), 38
Verdi, Giuseppe, 5, 82
"Viaje al infierno," 36
Vigil y Robles, Eduardo, 90, 91
vihuela, 27, 42, 46, 56, 89
Villa, Francisco "Pancho," 55, 87, 96
Villalpando, Fernando, 76
Villanueva, Felipe, 38, 73, 76, 95
Villarreal, B., 135
Villarreal, Manuel, 116
Villegas, Martín de, 50
violin, 26, 27, 28, 38, 40, 42, 43, 45, 84, 85, 89, 139

Waldteufel, Emile, 95
Walker, T-Bone, 139
waltzes, 16, 41, 47, 65, 71, 72–73, 82, 84, 101, 145
"Wasted Days and Wasted Nights," 141, 142
Waters, Muddy, 141
Wayne, Scotty. See Fender, Freddy
wedding songs, 60
western swing, 139
Wills, Bob, 139
"Woolly Bully," 119

XEB (radio station), 96, 108, 109
XEFA (radio station), 108–109
XELA (radio station), 110
XEW (radio station), 43, 47, 77, 97, 98, 102, 108, 109
XEX (radio station), 108

"You Belong to My Heart," 138
Yradier, Sebastián, 76
"Yucalpetén," 99

Zaizar, D., 117
Zamacois, Niceto, 37
zamba, 33

Zapata, Emiliano, 87
zapateado, 13, 19, 20, 25, 26, 36, 63
zarabanda, 13
Zarmeno, Alvaro, 117

zarzuela, 15–16, 91
zorzico dances, 27
Zúñiga, A., 61